I0531230

SON OF A POACHER IV

THESE HILLS HAVE EYES

"COMPARISONS TO FICTIONAL GAME WARDEN JOE PICKETT are inevitable but these tales of humans and human nature ring true because they're real-life accounts of daily challenges faced by Wyoming game wardens; all with a healthy dose of trademark Scott Werbelow humor. Fortunately, Werbelow's treasure trove of raw and authentic behind-the-scenes stories – and cast of characters – appears endless. Simply put, you can't make up this stuff."
-Joe Arterburn, Writer, Editor,
Former Director of Communications for *Cabela's*

"JUST WHEN I THOUGHT WYOMING GAME WARDEN SCOTT WERBELOW had exhausted all his wild memories in his first three books, *SON OF A POACHER*, he produces yet another. And this is a doozy. Scott pulls no punches when he reveals his most challenging confrontations with bad people. It amazes me that he survived throughout his 33-year career. Get this book. It's a winner."
-Jim Zumbo, Former Hunting Editor, *Outdoor Life Magazine*

"SPEND 33-YEARS AS A GAME WARDEN, and you're sure to see and hear enough outrageous stuff to fill a book. Luckily for us, Scott Werbelow has been able to fill four, and this might be the best one yet."
-John Taranto, Editor, *Game & Fish Magazine*

"*SON OF A POACHER* is down-right entertaining, providing a glimpse into the mind and day-to-day life of Wyoming's respected Game Wardens."
- Colton Heward- Managing Editor 1 *Petersen's Hunting*

SON OF A POACHER IV

THESE HILLS HAVE EYES

Scott C. Werbelow

Copyright © 2025 — Scott C. Werbelow

ISBN: Paperback: 979-8-9904166-4-2
ISBN: Hardcover: 979-8-9904166-5-9
Library of Congress Control Number: 2025925853

10 9 8 7 6 5 4 3 2 1

All rights reserved. No part of this book may be reproduced or transmitted in any form or for any means, electronic or mechanical, including photocopying, recording, or by any information storage and removal system, without permission in writing from the copyright owner.

To order additional copies of this book or other books, please visit my website at scottwerbelow.com

Books by Scott C. Werbelow
Son of a Poacher: Wyoming Warden in the Making
Son of a Poacher II: Blast From My Past
Son of a Poacher III: No Time to Rest
Son of a Poacher IV: These Hills Have Eyes

These Hills Have Eyes

Contents

Chapter 1

GAME WARDEN SUPERVISOR

It was Friday evening a little past 5:00 p.m. I had just received a call from Chief Game Warden Jay Lawson at Cheyenne headquarters. I had been waiting for this important phone call for over two weeks. Unfortunately, I had limited cell service and the call was dropped. My location was just south of Hoback Junction near Jackson Hole, Wyoming. My heart sank as I drove south into the canyon towards the tiny town of Bondurant. I think Mr. Lawson was going to tell me if I was selected or not for the Jackson/Pinedale game warden supervisor position that I had applied for several weeks earlier. I knew since it was Friday after 5:00 that I would probably not hear back from Mr. Lawson until Monday sometime. This was going to be a long weekend, worrying about if I was appointed the job or not. I could feel butterflies in my stomach. What if I got the job? Could I handle it? What if I didn't get the job? Would I feel embarrassed among my co-workers for not getting the job? I prayed that Jay would call back and leave me a voice message or call me during the weekend sometime.

The weekend passed and I never heard from Mr. Lawson. I swear it was the longest weekend of my life. I couldn't wait to get to my office on Monday morning to see if regional wildlife supervisor, Bernie Holz, had heard any news, or maybe I would get another phone call at the office. When I arrived at the office, Bernie stepped out of his office and asked, "Swerb, do you have second?" My stomach turned into butterflies again. Was this the moment that I had been waiting for? I nervously entered his office. Bernie had a concerned look on his face, but that was normal for most days.

Bernie said, "Sit down, Swerb. How was your weekend?"

I responded, "It was good, but the longest weekend of my life since I've been wondering if I received the game warden supervisor position or not."

I explained to Bernie how I had received a call from Jay on Friday but had poor cell service and had lost his call. Bernie pulled out a Cuban cigar and placed it in his mouth. I always knew when Bernie had something big on his mind because he would always pull out his cigar, lick it a few times, and roll it gently between his lips.

Bernie said, "I just got off the phone with Lawson and wanted to visit with you about our conversation." I took a deep breath. This didn't sound like good news to me. I prepared myself for the worst.

"It sounds like they are having a hard time making their decision. Right now, the job is between you and another game warden. Apparently, the other game warden is fighting a war in Iraq and won't return to Wyoming for about a year and a half. Please keep this information to yourself. His name is Brian Nesvik and he is currently the Elk Mountain game warden."

I replied, "Well, how is that going to work if Brian isn't going to return for over a year?"

"They are considering hiring you as an intern to fill in for Brian until he returns back on official duty."

I responded, "I can't see putting my heart and soul into this position for a year and a half and then go back to being a Feed Ground Manager/Game Warden. Who would do my job while I'm acting as a game warden supervisor? There is no way that we can leave that position vacant for over a year!"

2

Bernie said, "I agree with you, and I have shared the same concerns with Wildlife Administration. I will visit with Jay again and get back to you soon."

I thanked Bernie and stood up and shook his hand. I left his office very upset. I thought to myself, *Did I just blow my chance to become a game warden supervisor?* I really wanted this job, but it sounds like maybe they were just going to use me for a while and didn't have a care in the world about who would manage the elk feed grounds and do all that hard work! But if I didn't take the job, would they look over me the next time I applied for a promotion? I was so upset I just left the office and didn't even turn my computer on for the day to check emails. How long would it take them to make a decision? Would they hire Brian and just leave the position open until he returned to the States? I had never met this Brian Nesvik character before, but I had heard from other wardens that he was a top hand as a Wyoming game warden. I really didn't want to do this job for a year and a half and then return as a feed ground manager/game warden. I would be so far behind on feed ground maintenance that I may never catch back up. Who would purchase all the hay for the feed grounds this summer?

I stressed about it all week long. My wife Lana was getting tired of listening to me whine about the subject every evening. She said, "Quit worrying about it, honey; you don't want that damn job anyways! They want to hire yes-men and use the shit out of them and you are not a yes- man!"

I replied, "You're probably right, honey, but being a yes-man pays better than being a no-man! Right now, I need to be a yes-man!" My wife didn't agree with me, but that was pretty normal.

The week went by quickly. There was not a moment in any day that I didn't think about the game warden supervisor position and how they were going to handle the situation. It was Friday afternoon when my office phone rang. I thought, *could this be the call that I have been waiting for?* I took a deep breath and answered the phone. It was the Chief Game Warden Jay Lawson.

He said, "Hello, is this Swerb?"

I replied, "Yes, Mr. Lawson, it certainly is."

Jay responded, "Are you ready to become the Jackson/Pinedale game warden supervisor?"

I responded, "Yes, sir, I have been ready for quite some time."

Jay said, "Well, congratulations! The job is yours and is effective immediately. I will send out a statewide email in a few minutes."

I couldn't believe what I had just heard. WOW! I had just become the new Jackson/Pinedale game warden supervisor. Jay told me that they had decided to put me in the position and replace someone with my current position in the very near future. I was so excited! I thanked Jay and told him to have a great weekend. I would need to call Lana and tell her the good news. I would also need to call my good friend, Brad Hovinga, the Big Piney game warden, and tell him that I was now his boss. I wondered how it would be supervising one of my best friends. I heard my computer ding. The statewide email had already been sent from Jay. Bernie jumped out of his chair and came across the hall to shake my hand. He said, "Congratulations, Swerb; I look forward to working with you in the future."

As many thoughts raced through my head I thought, *Holy crap, I just became a game warden supervisor and was never an official game warden with my own district.* All I ever wanted to do is feed elk in the winter and they made me a Feed Ground Manager. All I ever wanted to do is become a game warden and they appointed me as a Game Warden Supervisor. Hopefully I could handle the job. I was looking forward to the many challenges ahead. Office manager Des Brunette came up and gave me a huge hug. She had tears in her eyes as she said, "Congratulations, Swerb!" I went home and celebrated that Friday evening, and may have even smoked a cigar or two myself.

Saturday morning my work phone rang very early. It was SALECS, our radio dispatch center. The lady's name was Jo. She had been one of our dispatchers for many years and was very good at her job.

Jo said, "Good morning, sunshine! I understand you are now the new game warden supervisor for the Jackson/Pinedale region."

I replied, "Yes, I guess my position became effective yesterday afternoon."

Jo replied, "Well, I have a report of a black bear trying to break into a cabin in the Hoback Ranches subdivision near Bondurant, and I can't get in touch with any of your game wardens on this beautiful Saturday morning. The lady's name is Helen, and she sounds like she may be elderly."

Jo gave me the lady's phone number and I thanked her for the information. I then tried to call the Big Piney game warden, but got no answer. I also tried the north and south Pinedale game wardens, same result. I then tried to call the South Jackson game warden, and again no answer. I became frustrated that none of the wardens answered their phones early on a Saturday morning. Maybe they were all out in the field and busy with something else. So, I left a voice message on each of their phones to call me back ASAP. I thought to myself, *Well I guess this was my first official call of duty.* I called the number that Jo had given me. A sweet, but panicked, little old lady answered the phone. I could tell she was very upset.

She was yelling, "GET OUT OF HERE, GO AWAY!"

I said, "Madam, this is Scott Werbelow with the Game and Fish Department. I received a report that you have a black bear trying to break into your cabin. Is that true?"

Helen replied, "Yes, the darn thing! I was baking an apple pie and looked up to see a bear sniffing the screen on my kitchen window. He has now torn a hole in the screen and has his head sticking through my window in the kitchen. GET OUT OF HERE!"!" she yelled.

5

I asked, "Madam, is there any way that you can go into the kitchen and close the window safely?"

Helen replied, "I'm here all alone and was just baking a pie for my grandkids. I'm afraid the bear is going to enter my kitchen any minute now."

I asked, "Do you have a gun to protect yourself?"

Helen replied, "My husband does, but he is not here and I don't know how to use the damn thing anyways!"

I was pretty sure that the bear was about to enter her kitchen. I wasn't sure what to tell her other than get the hell out of the house and into her car. I thought about telling her to put the freshly baked pie in the refrigerator to get rid of the nice apple smell and lock herself in the bathroom until the bear left the area. But what if the bear didn't leave the area and entered her cabin? The bear would tear the entire cabin apart, eating whatever smelled good.

About that time, I heard her say, "Hold on one minute, I have an idea."

I heard the sound of her putting the phone down on the table. I also heard her yelling in the background.

"GET OUT OF HERE! GET THE HELL OUT OF HERE!"

I then heard a loud crashing sound that scared the heck out of me. I thought, *oh dear God, the bear has entered her kitchen through the window!* I really needed to get headed that direction but it would take me over an hour to get to her cabin's location. I would be too late to help her in any way. About that time my phone started beeping. I was getting another call on another line. I didn't recognize the number as one of my game wardens trying to call me back. I didn't dare answer the phone because the lady had something very serious going on in her kitchen. I could still hear the sound of her yelling at the bear and I thought I even heard the bear growling back at her. About that time, I heard a loud noise (WHAP) and then it got really quiet. I was afraid something really bad had just happened.

6

I heard the sound of the phone being picked back up. I also heard the sound of heavy breathing. The lady said, "Sorry about that, I think everything is all right now."

I asked, "What just happened?"

She replied, "I noticed that I had a large cast iron skillet on the stove, so I whacked him right in the end of the nose as he was crawling through the window. I think it worked. He's gone now."

My God, this was one tough and brave lady. I told her to close the window and get rid of the fresh apple pie smell. I also gave her my phone number and told her to call me if he came back. I told her that I would head that direction and make sure that the bear was long gone. Besides, I wanted to meet this lady. That was about the funniest thing that I had heard in a long time. It wasn't funny, but it, kind of was. I wish I could have seen it happen in person. What a brave lady she was.

I finally got dressed and jumped into my new patrol truck and headed towards the Hoback Ranches subdivision. Oh shit, someone had tried to call me a few minutes ago. I checked to see if they left a voice message. I played the message and it said, "Hi, this is Cortney up in Jackson, I have a bear trying to break into my cabin. Please call me back ASAP." I thought to myself, *you have got to be shitting me right now.* How could this be happening to me, to have two different bears breaking into two different cabins at the same time? I could only be in one place at one time! I called the lady back and told her that I would have someone there ASAP and that I would be headed that direction. I almost told her to grab a damn frying pan and smack it in the nose. That's what the last lady did and it worked pretty well.

As I was headed to Hoback Ranches, I tried to call every game warden in the region but was not able to reach any of them. I finally got a hold of a biologist in Jackson and he agreed to handle the second bear call. I was thankful for that. I told him that I was headed that direction if he needed any assistance. Meanwhile my phone rang again.

7

It was Big Piney game warden Brad Hovinga, returning my earlier message. He told me that he was sorry that he had missed my call but was headed up to Hoback Ranches to deal with another call of a black bear trying to break into a cabin. After further discussion, we determined that this call had come in from a different lady who may have been neighbors with the little old lady and the cast iron skillet. I agreed to meet Brad at Daniel Junction and carpool with him to the cabin site.

I jumped into Brad's patrol truck. He smiled, shook my hand, and said, "Good morning, Boss Man; congratulations on your new promotion."

I smiled and replied, "Thank you, buddy. I bet you never thought I would be your boss."

Brad replied, laughing, "That's pretty scary, buddy. You know way too much about me to be my boss!"

I asked Brad if I needed to bring anything. He replied, "Nope! I got my rifle, shotgun, pistol and bear spray, so we should be good to go."

Brad went on to tell me that the lady who called him had locked herself in her cabin and was scared to death. I told him about the little old lady smacking the bear in the nose with the frying pan. Brad laughed and said, "It's probably the same damn bear and now he is really mad!"

It took us a while to find the correct address. There were a bunch of cabins in this area and many different two-track roads going everywhere. After locating the correct address, I noticed an old-looking station wagon car parked near the cabin. The car was completely full of crap: old clothes, shovels, axes, hand tools, and a twin-size mattress in the back of the car. It looked to me like someone had been living in this car for quite some time. The cabin looked like it was only about half done from being built. The windows had plywood over them and the roof was still unfinished. It appeared to me that someone had possibly been living in their car for quite some time while building their cabin. The car resembled the same car that Chevy Chase drove in the movie Christmas Vacation.

Brad and I sat in the truck for several minutes, looking for any bear activity in the area. It certainly didn't look like a bear was still trying to break into the cabin that Brad received the call from. Once it looked safe, we exited the truck and headed towards the cabin. As I walked up the steps to the front deck of the cabin, I noticed a shower head hanging up high on a dead pine tree. The shower head had a hose going up the backside of the dead tree. I also noticed a metal tub of water sitting on a large propane burner. It looked to me like someone had been taking showers out on their front deck in front of other cabin owners. I approached the front door of the cabin and noticed claw marks on the wooden door at about eye level. The claw marks were small and not very high up the door, indicating maybe a small black bear had recently been there.

I knocked on the door. Brad and I stood there for several minutes, waiting for someone to open the door. Finally, the door creaked open very slowly, to about six inches. I peeked through the crack in the door and observed a very large lady standing completely naked, holding a large frying pan in her right hand. She had the pan above her head as if she was going to swat something with it. She had a phone in one hand and a frying pan in the other. I wondered if she had maybe talked to the little old lady over the phone and was told to arm herself with a frying pan.

I said in a loud voice, "Good morning, Madam. We are game wardens with the Wyoming Game and Fish Department. We received a report that you had a bear trying to break into your cabin. Are you still having bear problems?"

The door slowly opened and the lady grabbed my arm and yelled, "QUICK, GET IN HERE BEFORE THAT BEAR GETS YOU! BOTH OF YOU GET IN HERE NOW!"

I looked at Brad and he looked at me with a crazy look on his face. We shrugged then stepped into the cabin with the naked lady. The lady quickly locked the door behind us. The next thing I knew we were locked in a cabin with a naked lady holding a frying pan over her head. She smelled horrible and had not shaved ANYTHING for weeks. If anyone ever thought they may have seen Bigfoot, it may have been her! I was starting to feel less afraid of the black bear. The lady was a nervous wreck and nuttier than a porta-potty in a peanut factory. She was scared to death. She apologized for being naked and claimed that she had been sleeping in her car when the bear tried to break into her car earlier that morning. She claimed that she had been living in her car for several months while building her cabin by herself. I admired the lady for her carpentry skills. She told us that she felt safer in her cabin, but forgot her clothes in the car when she made a break for the cabin while the bear was not looking.

For some reason the lady gave me the creeps. I looked at Brad and motioned with my eyes that we needed to get out of there right now. I thanked the lady and told her to be sure and call if she had anymore bear problems. I also told her that we would look around for the bear and remove it if found. Brad and I exited the cabin and jumped into his patrol truck.

Brad looked at me and said, "Oh my God, that lady is crazy! She reminds me of that lady in the movie, *Misery*. I thought she was going to thump us both in the head with that damn frying pan and tie us up and break our legs or something."

I replied, "That's why I motioned for us to get the heck out of there; I had the same feeling!"

We headed down the road a short distance and met the other lady who'd swatted the bear in the nose with the cast iron skillet. She was a very sweet elderly lady wearing a pretty flowered sun dress and sandals. Not someone that you would expect to swat a black bear with a frying pan at all. She invited us into her kitchen and showed us the damage that the bear had done to her window screen above the kitchen sink. She was laughing uncontrollably while telling us the whole story.

She said, "You should have seen the look on that poor black bear's face when that frying pan hit him in the end of the nose. He couldn't have gotten out of here any quicker if you had fired him out of a cannon."

She then opened the refrigerator and asked, "Would you boys like a piece of fresh baked apple pie?"

We both agreed and sat at her kitchen table with a fresh cup of coffee and an awesome tasting piece of apple pie. We told her to be "Bear Aware" and keep a clean cabin site. We also told her about the neighbor across the road who also had a bear try to break into her car and cabin.

The little old lady said, "Oh, she is crazy! I wish the bear had chased her plum out of the country. She is crazier than a pet coon! She doesn't shower very often either, but when she does it's quite a sight for the whole neighborhood to see. We have had nothing but problems with her since she started building that damn cabin. I just hope she gets it finished soon, so she can move out of that damn ugly station wagon; it's a damn eye sore for the whole neighborhood sitting over there!"

Brad and I thanked her for her hospitality and told her to be sure and call if she had anymore bear problems. She laughed and said, "I don't think I will ever see that bear again after he tried to break into my cabin."

Surprisingly enough, we never received any more calls on that black bear again. This was my first official call as a game warden supervisor. From this experience I quickly learned that it would be very important to have a schedule and have wardens available for calls on weekends to have adequate coverage in the region.

As Brad and I were headed back towards Pinedale, Brad said, "Hey, buddy, sorry I missed your call this morning. I kind of had a late-night last night and didn't get much sleep."

I replied, "Oh yeah? How come you didn't get much sleep?"

Brad laughed and said, "Man, I received the craziest call last night at 2:00AM. Some guy called me and wanted to know if he could keep a stringer of fish that was wrapped up in a Great Blue Heron's legs. I asked the man where he was at and he told me that he was at the Eagle Bar in La Barge. I then asked the man where the blue heron was located and he told me that he had the bird tethered to the bar stool next to him."

I laughed and said, "You have got to be kidding me right now!"

Brad laughed and said, "No, true story! The guy was out fishing on Fontenelle Reservoir and came across a blue heron with a stringer of fish tangled in its long legs. The man took the fish and the heron to the bar with him later that evening. While at the bar someone helped the man get the stringer of fish off the heron. They didn't know what to do with the heron, so they tied it to a bar stool. The bar was getting ready to close and the man didn't know what to do with the heron or the fish. The bartender told the drunk man to call the local game warden to see if he could get permission to keep the fish and figure out what to do with the heron."

I laughed and told Brad, "That's the funniest damn story I've ever heard!"

Brad laughed and said, "Yea, the damn phone rang at about 2:00 a.m.and I thought it might be an emergency, so I answered it. When I picked up the phone it was some drunk old man that wanted to know if he could keep the fish. So, I got out of bed and headed down to the Eagle Bar to rescue the blue heron and issue the guy a Wyoming Interstate Game Tag to legally possess the limit of catfish that was on the stringer. I didn't know what to do with the damn bird, so I put it in my patrol truck on the passenger seat and headed for the reservoir to turn it loose. The heron stood up nice and tall in the passenger seat and stared at me as I drove down the road. This made me nervous because it was dark and I couldn't see him very well. I was afraid that he may try and attack me while I was driving, so I turned on my dome light so that I could keep an eye on him. I only met one other person while driving to the reservoir who may have seen me in this situation at 2:00 a.m. So, if you get any reports that a game warden was driving around late at night with a blue heron sitting next to him, that would be me."

I laughed at Brad and replied, "Buddy, if the public only knew some of the shit that we get to deal with sometimes. Our job is not always about just catching the bad guys."

Brad laughed and said, "Boy, isn't that the truth!"

Chapter 2

WOLF LAKE COW CAMP

It was Monday morning, my first official day as the new game warden supervisor. Bernie informed me that he would like to have a staff meeting with me and our biologist coordinator every Monday at 8:00AM. I soon realized that if I was going to be an official supervisor, I would need to get rid of my small dirty day planner and buy the jumbo day planner with the leather cover so that I could fit in with all the other supervisors. I think this was a status thing that made you look busier and smarter than anyone else. So, I had Des order me a brand-new Franklin planner that was about the size and weight of a large Bible. This large planner meant that I could write more stuff down and look busier than anyone else.

I also learned that the Monday morning "Staff Meeting" was a meeting that Bernie could delegate much of his work for the week out to myself and the biologist coordinator. This was not a bad thing. It was great communication among the three of us to discuss the upcoming week and all the hottest issues. Bernie was a great delegator and let his people do their job. He did a superb job of delegating work to the right people to handle the job instead of trying to be in control and micromanage all his employees, as I have seen other supervisors do. I have always admired Bernie for this skill. Bernie would have me attend Forest Service and BLM coordination meetings on his behalf.

He would also send me to all the supervisor's meetings that were held somewhere around the state every other month. These meetings were very serious, and a great amount of work and planning happened during these two-to-three-day-long meetings. These meetings are "where the sausage is made", so to speak. They were also very fun. They were always planned at strategic locations that had great bird hunting or fishing for all the supervisors to enjoy during the evenings and early morning hours. Almost every regional supervisor and all of Wildlife Administration out of Cheyenne had bird dogs and fishing gear in the back of their vehicles. It was a perk to the job to get to stay at some very nice lodges in mountainous settings with great food and amenities. And if you carried a large Franklin planner and smoked a cigar you would fit in better with some of the higher-ups.

I felt very privileged to be at the same meeting table with twenty or more of some of the finest supervisors and wildlife managers in the state, if not the world. These supervisors were top notch and very knowledgeable about wildlife management, wildlife diseases, regulations, budgets, etc. You never spoke out of turn and you only spoke when requested by the Chief Game Warden or the Director. We would generally work through 30–50 agenda items in a two-to-three-day period. Some agenda items may take a half or full day to discuss. Difficult agenda items would almost always be assigned to a committee by the Chief Game Warden, Jay Lawson, to resolve the issue. If you spoke out of turn or interrupted someone at the meeting, you would almost always be assigned as the chairman of the committee. I quickly learned as the new guy at the table that sometimes it's better to go unnoticed and not stand out as the smartest guy in the room. Not that I was ever the sharpest knife in the sheath, but I always had an opinion and would often share it if I felt strongly about something. It seemed like anytime I shared my opinion, I got assigned as the chairman to some complicated committee that would take months to resolve. Director Terry Cleveland once stated, "Sometimes it's better to go unnoticed." This is some very sound advice! The higher you go up the ladder in life, the more your butt crack shows.

After attending the supervisor's meetings, I would return to Pinedale with 6–10 pages of handwritten notes. I would then hold a regional wildlife personnel meeting with Bernie to discuss everything with regional personnel and game wardens about what was learned at the supervisor's meeting. This regional meeting would generally take one to two days. The discussions were about fresh and hot topics that came from the top all the way down the chain of command to the employees working in the field. These meetings generally spiked some great discussions about the future of the agency and where we might be headed. Generally speaking, we were always looking for alternative funding for the department. The license sales from hunters and anglers were not keeping up with department expenditures. Back then, we were not allowed to purchase extra-cab trucks even though most people in Wyoming already owned one. Nobody wanted a regular cab truck anymore! We were afraid of what the public might think of our image if we had more expensive trucks. To this day, I don't know how we got everything required to carry for game wardens in a regular cab truck. We carried large black metal tool- boxes in the rear of our trucks to store most of our gear. Rifles and shotguns were stored in an overhead gun rack above your head to save on room. You could not get another item in your door pockets, glove box, or behind the seat. You had to be extremely organized to store all of your law enforcement equipment. If we were ever to arrest someone, there was never room to transport the suspect. It was also a safety issue to have someone in your cab with all of your department-issued firearms.

Many changes were happening fast. North Pinedale Game Warden Duke Early had recently retired and was replaced with a young and very energetic man named Hubba Healy, who had a blue flame shooting out of his ass almost a mile long. I had worked with this man while I was the feed ground manager/game warden and we didn't get along very well, or maybe even not at all. He rarely communicated with me, had no respect for me, and now I was his boss. This could end up being a challenge for me as a supervisor.

Hubba hadn't been in the North Pinedale warden district for even two weeks when he nearly totaled his game and fish patrol truck by hitting a deer in the Upper Green River area, traveling over 90 MPH in the dark. The patrol truck was absolutely trashed and probably should have been totaled. The bean counters at Headquarters decided to have the truck repaired for nearly $8000. This was a lot of money back then. The truck went into the repair shop during hunting season and Hubba had to borrow a spare truck. This is always a huge pain in the butt because we practically live in our trucks, and it's a pain to move all your law enforcement gear and equipment back and forth between trucks. The body shop was able to repair and repaint Hubba's truck in just a few short weeks. Hubba got the new-looking truck back and smacked a tree the very next day in the Upper Green River. Apparently, he took his eyes off the road while reaching down to get his coffee cup and ran off the road. Back to the repair shop it went the very next day, with several thousand dollars in repairs.

South Pinedale game warden Dennis Almquist had just announced that he would be retiring in early January of 2005. So, this would be his last fall hunting season. This meant that I would have another new employee to supervise in the South Pinedale warden district. It was always refreshing to get a young new game warden but very difficult to fill the shoes of a veteran warden who had been in one district for over thirty years. Institutional knowledge is very difficult, if not impossible, to replace. I was curious who would replace Dennis Almquist and be the next South Pinedale game warden.

It was summer of 2004. I was still doing many of my duties as a feed ground manager because they had not yet filled my position. I would end up purchasing all the hay for the elk feed grounds, performing feed ground maintenance, and looking after the draft horses at Soda Lake. I would end up sitting in on the interview board for the selection of the new feed ground manager. After interviewing a great group of candidates, Gary Hornberger was selected to fill the position, effective August 15, 2004. I was very relieved to finally have Gary on board so that I could focus on other work. Gary had worked for me earlier and certainly already knew everything about the feed ground manager position.

Hubba's patrol truck after hitting deer

Longtime South Jackson game warden Doug Crawford had also announced his retirement. I was also invited to participate on that interview board where Thermopolis game warden Tim Fuchs was selected to fill Doug's shoes, effective September 1, 2004.

With this being Dennis's last fall hunting season, I wanted to spend as much time as I could with him that fall. Dennis and Hubba had just solved a serious town deer poaching case involving two individuals who were killing mule deer in the town of Pinedale with a bow and arrow during July. It was a lengthy investigation with some great game warden work. At the end of the day, it was found that one of the culprits lived within two blocks from Hubba's warden station. Hubba was actually able to do surveillance of the man from his front porch of the warden station. The two men were later charged with poaching four deer, one moose, and an antelope. They were both charged with felony destruction of state property and fined over $15,000 each with jail time and loss of hunting privileges for 15 years. This may have been the first time in history that a poacher in Wyoming was charged with a felony for hunting violations. This poaching spree made the news big time in Pinedale, where the two individuals would later be named "The Pinedale Poachers".

Shortly after this case was solved, Dennis stopped by the office one day. He wanted to see if I would be interested in taking a couple of ATVs with a trailer into the Wolf Lake cow camp cabin. Opening day of rifle season was only one week away and Dennis wanted to haul some horse hay up to the cabin. He would then plan on riding his horses/mules the nine miles into the cabin the day before hunting season opened. This road was extremely rough and very difficult to get a pick-up truck into so he wanted to take ATVs. I agreed to go with him, as I hadn't ever been to this area before. Plus, I was always up for an ATV ride in the mountains no matter where we were going.

As I was leaving the office, Big Piney game warden Brad Hovinga showed up and I met him at the front door. He asked what I was up to and I told him that I was going up to Wolf Lake with Dennis to help him haul some horse hay. Brad asked me if I had an extra ATV around the office, as he would really like to accompany us on the trip. I told Brad to ask around the office and see if anyone would loan him an ATV so that he could go with us. A few minutes later he came back to my office with a smile on his face and said, "I just scored a brand-new Honda ATV from the fisheries biologist, so let's go, man!" Brad was really excited to go with us, as he had not spent any time in that area either.

We drove our patrol trucks as far as we could until the road got really rough. I hooked a snow machine trailer behind my ATV loaded with small bales of horse hay and other camping equipment. Dennis led the way in, with me in the middle and Brad taking up the rear. There were a couple really steep spots with huge ruts in the road, making it dangerous to pull the trailer loaded with hay. At one point Dennis stopped to talk to a hunter in the road ahead of me. I stopped behind him and started sliding backwards with all my brakes locked. I simply couldn't hold the heavy load on the steep hill. Dennis had no idea that I was sliding backwards down the road as he bullshitted with the hunter. Thankfully Brad saw what was happening and ran his borrowed ATV into the back of my trailer to hold me from sliding off a steep embankment to my right. It was all Brad could do to hold me, let alone get me going forward again after Dennis was finally done bullshitting with the hunter. Thankfully, we finally got moving forward again without having a serious wreck. Dennis never did know that anything was going wrong behind him.

We arrived at the cow camp cabin. The cabin was small but had two bunk beds and a wood stove. It was a nice little rustic cabin. I thought it would be pretty cool to come up with Dennis in a week and check hunters on horseback. I had never seen any of his high wilderness country before. The thought of riding a horse in the mountains all day checking hunters and returning to a cozy cabin in the evenings sounded fun to me. I always enjoyed sitting next to a warm woodstove in the mountains sipping a fine bourbon or whiskey before bed. Some of my best memories are sitting in a warm cabin in the mountains watching it snow big heavy wet flakes outside while sipping a whiskey next to a warm stove. If you have ever tried doing this in a cold tent, you know exactly what I mean.

We unloaded all of the gear and stacked the horse hay in a small storage shed so that the moose and elk couldn't eat it over the next week. I looked at Brad and Dennis and said, "I reckon we better make a mile; it's getting late in the day." They both agreed and we all jumped on our ATVs and headed back down the steep rough road. I was leading on the way down, with Dennis behind me and Brad in the rear. We only had about one hour of daylight left when I came to a junction in the trail. There was another two-track road that took off to my right, except it had a large cottonwood tree lying across the road as if to block the entrance to that road. I parked in front of the tree. Dennis pulled up beside me and said, "Don't go that way, that road is rougher than hell." I gave Dennis the thumbs up and went left on the road that we had used earlier.

I looked back several times in the nine-mile ride to see Dennis behind me. I only assumed that Brad was behind Dennis. I arrived back at our trucks just before dark and loaded my ATV into the back of my truck. I assumed Dennis and Brad would be there any minute. I waited for nearly an hour and still no Dennis and Brad. I knew something must be wrong so I unloaded my ATV in the dark and headed back up the steep rough road. I didn't make it very far when I looked up to see a red light coming around the corner towards me. I thought, *what in the hell is that?* As I got closer, I realized that it was Brad riding his borrowed ATV backwards. He was sitting on the front rack driving it backwards. I have never tried this before but I'm guessing it takes some real talent to drive an ATV off the mountain backwards using your taillight as a headlight. He pulled up next to me, laughing. The brand-new fish division ATV was all beat to shit, with both front and rear racks bent down along the tires. The handlebars were also bent, and the headlight no longer functioned.

I said, "What in the hell are you doing?"

Brad replied, "HOLY SHIT, BUDDY! YOU WON'T BELIEVE WHAT I HAVE BEEN THROUGH! Let's go back to the truck and I will tell you the story, Dennis should be along any minute."

Pretty quick, here came Dennis; shaking his head as he went around me. Once back at the trucks Brad told me the whole story.

Apparently, he had decided to jump over the large cottonwood tree and take the short cut home. He jumped over the tree after several attempts and heard a loud POP. Once over the tree he noticed that he no longer had any forward gears. Dennis had already gone the other direction and Brad could not get the ATV back over the large tree in reverse. So, he decided to ride the ATV down the mountain in reverse on the short cut road that was much worse than the road that we took.

He didn't go far when the ATV hit a rut and veered hard to the left and went flying over a steep embankment. Brad jumped off and watched the ATV roll all the way down into the bottom of a steep ravine. Stuck down in the steep ravine by himself he decided to un-coil all the cable in the winch and run the cable up the hill towards the road. He wrapped the cable around a sturdy pine tree next to the road. Since he had no forward gears, he would have to winch the ATV up the hill in neutral while trying to ride it. He nearly had it back to the road when the winch got hot and started smoking. He kept the button pushed and burned up the winch. Now, he was still off the main road on a steep hillside with winch cable running everywhere. He then turned the ATV around and finished climbing the hill in re-verse, dragging all of his winch cable behind him. Once back to the road he wrapped all the winch cable around the front rack that was all bent to shit and continued on down the road in reverse.

After a short distance he failed to negotiate another sharp corner. He and the ATV flew off the hill down into another steep ravine, off to his right side this time! Being stranded with no winch and unable to climb the steep hill in reverse, he just sat there in the dark. Dennis eventually went back looking for Brad, all the way back to the cot-tonwood tree. Dennis observed ATV tracks and leaking oil in the road and decided to take the short cut road down to find Brad. He eventu-ally located Brad and pulled his borrowed ATV back up the hill and sent him back down the road in reverse. I looked down at the mangled

ATV; the odometer read eighteen miles. This was a brand-new ATV that Brad had just trashed! I was Brad's supervisor, so I was responsible for his actions! How would I ever tell the cute little fisheries biologist that her ATV was now totaled? I was starting to wonder if Brad maybe hadn't found a bottle of scotch up at the cow camp cabin before we left to come home.

I told Brad to take the ATV to Rocksprings in the morning and get everything fixed and we would pay for it out of the warden's budget. We would not say a word about it to anyone!

I said, "Just get the damn thing fixed and get it back to the shop in Pinedale in new condition!"

Brad called me a few days later and said, "Hey, Boss, I got the ATV repaired, but you will never believe what happened on the way home."

I said, "Good God, what now?"

Brad replied, "Well, I had it on my snow machine trailer and had to drive through some construction. They had magnesium water on the road for several miles to keep the dust down. When I returned home, I noticed the entire ATV was covered in mag water and I can't get the shit off. Then I noticed the winch cable was all bound up and I couldn't get the cable to come out. So, I hooked the cable to my patrol truck and put the ATV in reverse to jerk the knot out of the cable. I finally got the cable all out and was winching it back in dragging the ATV so that it would be tight and the damn winch got hot and burned up again."

I couldn't believe what I was hearing. I replied, "Just get the damn thing fixed again and get it cleaned up and back to Pinedale, ASAP."

Brad responded with a laugh, "Yes, sir!"

Well, we eventually got the ATV back where it belonged and nobody knew anything had ever happened to it. I don't remember what the bill was, but I remember it wasn't cheap.

24

The next week came fast. Dennis had invited me to go ride horses back up to Wolf Lake, check hunters, and stay in the cabin. I was excited to do this. This would be my first official pack trip with just Dennis and me. We got the horses and mules unloaded and packed them up with all of our gear. Dennis was always very gentle with his pack mules and rarely cinched them up too tight. At some point in the trail a pack would generally slip and we would be re-packing. It was always generally the worst part of the trail when this happened.

We had only traveled a short distance and Dennis was cursing at his mule. He was riding behind me and all I could hear was, "EDDY, GODDARN YOU, LET'S GO! KNOCK IT OFF, EDDY!"

I turned around in my saddle and said, "Who are you talking to, Dennis?" Dennis always talked out loud, especially when he was upset.

Dennis replied, "Oh, this damn mule. He doesn't want to lead and is wearing my riding horse out, pulling him up the damn mountain. Can you see if you can drag him for a while?"

I dallied Eddy's lead rope around my saddle horn and gave my horse Champ a small kick in the ribs with my heels. Champ didn't like leading the mule at all. Champ didn't like mule's period, and had never led one before. That damn mule dug all four feet into the ground and would not take a step without being pulled. I dragged Eddy for several hundred yards and Champ was now getting tired as well. I told Dennis that this was not working and we would need to do something different. Dennis agreed. We unpacked Eddy and packed Dennis's riding horse with all of his gear. Dennis saddled up Eddy and away we went up the steep mountain.

At this point it started to rain and snow. The further we got up the trail the bigger the snowflakes got. It was now snowing so hard that it was difficult to see anything. It was actually beautiful out, but I was getting wet and cold. It snowed so hard that the brim of my cowboy hat was hanging down over my eyes with water running off the brim down the front of my coat. Dennis was behind me, cursing at the horses most of the way.

I finally heard Dennis yell, "SWERB, STOP FOR A DAMN MINUTE! I NEED A LITTLE TRAIL SHORTENER!"

I stopped and turned back in my saddle to see Dennis pull a bottle of Peppermint Schnapps out of his saddle bag and take a pull from the bottle. Dennis walked up to my horse and said, "You need a little trail-shortener, Swerb?"

I replied, "Trail shortener? I never heard of that saying before, Dennis."

Dennis said, "Yeah, when you get cold and are not at camp yet, this will warm you up make the trail seem shorter."

I took a pull off the bottle and, man, did it taste good. I could feel the taste of it go all the way down to my stomach. I was certainly looking forward to getting out of my wet clothes and starting a fire in the cozy little cabin just a few more miles up the trail.

As we got near the cabin, something didn't look right to me. There were other horses in the corral next to the cabin and I could see smoke coming out of the stovepipe. It appeared to me that someone else was already staying in the cabin.

I looked at Dennis and said, "Looks like someone is already staying in the cabin."

Dennis replied, "What the hell? I told them we would be using the cabin starting today. Maybe they are getting ready to pack up and head out in a bit?"

I replied, "I sure hope that is the case, because I didn't pack a bedroll or a tent and it's going to get damn cold tonight."

We tied our horses to the hitching rail out in front of the cabin and knocked lightly on the door. A short man with a wrinkled face and wearing a greasy cowboy hat opened the door. The cabin was full of cowboys. They were all drinking whiskey and the cabin was very warm. It felt good to enter the cabin. Dennis knew all of the cowboys pretty well and explained to them that we were planning on staying the night in the cabin. The head cowboy apologized and told us that they were planning on being out of the cabin, but the snowstorm delayed them from getting up in the high country to gather cows. He claimed that they would be out of there by tomorrow night.

One of the other cowboys, who had been drinking, yelled out, "Hope you game wardens brought a warm tent and bedroll, cuz it's going to get damn cold out there tonight when the clouds break and the wind picks up!"

I looked at Dennis and he looked back at me with a concerned look on his face. One of the other cowboys stood up and said, "Hell, if you didn't bring a tent or sleeping bags, we got some of that stuff out back in the shed that you guys are welcome to use."

I thanked the man and said, "I reckon that is our only option unless we ride all the way back out of here."

The cowboys all jumped up out of their chairs and offered to help us set up a teepee tent out back. One cowboy said, "Hell, I think we even have a few cots in that shed over there. If you want to grab them, go ahead! Beats the shit out of sleeping on the cold ground."

I was not impressed, but it was their cabin to use and was owned by the Cattleman's Association and not the Game and Fish Department. I was very polite and thanked the cowboys for their generosity. They all soon returned to their warm cabin and left Dennis and me standing out in a raging snowstorm with a teepee tent, a couple mouse-infested sleeping bags, and two ice cold cots for our sleeping enjoyment. I was pretty sure that they were all back in the warm cabin drinking whiskey and laughing their asses off at the two soaking wet game wardens trying to figure out how to set up a damn teepee tent in a snowstorm. Dennis handled all of this pretty well. I think he was just excited to get out of the wind and snow and crawl into an ice-cold Hantavirus-infected fart bag.

We got the tent and cots set up rather quickly. Everything went pretty smooth even though we were missing a few key items on the teepee tent. Luckily the tent did have a canvas floor, so at least we were able to place that on top of the fresh snow. We then made a fire ring with rocks outside the front door of the teepee. We positioned the fire ring so that the prevailing wind would blow heat through the front door of the teepee. Hopefully the smoke wouldn't be too bad, but we definitely were going to need some heat. We gathered up a bunch of nearby firewood and placed it next to the teepee. We also found two stumps that could be used as chairs to sit on next to the warm fire. Before we knew it, we had a raging fire next to the tent and, man, did the warmth of that fire feel good. My clothes were soaking wet and I was shaking like a dog trying to shit a peach seed as I sipped on some of Dennis's Peppermint Schnapps. I don't think I had ever had a better tasting drink that seemed to warm my body up pretty quick. Hopefully we would only need to spend one night in the teepee and have the warm cabin the rest of the trip.

I don't know what time it was, but it was dark and we were tired. We put a bunch of wood on the fire and entered the dark teepee. Man, was it cold in there when I took my clothes off to jump into my sleeping bag. We didn't even have a lantern or any other light source with us. I think I had drunk enough to fall asleep quickly, and that I did. I had never slept on a cot before. And after that night I have never slept in one since. I woke up at about 2:00AM, nearly frozen half to death. I laid there in my cot with my head in my sleeping bag so that I could exhale warm air into my rusted-out fart bag. I used my wet coat for a pillow. I heard Dennis grumbling something in his sleep. What I thought I heard was Dennis saying, "You god-darn zipper...damn it!"

Pretty quick Dennis rose up in his cot and said, "Dammit, Swerb, are you as cold as I am?"

I replied, "Yes, I'm nearly froze half to death."

Dennis replied, "Maybe we should stoke that fire up and stand out there for a while."

I agreed, so out the tent we went. We stoked up the fire and stood out there until the sun came up that morning. Thankfully we had packed some frozen breakfast burritos and had them wrapped in tin foil. We were able to throw them on some hot coals and warm them up for breakfast. No coffee that morning. We saddled up the horses early and headed up the mountain to check elk hunters on opening day of elk season. Thankfully the storm had blown over and we were able to enjoy a cool, blue-sky day in the high country.

As we were riding up the trail, we met a women coming down the trail on horseback. We asked her if she was hunting and she told us no, but that her husband had killed a bull elk and was behind her somewhere packing it out. As soon as the lady left, Dennis looked at me and said, "Swerb, I know her husband and he will be coming down the trail here shortly with an untagged elk. So, you might want to get your ticket book out and get ready to write a citation."

Dennis was a veteran game warden with over thirty years of experience. He knew that country like his own backyard and he knew who the hunters were and where they camped. Dennis was exactly correct. After about ten minutes we observed a man coming down the trail with a spike elk packed on his horses. Dennis greeted the man and asked to see his elk license. The man pulled his license out of his wallet and it was a "Slick License", meaning he had not filled it out. This is game warden terminology for failing to tag their animal properly. Dennis looked at the slick license and said, "Take that license over to Swerb and he can fill out the paperwork." The man knew he was in trouble, and had been in trouble before with Dennis. He brought his license over to me, as I was mounted on my horse Champ, and handed it to me. I issued the man a citation for fail to properly tag his elk and let him keep his elk meat. Primarily because I didn't have any way to pack his elk out if I confiscated it. This was the first and last citation that I ever issued while mounted on my patrol horse. The man was upset but shook our hands and thanked us for letting him keep his elk. Dennis rode up the trail a bit and turned around in his saddle and said, "I told ya, Swerb, to have your ticket book ready, and hell, you didn't even have to get off your damn horse for that case."

We saw some awesome country that day and checked a bunch of elk hunters. We even checked a hunter who had harvested a 350-class bull that evening. This was one of the prettiest bulls that I had ever seen. He had very heavy and dark horns with beautiful white tips on each point. We were nearly back to camp when we stopped by an outfitters camp just before dark. The outfitter was very friendly and knew Dennis well. He invited us over for a steak dinner and drinks later that evening. He said, "Hell, if you game wardens got any extra cash bring it over tonight, as we might even have a poker game!" This sounded like a really good time to me, as I loved steak, whiskey, and an occasional poker game.

Dennis checking large bull elk

We rode our horses back to the cabin. The cowboys were gone. I was happy to know that we would have a warm cabin to sleep in tonight. We fed our horses in the corral and took down the miserable teepee tent and cots and placed them back in the storage shed. I think the reason I got so cold is because my body was off the ground for insulation and the air was able to circulate around my entire body all night long.

Dennis said, "Damn, Swerb, I'm hungry; my belt buckle is scratching my backbone. Let's head over to the outfitter's camp and get some groceries in our belly. Did you bring any damn money for a poker game?"

I replied, "I got ya covered, Dennis! Let's head over there."

We would have to walk about 500 yards to the outfitter's camp in the dark with no flashlight. There were plenty of large boulders and a few small creeks to navigate between the cabin and their camp. We reached their camp and entered the large white cook tent out back. It was very warm inside and the food smelled delicious. The outfitter introduced us to four or five of his elk hunters. They seemed excited to meet a couple of Wyoming game wardens. Heck, I don't know, maybe they were nervous that we were having dinner with them? The outfitter grabbed a large bottle of Crown Royal off the top shelf and poured Dennis and me a glass of whiskey on the rocks. We all sat at the large dinner table and swapped stories. The non-resident hunters were intrigued about our jobs and asked us lots of silly questions about our day-to-day work as a game warden. One non-resident asked, "Have you ever had to shoot anyone? Have you ever been shot at? Another non-resident said, "Man, I don't know how you guys do it. Everyone you deal with has a rifle, pistol, knife, or even bear spray. You are always outnumbered and often times there is alcohol involved with hunting camps." I replied, "Do you mean like right now?" Everyone started laughing, as we were out-numbered in a camp full of weapons with whiskey involved.

The outfitter then served all of us one of the best beef ribeye steaks that I had ever tasted before in my life. It was cooked perfect and nearly two inches thick. It nearly covered my entire plate. We also had a salad and a huge, mashed potato with rich brown gravy. Once dinner was completed the camp cook brought us out a freshly baked apple pie with ice cream. I felt like I was living like a king and getting paid to do what I absolutely loved to do almost every day. Heck, the department bought me a new truck every three years and a new snow machine and ATV every five thousand miles. They paid for camp groceries and reimbursed wardens for horse expenses. It was a great deal of work to get to where I was at in my career, but I felt extremely blessed every day to have the job that I had. I couldn't believe that Dennis had been doing his job for over thirty years in the same warden district. He still worked his butt off every month and rarely ever took a weekend off. It was awesome to meet so many new people each year in the field. It was also pretty cool to have good relationships with outfitters that have your back and always have a warm place for you to sleep, and maybe even a horse to ride if needed. Dennis built these relationships over the years, and that is why we were invited to such a nice dinner.

After dinner we sat around the large kitchen table and told more stories and solved all the world's problems. I ate way too much and the whiskey was going down a little too smoothly. Pretty quick the outfitter brought out a deck of cards and asked if anyone wanted to play poker. Everyone was in agreement to play poker and most bought in for $100 or more. We didn't have any official poker chips so it was decided to use almonds, cashews, and peanuts for chips. One almond was worth five dollars, cashews were worth two dollars, and peanuts were worth one dollar. It was dealer's choice so we played many different poker games throughout the night. Dennis and I couldn't hardly lose a hand all night. Good cards were running us over; I think some of the non-resident hunters were starting to get upset with the game wardens winning most of the night.

At one point I reached over and took a handful of almonds, peanuts, and cashews, threw them in my mouth, chewed them up and swallowed them. One of the non-resident hunters laughed so hard that he pissed his pants and fell over backwards in his chair. Another guy asked him what was so funny. He replied while laughing uncontrollably, "Swerb just ate about $300-worth of peanuts!" SHIT, he was right! I forgot those were my poker chips and I had eaten a whole handful of them. I honestly think I ate several hundred dollars-worth of my chips. Everyone started laughing uncontrollably with tears streaming down their cheeks. I guess it was pretty funny, but not for me. I worked hard all night to gain that pile of almonds, cashews, and peanuts. We all decided it was time for bed after that and cash in our peanuts. One of the non-resident hunters was still laughing and said, "It won't surprise me to see ol' Swerb picking through his morning poop to try and recap some of his winnings." I thought to myself, *That's actually not a bad idea, especially with the almonds at $5.00/ piece.* Just kidding!

I will guarantee you that those non-resident hunters will never forget that night playing poker with the game wardens. Dennis and I had won most of everyone's money, except I didn't have much to show for it. It was a long walk back to the cow camp cabin, stumbling along in the night, tripping over boulders and navigating small creeks. We finally arrived at the very cold cabin. We fumbled around in the dark and eventually got a propane lantern lit.

Dennis said, "Damn, Swerb, A good supervisor would have come over earlier and built a nice warm fire so that I don't have to freeze my ass off again all night."

I replied, "You're right, Dennis, and a good supervisor probably wouldn't have eaten all his poker earnings either."

I poured Dennis and I a light night cap whiskey. We didn't have any ice cubes so I filled two coffee cups full of snow and had a Black Velvet slushy. I don't think Dennis was very impressed, as he preferred bourbon on the rocks. I handed Dennis his drink and he said, "Damn, Swerb, when you get done treating me like royalty would you build a damn fire? I'm cold!"

We both slept well that night in a warm cabin. We set the alarm for 5:00AM. Over the next few days, we covered some really beautiful country and checked more hunters and camps. We didn't come across any other violations, but we had contacted nearly every hunter in the area. This was Dennis's last fall as a Wyoming game warden. I felt very grateful and blessed that I was able to make this trip with him and many others over the years. Even though we totaled out a fishery's ATV, nearly froze to death at night in a teepee tent, and I consumed all my poker winnings, it was well worth it.

Thank you Dennis for 33 years of service to the State of Wyoming

Bernie Holz thanking Dennis Almquist for 33 years of dedicated service

Chapter 3

WILD BILL

If you have read my previous books, you have heard me mention the infamous Wild Bill of the Upper Green River. Well, here we go, it's story time!

Retired north game warden Duke Early first told me about Wild Bill. Duke claimed that he was a mountain man who lived in the Upper Green River area. The man built his own log cabin by hand. He wore handmade rawhide clothing and moccasins. The man wore a beaver skin hat and had a long gray beard that was sometimes braided with elk ivories. He was often seen with a large bowie knife strapped to his waistband; sometimes with an ax on one side and a knife on the other. He had no telephone or power and rarely got along with his neighbors. Duke told me that he raised a pile of German Shepherds, and was illegally feeding them roadkill wildlife. Duke told me that he didn't feel comfortable approaching the man alone, as he or one of his dogs might just kill you! As Duke said that with a laugh, his eyes got bigger! I got the impression that Duke didn't care for him breaking the law, but didn't want to deal with him for fear of getting injured or killed.

This issue never really got resolved, and Duke retired. Hubba Healy was hired a short time later and received word that Wild Bill was feeding his dogs roadkill wildlife. Hubba was not going to tolerate this sort of activity in his warden district. Hubba was a warden that never asked for any help, and by God there was nothing on this green earth that he couldn't handle alone. Hubba could quite possibly be the real Joe Pickett of the Wyoming Game and Fish Department, except he shot his pistol very well.

One day Hubba walked into my office and said, "Swerb, I got a problem that I'm not sure how to handle."

I replied, "What's that, Hubba?" I about fell out of my chair that Hubba Healy was actually asking for advice from his supervisor.

Hubba said, "I have this mountain man living in my warden district who is feeding roadkill wildlife to about 15-20 German Shepherd dogs. I don't really feel comfortable approaching him at his home alone with all them warden-eating dogs running free around the place."

I scratched my head and replied, "Why don't you write him a letter to come meet us at the regional office on a specific date and time, and we will just see if he shows up. Just type up a letter and place it in his mailbox along the highway."

Hubba replied, "That might work, but I don't think he has a driver's license or vehicle insurance for that matter. I guess it's worth a try."

Hubba got up and left my office. He was a man of few words and didn't care to waste many of them visiting with me about anything. Hubba was a very serious and dedicated game warden. He did his job very well and was thorough with his investigations. He pissed a lot of people off, but sometimes that happens when you are doing your job as a game warden.

About two weeks later I heard our office manager Des screech out at the front desk. She yelled, "Oh shit! Wild Bill is headed for the front door!"

I had never met Wild Bill before in person but had heard so many crazy stories about him that I felt like I should know him. I quickly called Hubba and told him to get over to the office right away, as Wild Bill had showed up. Hubba lived in a warden station right across the street from the regional office. I jumped up and looked out the window of the regional office and observed Wild Bill petting one of many German Shepherds in the back of his Toyota truck. Wild Bill then headed for the front door of the office with Hubba trailing right behind him. They walked into the office together. Hubba introduced Wild Bill to me and we stepped into my office and closed the door. My back was against the far wall as I faced Hubba in one corner and Wild Bill in the other corner of my office. I felt uncomfortable being in my office with Wild Bill with my door shut. The man looked plumb crazy to me.

Hubba started out and explained to Wild Bill why we had invited him to the office to speak with us about feeding roadkill wildlife to his dogs. While explaining this, Wild Bill interrupted Hubba and said, "When I was in the war, I swam out into this large river to rescue a man's life. As I got my hands around the man's body to save him, I recognized that he was the enemy." Wild Bill then flew out of his chair towards me and pulled a large bowie knife out of the sheath attached to his belt and held the knife to my throat. He yelled, "I CUT THE MOTHER F-------S THROAT LIKE THIS AND WATCHED HIM FLOAT DOWN THE RIVER, DEAD!"

Wild Bill was in a rage with a knife to my throat, and I nearly shit my pants. Hubba started to draw his pistol in the opposite corner. I looked Wild Bill in the eyes and calmly said, "Wild Bill, please put your knife away and sit back in the chair and don't ever, ever do that again." Wild Bill complied and walked back to his chair to sit down. I noticed Hubba holstering his pistol. I told Wild Bill, "Let's get back to the issue of feeding roadkill wildlife to your dogs". Throughout the conversation Wild Bill would go from topic to topic. At times he was very calm and hard to hear, and then all of a sudden, he would go into a rage about something that we weren't even talking about. He was not making any sense, as if he might be schizophrenic. Hubba and I were getting nowhere with this guy and he was not going to agree to quit feeding his dogs wildlife meat. Wild Bill went on to tell us that he utilized every ounce of the roadkill wildlife. He tanned their hides. He used brain material to tan their hides. He made rawhide clothing out of the tanned hides. He fed the inedible meat to his dogs and ate the edible meat.

I sat patiently and listened to all of this. Personally, I was happy to see that the road-killed animals were not going to waste. I really didn't care about what he was doing, but it was against the law. I actually admired the guy for his way of life and some of his beliefs, but he was certainly a bit crazy. I never figured out if he was trying to intimidate us or if he was crazier than a pet raccoon. Maybe a little bit of both. We finally ended the conversation with him telling us that he was going to write a letter to the chief game warden, Jay Lawson, and get permission to pick up roadkill wildlife to feed his dogs. He said, "Hell, Jay will understand. He was in the Vietnam War himself." We both told him not to do it anymore or he would be cited for it. He said, "I will get permission from the Chief, you will see!" We both shook his hand and escorted him back to his truck. We walked back into the office and Des said, "Well, how did that go? Hubba responded as he looked at me and said, "I told you he was f-----g crazy!" I said, "Yeah, I'm just glad he didn't slit my throat."

A few weeks later I received a copy of a two-page, handwritten letter in the mail that Wild Bill had sent to our chief game warden Jay Lawson. The letter discussed how Wild Bill had seen two albino grizzly bears near his cabin in the Upper Green. He felt like they were spirits from up above. He also discussed a white buffalo on the property. In the letter he stated that he used every part of the animal that he picked up and nothing went to waste. At the bottom of the letter Chief Lawson wrote, "Please contact Bill and give him my authorization to pick up roadkill wildlife in the future, as long as he has them tagged with a Wyoming Interstate Game Tag. Wild Bill was correct. The chief game warden gave him permission to collect roadkill and feed it to his dogs. Hubba was not going to like this news, but it came directly from the Chief. The game tags cost eight dollars, and I doubted that Wild Bill would ever make a special trip to town to have the roadkill legally tagged. But it was what it was, and that's the way it would be.

My phone rang early one morning and a lady said, "Excuse me, sir, but I wanted to call you to get permission to pick up a roadkill moose that was killed on the highway close to my house." I scratched my head for a minute and said, "Is Wild Bill standing in your house right now, putting you up to this?" The lady got really quiet and replied, "Uh, yes, he is."

I said, "Please put me on the phone with him."

Wild Bill answered, "Hello."

I responded, "Wild Bill, you can't have that moose unless you get it tagged with a Wyoming Interstate Game Tag. If you don't get it tagged first, I will cite you for possessing wildlife parts without the proper tag or prior authorization. Leave your neighbor alone about this damn dead moose!"

Wild Bill responded, "I have no driver's license or insurance, and I can't legally get to town to buy the Interstate Game Tag." I then authorized Wild Bill to possess and transport the moose and told him that I would either come out or send Hubba out to get everything legal for him. He was very thankful and hung up the phone. I couldn't believe it! Now he was trying to get his neighbors to pick up the dead wildlife for him!

The next morning, I was in my office when I heard Des screech again, "Wild Bill is here and coming to the front door!"

I got up and met Wild Bill at the front office. I shook his hand and invited him into my office. I didn't close the door this time and asked Des to fill out an affidavit for him to legally possess a roadkill moose. She asked for his driver's license. He responded, "I will have to just give you the information, because I have no driver's license." I waited for this to happen and then invited him back into my office. He sat down in the same chair that he had sat in before. I could not get the thought out of my head from the last time when he sat in that chair, charged me, and put his large bowie knife to my throat. He sat down in the chair and put both hands over his face and began crying. He looked up at me and said, "Could you please close that door for a moment?" I thought, *oh shit, here we go again! I'm back in my office by myself with the crazy mountain man!* I got up and gently closed the door. I started wondering if my pistol had one in the chamber or if maybe I had forgotten to do that the last time that I cleaned it.

I sat there and watched Wild Bill sob for a few moments. I finally asked him what was on his mind.

Wild Bill responded with a faint and crackly voice as he sobbed, "I have no money to feed all my dogs. I have whacked most of them in the head with a pair of fencing pliers. I have one of the most beautiful German Shepherd pups that I have ever raised before in my truck. Scott, I want to give that pup to you, or I will be forced to knock him in the head with my fencing pliers as well."

Wild Bill started sobbing even harder and put both of his hands over his face and placed his head and hands nearly in his lap as he sat in the chair next to me. I didn't know what to say so I just sat there for a few minutes with no reply. Finally, I said, "Wild Bill, I already have four dogs and can't take care of another one. Please don't kill the pup with your fencing pliers. We will find a good home for that dog, I promise."

Wild Bill looked up with tears in his eyes and replied, "Scott, this is the most beautiful dog that I have ever raised before in my life and I want you to take him, PLEASE!" Wild Bill got up out of his chair and said, "Come with me, you need to see this dog." I got up and followed Wild Bill out the front door of the office to his Toyota truck. The dog was in the back of the truck. I reached out and petted the dog on the head. The dog wagged his tail and licked my hand. This dog was only six months old and weighed nearly 100 lbs. He was absolutely the prettiest marked German Shepherd that I had ever seen before in my life. It absolutely broke my heart to not to take this dog. I told Wild Bill what a beautiful dog he was, and that I would work to find him a good home. Wild Bill thanked me and shook my hand.

I thought to myself, *what have I done to earn the confidence and respect in Wild Bill's mind for him to give me his favorite dog?*

Wild Bill grabbed a small brown bag out of the front seat of his truck and asked if we could go back into my office. I said, "Sure, what do you have in the bag?" He replied, "I will show you in a minute, please let's go back to your office." I thought to myself, *here we go again, I'm not sure what is in the bag and we are going back into my office.*" I just never could fully trust the man after he had put a knife to my throat several weeks back.

We stepped back into my office. I was very cautious and watched his hands closely as he reached into the brown paper bag. He pulled out several obsidian arrow heads that he had recently knapped himself. They were absolutely gorgeous points. We then had quite a discussion about Indians and artifacts that were in the Pinedale area. Wild Bill also pulled out a perfect hammer head stone out of the paper bag. He proudly showed it to me and told me that he had found the stone while digging the foundation for his cabin. I told Wild Bill that I also knapped arrowheads and had spent a great deal of my life searching for artifacts. This news really excited him. He got a huge smile on his face and said, "Wait right here, I will be right back!"

He jumped up and went back out to his truck. He returned with another bag full of obsidian chips that he had flaked off a large piece of obsidian. He said with a huge smile on his face, "Scott, please take these beautiful obsidian rocks home with you and see what you can make out of them."

I couldn't believe what I was seeing. Wild Bill showed a different side of himself, and I really started to kind of like the guy. I was fascinated with his lifestyle and how he lived off the land. I actually greatly admired the man, even if he was a little crazy. I thanked him for the obsidian chips and told him that I would try and make him an arrowhead someday with the chips and bring them up to him at his cabin. I didn't know how many of his dogs he had actually killed with fencing pliers, but I had heard rumor that he had around 17 German Shepherd dogs at his home. Wild Bill told me that there were a number of poachers living in the Upper Green River valley and that he would keep an eye out and patrol the valley for me. I thanked Wild Bill and shook his hand firmly as I looked him in the eyes. I thought, *oh dear God, what have I started with Wild Bill being my Deputy Game Warden in the Upper Green? He doesn't even have a phone to call me if someone is violating the law up there. Nor does he have a driver's license to be driving back and forth to town to report violations.*

North Pinedale game warden Hubba Healy absolutely despised the man and would never befriend him to gain any information on anyone. So, there was that. But I always believed as a game warden that you should always keep your friends close and your enemies even closer. If you have a good relationship with your enemies, it makes it that much easier to deal with them when they are caught poaching. Some game wardens have never figured this out, and probably never will. I always believed that a successful game warden needs respect and help from the entire community to catch poachers. Once the public believes in you and respects you, some quit poaching themselves and actually turn in other poachers they know about. I have seen this happen many times in my career. The warden who runs around harassing the public and treating them with disrespect each day gets nowhere in their career. The community ends up disliking them and some people will poach out of spite just because they dislike the game warden so much. A single game warden can't catch every poacher in their district, ever! They need the help of the entire community to patrol for them and report violations.

I even had a known poacher from Pinedale who came up to me one day and shook my hand as he said, "Scott, I just want you to know that I have poached my share of animals in my lifetime. I respect you so much that I would never want to put you in the position of catching me poaching something. Therefore, I have quit poaching altogether, and I have a much deeper appreciation for wildlife and what you do out there every day. I can also tell you that there are others in the valley who have quit poaching due to the respect that they have for you." This was probably one of the best compliments that I ever received from a known poacher.

Fall hunting seasons were now upon us once again. It seemed like I was never ready for hunting season, but it always showed up ready or not. This was my first official hunting season as a game warden supervisor. I found that I was spending less time in the field and more time in the office. We also had just received a new regulation in Western Wyoming making it illegal to collect shed antlers from January 1st through April 30th. This would be a huge workload in itself for the wardens to patrol the entire winter range, looking for illegal antler hunters starting in January. This season would be almost just as busy as the hunting seasons that started September 1st each year.

I was having a long day running from one call to another. I always knew when Hubba was out of town or out of radio signal, because our dispatch center—SALECS—would call me if they could not reach Hubba. I had spent about three days off and on watching a large four-point mule deer that had been standing on private property right next to the main highway between Pinedale and Daniel. The buck was very nice, and I was certain that someone was going to shoot him on private property without permission. Whoever did this would probably also end up shooting from their vehicle and from a public road, which were both illegal. Wardens often utilized wildlife decoys to catch poachers in similar situations. Decoys work very well because it puts the warden, the animal, and the poacher in one spot at one time. I felt like live decoys always worked the best. I had sat hidden in cover at a long distance away watching this live buck for several days. Hubba had also kept an eye on this buck for the past several days, but nobody tried to poach it on private property.

I was in the Daniel area when the call came. "Pinedale, GF-14," blurted my radio. My new call number went from GF-84 to GF-14 when I became supervisor.

I grabbed the mic and replied, "Pinedale GF-14, go ahead with your traffic."

"GF-14, we just received a report that someone has poached a large mule deer buck on private property near the Cora Junction. The RP (Reporting Person) indicated that the suspect is still in the area trying to load the deer."

I responded, "10-4, I'll be en route to that location. I'm only about ten minutes away. Please get the RP's contact information and let him know that I will be there as soon as I can."

"10-4, GF-14, I will pass the information along, thank you," replied SALECS.

I thought, *Damn I missed it! Someone finally poached the large buck deer I've been watching.* I knew exactly what deer had probably been poached. I turned on my red and blue lights and gave it the onion! I was passing cars left and right with the sound of my sirens wailing. I literally arrived at the location in a matter of minutes. As I approached the area an older white truck was just leaving the area. This was a Wonder Bread truck. I also observed drag marks and blood in the snow next to the highway where the white truck had been parked. I pulled in behind the truck and pulled him over. I radioed my location and the license plate number of the truck to SALECS. As I approached the driver's side of the truck, I observed a very tiny man

44

sitting in the front seat driving the truck. The man had a long, braided ponytail nearly down to his ass crack. He looked to be about 5'6" and about 140 pounds.

The man rolled down his window and said, "Can I help you with something?" He was very nervous, and I observed that he had some blood on his hands. I asked him if he had just harvested a deer.

The man replied, "Yes, sir, I did."

I then asked the man for his hunting license. The man showed me his deer license that had been properly filled out. I asked the man if I could look into the back of his bread truck to age the buck deer and record its harvest. He jumped out of the truck and lifted the rear door of the bread truck. The large buck deer had been loaded whole and was not gutted out. I don't even know how to this day that the little man loaded this deer guts and all into the back of that bread truck.

I asked the man, "Why haven't you field dressed this deer yet?"

The man responded, "I'm supposed to be working and I was in a hurry. I will dress it out when I return home tonight.

I responded, "Where's home?"

The man replied, "Evanston."

So, this man was going to deliver bread with an un-gutted buck deer in the back of his bread truck once he returned to Evanston several hours later, and in the dark?

I asked the man where he had killed the deer. He pointed to the other side of the highway and told me that he had initially shot the deer on public ground and that it had jumped the highway right-of-way fence, crossed the highway, and jumped another right-of-way fence and died on private property. I then asked the man to show me his rifle. He produced a .300 Winchester Mag from his passenger seat. I looked at the buck deer and determined that it had been shot right behind the shoulder. I told the man that I didn't buy his story, as I have hunted my whole life and doubted that a deer shot behind the

45

shoulder with a .300 Winchester Magnum could jump a highway fence, cross a highway, and then jump another highway fence.

The man replied, "Well, you can believe whatever you want, but that's what happened."

I asked the man where he shot from.

He responded, "Right over there, from that public ground."

I responded, "So, in order for that to happen you would have had to park your truck alongside the highway. You would have then had to cross the fence onto public property and shoot that deer at a range of approximately 20 yards?"

The man replied, "Yes sir, that is exactly what happened. Now, can I get down the road? I have work to do."

I told the man to sit in his truck as I further investigated the tracks in the snow to try and figure out just what had happened for sure. I knew in my heart that the man had shot from his truck while it was parked in the middle of the public highway and killed the deer on private property without permission. He then loaded the deer as quickly as possible with the guts still in it to get out of the area quickly and not leave any evidence of a poached deer. And yes, this was the buck that I had been watching for several days, and now I'd missed it all and would have to prove my case.

After looking the area over, I could not find any evidence that the man ever got out of his truck. I also could not find any evidence from blood or tracks in the snow that the deer was first shot on public property and jumped the fences while wounded. I went back to the man and interviewed him some more. I told him exactly what I thought had happened, and he denied everything and became agitated with me. The man was right in my face, yelling at me, when I looked up to see another man park alongside the road. The man exited his truck and came walking down the hill towards us. I stepped away from the braided bread boy for a moment. The man looked huge, like he was a weightlifter or something.

The man said, "Hi there, sir, I'm the one who reported this incident. I manage the ranch on which this deer was poached on. I would like this guy charged with trespassing and the deer confiscated."

I told the man that I was in the process of trying to figure out exactly what had happened, but the man was not being truthful with me. I then asked the guy if he had seen anything.

He replied, "No, I did not see anything except the man trying to drag the deer under the right-of-way fence with its guts still in it. That's when I called and reported the incident to your dispatch center. Hey, is this guy giving you problems? I saw him yelling in your face. If he is giving you any problems, I will shove that sawed-off little pony-tailed bastard into a post hole for the rest of his life." I thought, *Wow, it's good to have some backup if needed.* I told the man to head on down the road and that I would call him if I needed any backup. I also thanked him for reporting the incident and checking up on me. We shook hands and he drove off.

I walked back over to the pony-tailed man and said, "Listen, the man who just drove off is the man who reported this incident to me. He also observed everything that you did wrong and just told me the entire story. So, you need to quit telling me your lies and tell me exactly what happened, or I'm hauling your skinny little ass to jail for poaching and I will call your boss for poaching out of the company bread truck!"

The man looked at the ground and said, "I'm sorry, yes, I shot from my truck from the highway and killed the buck in one shot on private property. I'm sorry for not being honest with you, and please do whatever you think you need to do."

I thanked the man for his honesty in the matter and issued him a citation for hunting private property without permission, shooting from a public highway, shooting from a vehicle, and then I confiscated the buck. The whole incident cost the man about $1200. I later gave this buck to a local taxidermist in Pinedale and they agreed to make a life-sized, remote-controlled deer decoy for the department. I couldn't wait to see it when it was done and try it out, hopefully by next fall.

I have learned over the years that sometimes even the game warden may need to fib a bit in order to get the truth when dealing with poaching dirt bags.

I jumped back into my patrol truck and cleared my stop with SALECS. About that time my bag phone was ringing. It was Des, our office manager in Pinedale. I answered, "Hello, Disney, what's up?"

"Hello; have you seen or heard from Hubba for the last few days?"

"No, I haven't."

"Well, we have a situation going on right now in the Upper Green with Wild Bill and I can't get in touch with Hubba. Can you take the call?"

"Sure, what do you have going on?"

"Apparently, Wild Bill is holding a couple of people at gun point on the Circle S Ranch. They are in a tractor and he won't let them leave the area."

I thought, *Oh, dear God! I knew something like this was going to happen when he told me that he would patrol the Upper Green for me.*

I flipped the switch to my tiny little red and blue lights that were mounted on my front grill guard and gave it the onion to the Circle S Ranch, which was located approximately twenty miles to my north. I then flipped the switch to turn on my sirens. I could barely hear them. *My speaker must be packed full of mud again.* It was elk season and the Circle S Ranch did not allow any hunting ever! I had purchased hay from the Circle S Ranch for many years for the elk feed grounds but had not ever met the owner of the ranch. Apparently, the owner was a female and had ownership in the Indianapolis 500 Speedway. I had always wanted to meet this lady someday; she seemed very nice over the phone during our conversations regarding purchasing hay.

I drove past the Circle S Ranch and turned left onto a narrow two-track road. The road had tall willows about 8'-10' feet high on both sides and was just wide enough to drive down the road without scratching your truck. After a short distance I noticed a man wearing buckskin clothing standing in the middle of the road with a rifle pointed towards a tractor. The tractor had two male occupants in the cab and a large six-point elk loaded in the front-end bucket. I drove up next to Wild Bill.

Wild Bill looked at me with his rifle still pointed at the men in the tractor and said, "I got them poaching sonsabitches! They poached that bull elk on the Circle S right out in the hay meadow. They shot from that fence over there across the Green River."

I thanked Wild Bill for his great deputy game warden skills and told him to return back to his cabin and I would meet up with him later. I wanted Wild Bill out of the area so that he didn't escalate the situation any more than it needed to be. Wild Bill agreed to go back to his cabin as he lowered his rifle and flipped off both men in the tractor and yelled something at them that I couldn't understand. The rifle that Wild Bill was holding appeared to be a .50 caliber black powder rifle. So, he was only going to get one shot off but I'm sure the men in the tractor did not know what kind of rifle was being pointed at them.

I approached the tractor on foot and moved up the steps of the tractor to visit with the men inside. As I opened the door on the cab of the large John Deere tractor, both men's eyes were the size of silver dollars.

The driver of the tractor said, "Who in the f--- is that crazy bastard?"

I replied, "That's Wild Bill; he is a mountain man who owns a cabin just up the hill in the trees. He is the one who reported you guys for trespassing and killing this elk on the Circle S property."

The driver of the tractor replied, "Well, that is one crazy son of a bitch! He came running out of the willows over there with a bowie

49

knife in one hand and a rifle in the other. He told us to back away from the elk while we were gutting it out. We put our hands in the air and backed away from the elk. He then took his bowie knife and cut the heart and liver out of the elk and took a bite out of each one of them. He then cut up the heart and liver into small pieces and shoved them into the pockets of his rawhide coat."

I almost crapped my pants when I heard that story. I replied, "Yeah, that's Wild Bill and that sounds about right."

I asked the men to get out of the tractor and show me their hunting licenses. I learned that they were brothers and only one brother had a coveted limited quota elk license valid for the area. This brother was from out of state and staying with his brother who lived a short distance up the hill. I also learned that the brother who lived in the area was a taxidermist and the father-in law to a newly hired game warden trainee stationed in Cody, Wyoming. The men told me that they had shot from their private property across the river and killed the large six-point bull elk. They also told me that they had permission to hunt the ranch property. I knew they didn't have permission because I had just spoken with the ranch manager the previous week and he told me that nobody has permission to hunt the ranch EVER! I told the men to take the elk up to their house and hang it in the shop while I finished conducting my investigation. They agreed and left the area in the large tractor. I never did figure out who the owner of the tractor was.

I got back in my truck and headed down to visit with the ranch manager at headquarters to make sure that the men didn't have permission to hunt the ranch property. I didn't know the ranch manager well at all, I had only talked to him once before. I walked up on the porch of the beautiful log home and banged on the door. The ranch manager opened the door and shook my hand.

He said, "Thanks for coming over! I'm glad you caught them poaching bastards; please come in and sit down if you have a minute."

50

I entered the beautiful home and followed the man into the kitchen. Sitting at the kitchen table was Wild Bill.

Wild Bill looked at me and said, "Well, did you confiscate that elk and issue them bastards a citation? If you confiscate that elk, I would like to have it! That is a beautiful bull elk."

I replied, "Wild Bill, you already stole and ate their heart and liver, what more do you want?"

Wild Bill did not reply. He pulled his bowie knife out of the knife sheath on his left side and began sharpening it on a smooth rock at the kitchen table.

I looked at Bill and said, "Dammit Bill, could you please put that knife away until we're done visiting?"

Wild Bill slowly put the knife back in his sheath and mumbled, "Sorry."

I noticed he still had blood in his long gray beard and around the corners of his mouth from eating the heart and liver. I didn't push the theft of their heart and liver. I figured that was Wild Bill's reward for catching them and turning them in. After visiting with the ranch manager, it was made very clear to me that the two men did not have permission to hunt the ranch property. I returned to the area where the bull had been killed. After about an hour of looking around I discovered where the man had shot from. He'd leaned over a fence post on someone else's private property and shot the elk across the Green River. I located two spent .270 shell casings in the grass at the base of the fence post in the tall grass. I was very lucky to have found the brass from the man's rifle. I would have never found them without Wild Bill telling me where the man had shot from. Not only did they trespass on the land where the elk was killed, they also trespassed on private property to shoot. I collected the shell casings and headed up to the house where the elk was supposed to be hanging in a large metal shop building.

Upon arriving at the man's house, both men were standing outside and the elk was hanging in the large shop by its antlers with the shop door open. I questioned both men and asked the hunter where he had shot from and what caliber of rifle he used to kill the elk.

The non-resident hunter replied, "I used a .270 caliber rifle and shot from my brother's property boundary right down there." He pointed down the hill towards the river.

I then asked the man, "How many times did you shoot, and can I see your rifle?"

The man responded, "I shot three times" as he handed me the scoped rifle.

I grabbed the bolt of the man's rifle and ejected a spent cartridge that was still in the chamber of the rifle. I then grabbed the two empty shell casings out of my pocket and handed all three empty shell casings to man.

I said, "You are correct. You shot three times, but you didn't shoot from your brother's property boundary. You trespassed on someone else's property down by the river when you shot that bull elk."

The man later admitted to lying to me and fessed up to where he had actually shot from. Both brothers were very nervous during the interview.

I requested the non-resident hunter to come over to my patrol truck, away from his brother. He agreed and sat in the passenger seat of my patrol truck. I explained to the man that I was going to confiscate the bull elk and issue him a citation for $450 for hunting on private property without permission.

The man began to cry and said, "Sir, you can't do that! You see, this is the first bull elk that I have ever harvested and I'm dying of cancer!"

I replied, "I'm sorry to hear that but I'm going to confiscate the bull elk and issue you a citation. You simply can't just shoot an animal on someone else's private property without permission. Besides that, you even lied to me about where you shot from."

The man started weeping even harder. He was having a hard time breathing. He said, "Sir, you don't understand. My house recently caught fire and burned to the ground. I lost everything I own except this elk license." The man pulled out his elk license from his wallet and said, "Look at the edges of this license; you can see the charred burn marks around the edge of the license. The only reason it survived was because it was in my leather wallet."

I looked at the license; it did appear to have burn marks around the top edges. I explained to the man that I was sorry for everything that he had been through but I was still going to confiscate the elk and issue him a citation. The man started crying again and exited my patrol truck. He walked over and joined his brother. I grabbed my citation book and headed over to the two brothers, as I would need the man's driver's license to issue the citation. As I approached the men, the other brother was on the phone with the owner of the ranch. He was pleading with her to not file trespass charges against his brother, as they had just made an honest mistake. He asked the lady if she would please talk to the game warden and handed me his cell phone.

I said, "Hello, this is Scott. How are you doing today?"

She responded, "I'm doing well, but if these guys made an honest mistake, I don't wish to have them cited for trespassing. I just want to be neighborly, if you know what I mean?"

I responded, "You need to understand that they didn't make an honest mistake. They very blatantly trespassed on your ranch to kill a trophy-class bull elk right in your hay field by the river."

She said, "I know, but they are my neighbors and I don't wish to have them fined. But they know from here on out that I don't allow any hunting on my property in the future."

I replied, "Okay, if that is what you want, I will let the man keep the trophy elk and issue him a written warning to document the violation."

She replied, "Thank you, Scott, and I'm sorry, I look forward to selling you more hay this coming spring and maybe we can actually meet sometime. Good-bye."

I couldn't believe what I had just heard. These men blatantly poached a trophy bull elk right in her hayfield and she didn't want them trespassed! Two men could have been killed that day by Wild Bill and I wasted four hours of my life dealing with the mess. At this point, I was sure wishing that the North Pinedale game warden Hubba Healy had been available to take this call. As for Wild Bill, we became closer friends after this event. He even got to where he would occasionally bring cinnamon rolls to the office. Office manager Des Brunette would look at me with a smile and say, "Are you actually going to eat those?"

Chapter 4

ROCK CREEK

I received a tip one day from a man who had probably been drunk since the 6th grade. He told me that he had information on a man who was scab-outfitting (illegally guiding hunters without an outfitters license). He told me that the man operated alone and that he would be in the Water Dog Lake/Rock Creek area around mid-October. He said that he thought the man's name was Jake and that he was from Rocksprings. I didn't know how credible this man was because I had never seen him sober before. Anyhow, I gathered the information and kept it in my jumbo planner for a later date. I also drew a coveted deer license that fall that was in the same area that the illegal outfitter may be camping in. This area was known to produce huge mule deer over the years. Several large buck deer are currently in the Boone and Crocket record book that were harvested in this area. My wheels were starting to turn. I thought maybe I could plan a wilderness deer hunt in this area and go horseback in plain clothes and pose as a hunter to catch this guy that was allegedly illegally outfitting. Game wardens in Wyoming rarely wear their red shirts while patrolling horseback in the high country. We do this so that we can blend in with the rest of the hunters, as our bright red shirt can be seen for miles from other hunters.

I had never been in this area much before. I would have to do my homework about how to get in there on horseback and learn the lay of the land and the trail system. I had a friend who worked for the Forest Service who knew that country very well. He was also an avid deer hunter who had spent many days chasing large bucks around in the high country. I met him at his office one day during the noon hour. He was happy to tell me everything he knew about the area. He also told me that there was only one good camping spot at the end of the trail before you drop off into Rock Creek drainage. He pulled out a map and drew a circle where the camping spot was. He also got really excited and told me that he had seen a true 40" wide mule deer buck in this area earlier that summer. He said the buck had a lot of trash and a drop tine. This got me really excited. I then told him that I had drawn a deer license for that area and was planning on doing some hunting up there. He grabbed his map and made a red circle right where he had last seen this buck. Apparently, he had seen the buck in a small grass clearing surrounded by heavy pine trees. He got so excited to hear that I had a license that he even agreed to go with me to try and find him. I appreciated that but didn't want anyone with me while I was investigating the illegal outfitter. If there even was such a thing. The last thing that he said was, "Be careful up there; I swear there is a grizzly bear behind every tree. I run into them every time I go up there." *OH GREAT!* I thought to myself.

I sat down with my wife Lana and started planning my trip. The more I thought about it, I decided to have Lana take me in with horses and leave me somewhere for a week. This way I would be less noticeable with a camp in the trees somewhere and no horses to take care of or be seen by others. I would take my rifle and orange hat and blend in as a hunter. And I might get a chance to shoot a 40" wide deer. Lana would then come back with horses in a week and pack me out. I was really getting excited about this trip.

The day before we were going to pack into the area, Lana got a call from her parents in Shell. They requested her help on their guest ranch to assist with some dudes that were staying there. Lana hung up the phone and said, "I guess you will need to pack yourself into Rock Creek because I need to go home and help Mom and Dad tomorrow with some dudes." This threw a wrench into my plans. I didn't have any of my camping gear ready, and didn't even know which horses to take now that Lana would be taking some of our horses with her to Shell. She also told me that she really needed the horse that I had planned on packing my stuff in with.

I said, "But honey, what horse will I use to pack all my stuff in with? We don't have another pack horse!"

Lana responded, "Just take Trooper; he has never packed before but he is a good horse and will do just fine."

I thought, *oh good Lord, here we go again! Just pack a horse that has never been packed before into the rugged mountains of Wyoming. What could go wrong? It will be fun!*

My wife and I had bought a lot of cheap horses over the years. She would ride them daily, moving and roping cattle; this made good horses out of them over time. We would then eventually resell them for more money. Because most of them were young and green broke I'm not sure I ever knew what a good horse actually was. But I did know that I didn't have any patience for horse nonsense in the mountains. To be honest, I never really cared for horses or had the patience to deal with them. They were just another tool to me to get me around the mountains and pack out harvested animals. A tool like a motorcycle, snow machine, or an ATV. Lana would go on most pack trips with me and take care of the horses while I worked. She loved everything about taking care of and riding horses. She generally wasn't happy with life unless she was on a horse seven days a week. I grew up riding a motorcycle and always had a reliable engine under my ass. If you got bucked off your motorcycle it was generally your fault. Horses can blow up for no reason and leave your ass sitting on the ground within seconds of you thinking what a wonderful horse you were just riding. Don't ask me how I know!

So, I spent all the next morning packing differently than I had planned and hoped that Trooper still had all his shoes on and that I could catch him. I didn't know Trooper very well, as we had only owned him for a short time. He was actually easy to catch and seemed eager to get into the trailer with Champ. By the time I got everything organized, packed, and horses loaded it was after lunch. I had to remember all my camping equipment, food, law enforcement equipment, and hunting equipment. I knew in my mind that I was getting too late of a start and may be riding in the dark before I reached the only good camping spot up there. I also remembered to bring my map with the marked circles of the camping spot and where the large mule deer buck was last seen by my friend.

I finally reached the north Beaver Creek trailhead early that afternoon. As I drove to the end of the road I noticed several hunting camps in the area. I was hoping that there would be no camps, as I didn't want other hunters to see my green patrol truck and horse trailer at the trail head for a week and know that a game warden was in the area. This was also why I wanted Lana to pack me in, drop me off and leave the area. If someone was illegally outfitting, they would know that the game warden was in the area, making it even harder to catch them. To prove an illegal outfitting case was always very difficult. You had to prove that money was exchanging hands and it wasn't just a friend taking another friend hunting for no compensation. This often resulted in obtaining search warrants to look at bank accounts to prove your case. You also generally needed a great deal of probable cause to get a judge to sign off on the warrant to look at someone's bank accounts. So, these cases were a lot of work that sometimes took years of investigation to solve. The Outfitter's Board had hired two investigators who did nothing but investigate this sort of illegal activity. And since all the licensed outfitters in the state had to pay an annual fee for their license, it made them very upset when someone was "scab outfitting" in the area that they are allowed to hunt in. Generally speaking, wardens would determine if they thought someone might be illegally outfitting and then turn the case over to the investigator working for the Outfitter's Board. Some cases were much easier when the hunter being interviewed admitted to paying for the service offered by the illegal outfitter.

So, there I was at the trail head in my green truck and personal horse trailer. The department would not buy me a horse trailer because I didn't use one as much as the other wardens. They would pay me for renting my horse trailer at $35.00/month. I can tell you that $35.00/month is not much money to beat your brand-new horse trailer up and down nasty rutted up roads with huge rocks in them. It also doesn't pay much for a new set of tires and an occasional broken axle and flat tire. But it was something, and I was happy for that.

I tried to park out of sight from other hunters and hide my truck in the trees the best that I could. I unloaded my horses and tied them to the side of my trailer. I was hoping that Trooper would behave himself while I tried packing him for the first time. I was actually a little worried about it. What if he threw a walleyed fit and I wasn't able to get all my stuff packed on him and into the mountains? Well, that's exactly what he did! I could not get anything on him. He was afraid of the panniers every time that I approached him. He was being an absolute spoiled little jerk! He pulled back on the lead rope, struck the side of the trailer with his front foot several times, then whirled around and tried to kick me. I was getting nowhere and was starting to get concerned.

A heard a voice from behind me yell, "What kind of hitch ya gonna tie today?"

I turned around and observed a very short man with a huge cowboy hat and a beer belly. He had a southern accent, short red goatee, and a big ol' belt buckle. He was also smoking a stubby little cigar. I thought, *Hell, I don't know what kind of hitch I'm going to tie! I will be happy to just get the son of a bitch packed.* I also thought this sawed-off little guy was probably from Texas.

I don't think the man had seen the earlier problems that I was having trying to pack ol' Trooper. I kindly responded with a smile, "Heck, I don't know; probably a standard box hitch."

The short man responded with a southern drawl and the cigar still in his mouth, "You all ever tried a Tennessee box hitch?"

I responded, "Nope, I don't believe I have ever seen that hitch before. I would love for you to teach a Wyoming game warden your Tennessee box hitch."

The man yelled back toward his camp in the nearby trees, "HEY GET OVER HERE, WE NEED TO TEACH THIS WYOMING GAME WARDEN HOW TO TIE A DAMN TENNESSEE BOX HITCH; HE'S NEVER SEEN ONE BEFORE!

About that time three other guys came over, wearing cowboy hats and their pants tucked into their boots. I thought, *oh good God, this is going to be a rodeo with four city slickers or super punchers trying to pack a horse that has never been packed before.*

I introduced myself to all of them and told them the horse was acting a little skittish this afternoon and hadn't been packed much this year.

The short guy responded, "That's all right, we will get him packed; just stand back and learn a new hitch that you are going to love."

Hell, I didn't care about no new hitch. I would use bungee cords, if need be, just whatever got the job done. It's not always about just looking cool as the High Country Ranger in your red shirt! Champ was already saddled, so I just climbed up in the saddle and got some distance from them so that we didn't have a big wreck with Champ tied to the horse trailer.

I never laughed so hard in my life. Those four yee-hawers got the shit kicked out of them by ol' Trooper before they finally got him packed. Hell, two guys had Trooper in a headlock and were biting down on both of his ears while the other two tied down the pack. When the dust cleared there were sunglasses, cigars, and cowboy hats lying everywhere on the ground. One ol' boy had a bloody nose and his hair was hanging down in his eyes as he looked for his glasses. Trooper was done being an asshole and just stood their wide-eyed with his nostrils flared. He was like *DAMN, WHAT JUST HAPPENED*!

I said, "Looks good, men; I'll damn sure give your hitch a try and see how it holds up today with ol' Trooper. If you could just hand me his lead rope quick, I can get headed up the mountain before it gets dark."

The little fat guy handed me the lead rope and said, "I think yer gonna like that hitch."

I headed up the trail with a smile on my face. There was no way that I would have ever gotten Trooper packed alone. And there was no way that I could tie the hitch that they had just done because there were too many guys flying around to even see how they tied it. I was hoping Trooper would be broke to pack by the time we got to camp. I had packed two bottles of trail shortener: One bottle on my pack horse and one bottle on my riding horse in the saddle bags. I learned over the years to not put all of your whiskey on one horse just in case you have an accident and get separated. Don't ask me how I know.

Everything was going just great as we neared Water Dog Lakes. I pulled my flip phone out of my rear pocket and discovered that I had one bar of cell service. I thought, *I'll call Lana and let her know that everything is going all right.* This would be the only area that I would have a cell signal for the rest of the trip.

I called Lana and she actually answered. I told her that everything was going just fine and that we had reached Water Dog Lakes with no issues.

Lana responded, "That's great; how was Trooper to pack?"

I responded, "He did just fine, honey, and I learned a new hitch from some Texas hunters."

I didn't want to waste my one bar of cell signal telling her that people could have died or been seriously injured packing ol' Trooper. I told her that everything was going just fine and that I was getting close to where I would camp for the night. I told her that I loved her and said goodbye. Just as soon as I got my cell phone back into my rear pocket an antelope came running out of the trees to my left. It stopped about twenty yards from us and snorted and quickly ran off over the hill, out of sight. This all happened very fast, which spooked Champ; and me for that matter. There should not be any antelope at 9000 feet elevation running out of a thick patch of lodgepole pine trees.

Champ snorted back at the antelope and veered hard to his right with a small buck. This got me out of my saddle and I landed face first in the fresh soft black dirt of a newly constructed gopher mound. I held onto Champ's reins and he only dragged me for a short distance. I was uninjured and thought *holy shit I just hung up the phone with Lana telling her that everything was alright and within ten seconds of that I was bucked off and lying face first in a gopher mound.* Champ was still snorting and his nostrils were flared, but I was able to get back on without incident. Trooper was pretty buzzed up as well but behaved pretty well, considering what had just happened.

It was getting near dark as I continued up the trail. The trail was very rough and steep and faded in many areas. Sometimes I had to use my imagination to find the horse trail. I had reached the summit of the mountain and was getting close to the area where my Forest Service friend had told me to camp. As I rode out of the trees and into a grassy meadow, I noticed several large wall tents in the area that I was planning on camping. This was not good, as it was now almost dark and this is where the trail ended.

I noticed about eight horses tied to various trees in the camp. There was a pile of riding saddles piled up un-professionally on the ground by one of the wall tents. There were pack saddles and bridles hanging somewhere in almost every tree in the area. It was a very sloppy-looking camp to say the least. I thought, *I wonder if this is the camp of the illegal outfitter.*

A slender young man came walking out of his tent with his hair a mess and standing on end. He had no hat on and it looked like maybe he had just woken up from a nap. The man approached me and said, "Good evening, can I help you with something?" I replied that I was just doing some deer hunting in the area and looking for a place to camp.

The man replied, "Well, you are at the end of the trail here and you're welcome to pitch a tent for the night in my camp if you would like."

This all happened fast and caught me off guard, especially if this was the illegal outfitter's camp that I was looking for. I replied, "Thanks for your generosity, but I don't feel good camping right on top of you. I will head down into Rock Creek and find a place to camp down there for the night."

The man responded, "Well, if I was you, I wouldn't try that in the dark. There is a lot of down-fall and no trail. I can cook you some dinner while you unpack and set up your camp if you would like."

I responded, "Thank you very much, I really appreciate that, but I'll make a mile on down to the bottom of Rock Creek and camp there tonight."

The man responded, "Oh, by the way my name is Jake" as he reached out to shake my hand.

I responded, "Nice to meet you, Jake. My name is Steve and I'm from Baggs, Wyoming." I pulled that out of my ass and would probably have to make up some more bullshit if Jake asked me a bunch of questions. I thought this might be a good opportunity to ask him some questions as well.

I said, "Well, nice to meet you Jake, are you up here doing some hunting? Where are you from?"

Jake responded, "No, I'm not hunting; I'm just waiting for some friends to come up and stay with me in a few days. One of my buddies has a deer tag for the area. I live south of Rocksprings."

I thought to myself, *Eight horses and three wall tents for one friend with a deer tag?* Not to mention whoever was coming in would probably have their own horses to get into this remote area. Maybe this man would be meeting them at the trailhead and bring them in himself? What if they saw my green patrol truck parked in the trees at the trailhead? This was probably the guy I was looking for, as the drunk had told me that the guy's name might be Jake and that he was from Rocksprings. I didn't have time to visit with the man at the moment because it was dark and I still needed to bushwhack my way down into Rock Creek and get my camp set up. I told Jake that it was nice to meet him and that maybe we would run into each other again over the next few days. I shook his hand and started to leave on Champ.

Jake said, "Nice Tennessee box hitch; I haven't seen that much in this country before."

I almost crapped my pants when I heard that comment. Maybe the hunters that helped me get Trooper packed were the same guys that this guy would be guiding illegally. They would know that I was a game warden and tip Jake off, probably in the morning. Jake would then know that I was lying to him and wasn't a hunter from Baggs, Wyoming. What had I gotten myself into? If Lana had just hauled me in and dropped me off, we wouldn't be having this problem right now. But heck, maybe these people didn't even know one another and I was over-thinking things again.

I responded, "Thanks, I just recently learned it and really like it so far."

I left his camp and headed into the thick timber ahead. It was only about one hundred yards later that I found myself in a tangled mess of trees and could not see anything in the night. I jumped off Champ and started working my way over down trees and thick timber. I was worried that a horse might jump over a dead tree and land on my foot or leg and break it in the middle of nowhere. Champ and Trooper were literally walking on top of dead trees to get through the mess. Some of the dead trees were on top of other dead trees and at times we were four feet above the ground, trying to work our way down the mountain. At one point I had a sheer cliff on my left and straight up to my right with down timber. I would have to jump over three dead trees in a row while climbing straight up. I took off running as fast as I could, leading Champ to gain momentum up the hill to jump the first of three trees. I cleared the first tree and was quickly running out of energy to jump the next tree. Champ and Trooper were lunging forward behind me, digging all four feet into the ground at once to get traction to go up the steep hill. I tripped over the second tree and fell to the ground. Champ and Trooper went right over the top of me, lunging with all they had to get up the steep hill or fall off the cliff a short distance to our left.

Both horses made it to the top and stopped and waited for me to catch up. We all nearly went off the cliff to our left, which would have been hundreds of feet to fall to the bottom of the canyon. How two horses ran over the top of me in the night without stepping on me was a miracle in itself. To this day I don't know how I made it through that mess without injury. I must have had another guardian angel working overtime.

I finally came out of the trees into a small meadow near a creek. The grass was waist-high and water was close for the horses. I decided to set up my camp on the edge of the trees near the meadow and creek. This would also be a good place to highline the horses for the night and plenty of room to hobble them in the morning.

For those of you who have experienced this sort of trip by yourself, you know how much work it is. The horses needed to be watered and fed after unpacking Trooper in the night with a headlamp. A highline between two trees would need to be set up to tie the horses to at night. This generally meant limbing and climbing trees. You would also need a couple of trees that were far enough apart for both horses to stand comfortably and not get tangled up with one another. Rocks would need to be gathered for a campfire and wood collected. I refused to be on a pack trip in mountains without a campfire. Especially with grizzly bears and wolves in the area. It took me a couple hours to get organized but I finally had a fire going and dinner cooking. I would need to hang all my food high up in a tree to keep the grizzly bears out of it at night. I put everything that was edible in my soft pannier and threw my lash rope over a tree branch about twelve feet high and hoisted it up as high as I could get it. The food would be high off the ground and about 100 yards from my sleep tent. I had a simple canvas teepee tent to sleep in, with no cots this time.

My belly was full, the fire was crackling and popping, and the stars were absolutely beautiful. I finally had time to pack my small metal cup with snow and pour some Jack Daniels in it and enjoy the fire. I was lying on my back next to the fire with my head propped up on a rotten log gazing at the stars and sipping my drink. I thought, *This is what life is all about, not many people ever get to experience something like this. This is one of the most beautiful nights that I have ever spent the night out in.* About that time the horses started to whinny and snort while tied on the highline. They were looking off into the dark, as if they had spotted something. Horses have an excellent sense of smell and are generally pretty good at letting you know if you have any intruders coming into camp, well before you know it.

It was at this time that I heard my first official wolf howl. The wolf was only about fifty yards away and extremely loud. It was one of the most amazing and loud sounds that I had ever heard before. It was really similar to having a large bull elk bugle right next to you in the trees. It literally made the hair on my entire body stand up.

I thought it was pretty cool, until I heard another wolf howl behind me and then another one off to my left. I didn't know what was going on but it was getting kind of eerie. I stoked the fire and poured another whiskey. By now I estimated that there were about ten to twelve wolves that had me circled and were all howling at the same time. The howling was very loud and echoed down the canyon below. I thought, *if your one of those people from New York that supported the reintroduction of wolves just to hear a wolf howl, your damn sure welcome to join me right now!* This was one of the scariest moments of my life. I didn't know much about wolf behavior and they didn't seem very concerned about my fire, my horses, or even me for that matter. I grabbed my bear spray and my .270 rifle. I also made sure my duty pistol was locked and loaded. We had just traded in our 9mm Beretta pistols for a .40 caliber Glock. I felt much better about packing the Glock than the 9mm. I wanted to shoot my pistol in the air and yell and scream like a little school girl. But I also wanted to hunt for the 40" deer in the morning and didn't want to scare everything out of the entire drainage. The wolves came within about thirty yards of my fire. I turned on my headlamp and could actually see the eyes of several wolves glaring a red color in the night. They were constantly moving and never stood still.

I don't know if it was me or the Jack Daniels talking, but I jumped up and ran straight towards one of the wolves yelling, "GET THE F—K OUT OF MY CAMP!" as I threw a large rock towards the wolf. I was relieved that the wolf turned around and ran off into the night. After that I never heard another wolf howl and that was okay with me. I didn't sleep very well that night.

The next morning, I awoke at daylight to the sound of my horses whinnying. They were probably hungry or thirsty, or both. I did not see any bears or wolves in the area. But as I was glassing the hill north of the creek, I located several nice buck deer high up on the mountain side. These were very nice bucks, possibly bigger than anything that I had ever harvested before. I got so excited glassing the large bucks that I walked away from camp and sat down next to the creek where I could see them better. They were high up on the side of the mountain above me. The mountain side had scattered pine trees with waist-high sage brush. It was perfect habitat for large mule deer and absolutely some of the most beautiful country that I had never seen before.

After glassing the deer for nearly thirty minutes I observed something interesting. I started seeing deer running everywhere through the trees and sagebrush high up on the mountain side. All of the deer were headed down the mountain, kind of towards me but further down the creek. I observed a hunter wearing orange, walking and carrying a rifle towards the deer. There were deer jumping up way out in front of the hunter. The deer couldn't even see the hunter, as he was so far away. I finally figured out that the wind was blowing towards the deer and the deer were smelling the scent of the hunter as he moved towards them. This caused over one hundred deer to haul ass off the mountain. And they were headed in my direction!

I grabbed my backpack, rifle, and orange hat and hauled ass down the creek bottom to get a better look at all the deer. Once in position I observed one of the coolest things that I had ever seen before. I counted over one hundred deer, with twenty-three of them being four-point bucks or bigger that walked right by me single file. Several of the bucks were larger than anything that I had ever harvested before, and I have harvested some nice deer over the years! Hunting large mule deer was a passion of mine growing up as a child on Bear Creek Ranch. One hunter had single-handedly moved every deer off that mountainside because the wind was at his back. I doubt he'd even seen a single deer run off ahead of him because they were so far away. The deer went by me less than one hundred yards away. I thought really hard about shooting one of the bucks that was about thirty inches wide and would score well over 180 Boone and Crockett points. But I still had hopes and visions of seeing the buck that was 40 inches wide and supposed to be in that same area, as reported by my friend. This was so cool to watch all of these large four-point bucks so close. I was very excited about hunting in this area. I decided I had better get back to camp and let the horses feed and drink.

I put the horses out on their hobbles next to my tent. They were hungry and the grass was tall. I crawled back into my tent to look at my map and try and decide where I might want to hunt in the evening. While in the tent I thought I heard the distinct sound of horses running off with their hobbles on. Don't ask me how I know this distinct sound, but I do and it's not a good sound.

I poked my head out of the tent and the horses were gone. I figured they were thirsty and maybe headed down to the creek for a drink. I walked a short distance from camp to look down into the creek. No horses anywhere! I thought, *damn where did they go so quickly to get completely out of site?* I started to panic because they were flat gone out of sight in a matter of seconds. I grabbed their lead ropes and walked over to look for tracks in the snow along the tree line south of my camp. While over there I found tracks of horses headed up through the thick timber in the direction of the illegal outfitter's camp. I followed the horse tracks the best that I could up the steep mountainside through the downed timber. There were places that I could actually see hoof marks on top of the downed trees were a horse had stepped onto the dead trees to get over them. I had not yet eaten anything that morning because the large mule deer got me excited. I had no food, no coat, no water, and was headed up a steep mountain slope with two lead ropes in my hand. I was bound and determined to catch up with the horses before they made it all the way back home. The tracks in the trees were headed towards home. Not a good sign.

I broke out of the trees at the top of the mountain into a large grassy meadow. I lost the horse tracks in the meadow but they were last seen headed towards the outfitter's camp which was just up the mountain a short distance away. I was absolutely exhausted and hungry. I thought to myself, *those damn horses will be at the outfitters camp because there are other horses there and they have been there before.* I said a few prayers and headed for the outfitter's camp.

I arrived at the camp and it looked like there was nobody around. Except all of Jake's horses were still there and mine were not. This made my heart sink as I knocked on the tent flap of one of the large wall tents. To my surprise, Jake came out, with his hair standing on end, rubbing his eyes as if he had been sleeping again.

Jake looked at me standing there with the two lead ropes and said, "Are you looking for a couple of horses?"

I don't know why I replied the way that I did, but I said, "Nope, just jump-roping in the wilderness, Jake." (Here's your sign.)

Jake rubbed his eyes and said, "They haven't been here that I'm aware of."

But how would he know, if he was sleeping? I told Jake that they were wearing hobbles and that I had tracked them up through the trees into a grassy meadow until I lost their tracks.

Jake responded, "Wait, where did you come up through the trees?"

I explained everything to Jake and he replied, "Those weren't your horse tracks, those are mine from yesterday. I led a couple of horses right up through all that downfall and came out into that meadow."

I said, "Well, heck, maybe I'm on a wild goose chase. I will go back down to camp and look for different tracks in the snow."

I thanked Jake and headed back down the mountain. I got back to my camp and went back to the area where I had found the horse tracks. I walked another twenty yards along the tree line and observed large grizzly bear tracks in the snow with another set of horse tracks going back up the mountain in the same area that I had just hiked up previously. Heck, this is why the horses left in the first place, because a grizzly bear came out of the trees right next to them. It all made sense to me now. I followed the horse tracks all the way back up through the trees towards the large grassy meadow again. The tracks came out in the meadow again and I lost them, but they were last seen headed in the direction of the trailhead. I frantically hiked back over to Jake's camp and told him what I had discovered.

Jake said, "Well, hell, if they are headed home, we will go find them, even if we have to ride all the way out. Grab a saddle and a horse and we will go find them."

I looked at the pile of saddles on the ground and said, "Does it matter what saddle or what horse I use?"

Jake replied, "No, just grab a saddle and a bridle off the tree branch and fit it to whatever horse you prefer."

So, I picked the horse closest to me and fitted him with a saddle and bridle. Everything was completely out of adjustment. This was a very tall and lean looking horse. I put a foot in the stirrup and mounted the horse. The horse reared up and was ready to go; he nearly went over backwards with me and scared the shit out of me. To keep from getting bucked off I walked the horse in tight circles while Jake saddled his horse. It took Jake forever to get mounted on his horse! The whole time I was trying to keep my borrowed horse from bucking me off.

Jake finally came up to me as I was pulling back on this crazy horse and said, "Why don't you go ahead and lead."

I said, "I don't think that will be a problem, this horse wants to go!"

Jake replied, "Oh, shit, I should have told you that's an ex-race-horse from Texas."

I thought, *a race horse in Texas? Did this horse belong to the guys at the trailhead that helped me pack Trooper? I'm pretty sure they were all from Texas. Shit Swerb, now you are on a runaway ex-race horse from Texas while investigating an illegal outfitter.*

71

I gave the horse some rein and that son of a bitch took off like he was coming in first place in the Kentucky Derby. I had never seen such a thing! Every time that I pulled back on the reins to stop him, he would go to bucking and try to unload me. He was uncontrollable and running through thick trees, trying to knock me off with the tree branches. Jake was running his horse on the trail next to me yelling, "Get him back on the trail before he kills you!"

I finally got him back on the trail, but he was still running very fast. If you have heard the saying "Like a horse headed for the barn", well, this was him and he thought he was headed home. I'm sure deep down inside Jake was laughing his ass off. He knew exactly what horse I was saddling and never said a word. He would really be laughing if he knew that I was a game warden investigating him for illegal outfitting. Maybe he already knew this. This horse was probably used as a pack horse and hadn't been ridden since his last horse race. We finally busted out of the trees near Water Dog Lakes. I looked to the south and observed Champ and Trooper moving quite well with their hobbles on, headed home. I was excited to see them, but really wanted to choke the hell out of them for leaving me in the mountains. I ran up alongside of them on my racehorse and grabbed Champ by his bridle and got my racehorse stopped for a moment. Now I needed to remove the hobbles from my horses so that I could lead them back to camp. I was trying to hold on to the crazy racehorse while he was trying to kick the shit out of both of my horses. Now all three horses were going nuts, trying to kick one another. Remember when I told you that I have no patience for horse nonsense in the wilderness? Well, this was one of those moments!

Jake finally showed up to help. He grabbed Champ's lead rope and offered to lead him back to camp while I led Trooper, riding the racehorse. I was thankful for that because I had my hands full. We turned the horses around and headed back to camp. The racehorse threw a tantrum because we were no longer headed in the direction of home. He started bucking and kicking Trooper in the head and chest with both barrels. Jake was getting further out of sight as I fought with this damn horse. Finally, the horse decided that Jake was getting too far away and took off in a dead run headed for Jake and Champ while still kicking the shit out of poor Trooper. I lost my patience and jerked hard on the reins and yelled at the horse, "Knock it off, you little piece of shit!" I tried to line the horse out and he decided to line me out. He went into a full walleyed buck right towards Jake. As the horse ran up behind Jake, he quit bucking.

Jake heard us approaching and looked behind him in the saddle. He said, "How is everything going back there?"

I replied, "Great, really great, but I'm going to just let Trooper follow us the rest of the way so that he doesn't get kicked anymore." I reached over and un-hooked Trooper's lead rope and let him free of the crazy racehorse. Trooper followed for a while until we started to drop back down into Rock Creek. We were all going down the trail and Trooper just stopped in the trail behind us. I wasn't worried, because he was a young horse and would get worried once he knew he was all alone. We kept riding for another couple hundred yards until we were almost out of sight of Trooper. I was sure he would get worried and come running to us. Nope, Trooper turned around in the trail and headed back towards home, running just as damn fast as he could. I quickly turned the racehorse around and kicked him hard in the ribs with both feet and said, "You want to run, you little bastard? Well let's run, dammit!" That horse took off like we were just crossing the finish line in the Kentucky Derby. The Man from Snowy River would have been proud of me, and my wife Lana may have actually called me a man that day.

I was gaining on Trooper quickly as we broke back out of the trees. I ran up alongside Trooper traveling about 30 MPH and clicked the lead rope onto his halter. I then dallied the other end of the lead rope to my borrowed saddle horn and turned the racehorse back towards our camp. Of course, the racehorse threw another fit and started bucking and kicking Trooper in the head and chest. I was so mad I didn't even care anymore. I whipped and spurred that damn racehorse into another bucking run, headed for camp. We flew over the ridge and headed back down the trail. We had traveled about another mile down the trail and met Jake standing in the trail with Champ.

Jake said, "Glad you got him caught again. Would you like to come to my camp for dinner and a cold beer?"

This sounded really good to me, but it was nearly dark and I needed to get the horses back to camp and get them fed and watered for the day. I had not eaten anything all day and was pissed off and starved and starting to get cold with no jacket.

I replied, "Thanks for the offer, Jake, but I better get back to camp and take care of business. Thanks again for all your help today, and thanks for loaning me your fastest horse."

Jake responded, "No problem, just let me know if you need anything else while you are in the area. And by the way, I can't believe you made it down to Rock Creek last night the way that you went. I know many that have tried that and never succeeded. You must be quite a hand with horses to do that in the dark. Nobody that I know has ever made it through there, let alone in the dark."

I replied, "Thanks, Jake; a lesser man may have died." And I damn near did die! I will never go that route again.

How could I continue to investigate and later prosecute this man for illegal outfitting after all that he had done for me today? Hopefully, he was not illegally guiding hunters without a license.

I grabbed Trooper and Champ and walked them back down through the grassy meadow and into the thick timber. I didn't dare try and ride them through the thick downfall in the dark. Once I reached the down-fall they both acted up and started pulling back and trying to get away from me. This had me really stressed, as I knew if one of them got away from me both of them would get away. I wasn't strong enough to hold them if they really wanted to go home. If they got loose, they would leave me alone in the mountains and go all the way back to the trailhead. And I did not want to ever have to ask Jake for help again. I definitely wouldn't ever ride that damn racehorse again.

Luckily, I was able to hold on to both horses all the way back through the heavy timber. It was definitely a challenge at times. Once I returned to camp, I put both horses on the high-line. They were acting up and pulling back. I didn't dare try and hobble them again to get them fed, as they would probably run off again. These horses had never acted this way before. My guess was that there was a grizzly bear close to camp and they didn't want to be there anymore. That is the reason they left in the first place. I was tired, hungry, and cold. All I wanted to do was sit down and relax for one moment.

I entered my tent and placed my headlamp on my head. I would need to go down to the tree where I had my food hung high in the air. The horses were snorting and pawing at the ground on the highline. They were looking in the direction of where my food was hanging. I thought, *Is that damn grizzly bear is down there, trying to eat my food?*

I grabbed my bear spray and noticed that the top was broken off. There was no way that it would spray. I was just glad that it didn't go off in my pannier or the tent. I wasn't sure how or when it had got broken. I was hungry and pissed off at the day. I grabbed my .270 and chambered a round as I walked down towards the tree where my food was hanging. As I approached the tree, I heard a loud "WOOF-WOOF". I picked my head up to shine my headlamp further back in the trees. I could see a very large grizzly bear staring right back at me. He woofed one more time and charged me. I nearly shot him from my hip, but he veered off to my right and disappeared into the dark. I think this may have been the most scared that I had ever been in my entire life. I may have soiled my shorts just a bit.

I didn't even take the time to lower the pannier full of food down out of the tree. I grabbed my knife and cut the rope. The entire pannier full of food and supplies came crashing down to the earth in about two seconds. I grabbed the rope and dragged the pannier full of food back up the hill to my tent. I quickly built a large bonfire and cooked a large ribeye steak over the fire. It was charcoaled on the outside and absolutely raw on the inside. (Just the way I liked them.) I poured a stout Jack Daniels slushy and nervously ate my steak dinner over the warmth of the fire. I also placed a can of baked beans in the fire to warm up. I had forgot my can opener so I opened the can with my hunting knife and drank the warm beans straight out of the can. There was no salad that night, just meat and beans. This would end up being one of the longest nights of my life, as the grizzly bear would not leave my camp. He kept circling the entire camp all night long. The horses would not calm down throughout the night. I was afraid to crawl into my tent and fall asleep, fearing that the grizzly bear might kill me in my sleep. I ended up drinking copious amounts of Jack Daniels that night and slept by the fire. This was probably the longest night of my life. I would have welcomed twelve howling wolves that night.

Daylight could not come soon enough. I stoked the fire and made some strong sheepherder coffee. As soon as it was bright enough to see I spotted three buck mule deer right out in front of my camp. Every one of them was larger than anything I had ever harvested before. They were literally right in my camp. I considered shooting the biggest buck in the group, as he was right near camp and would require no dragging. I wondered, *If I shoot my rifle in camp and kill this deer, will my horses spook at the sound of the rifle and tear down my highline and head for home?*

I nearly pulled the trigger on the larger buck, but I still hadn't spent anytime hunting the 40" buck that my buddy had told me about. I decided to grab my shitty department binoculars and glass the side of the mountain where I had seen all the nice bucks the day before. I observed several deer scattered across the high mountainside.

As I was glassing near the very top of the mountain below a group of trees, I spotted the largest mule deer buck that I had ever seen in my life during a hunting season. This buck was at least 32" wide. He was heavy and had very deep forks with a long brow tine on each side. The rack came straight out and went straight up like a box. This buck would definitely score over 200 Boone and Crockett points. I absolutely couldn't believe that I had this buck in my binoculars and a license in my pocket. This buck had no trash and was a very symmetrical 5x5.

This buck would be extremely difficult to stalk. There was no cover all the way up the mountain to get close enough for a shot. The wind was blowing slightly straight up the mountain towards him. The buck could see and smell me coming for a very long way. I glassed the entire mountain, trying to formulate a plan to get close to the buck. It looked impossible. There were several small patches of trees on the mountainside that I could gain cover in, but I would have to figure out how to jump from one patch of timber to the other without being seen. I gathered all my hunting gear and threw my backpack on. It looked like I could use the cover of the creek below me to hike up the creek nearly a mile and then jump into some trees and slowly work my way to the top of the mountain, jumping from tree patch to tree patch. I started the journey of a lifetime with a high expectation of getting near this buck. I had hunted large mule deer bucks my entire life and quickly learned that they didn't get that big from being stupid. To get within 200 yards of a buck like this can be very difficult and challenging, to say the least. And definitely fair chase for the deer. Back then we didn't have long-range shooting rifles like we do now. Even if we did, I would never take a shot over 1000 yards. This is not fair chase for the animal.

I couldn't believe it, but after about an hour I was almost halfway up the mountain slowly working from one tree patch to the other. I was curious if the buck was still in the area where I had seen him from camp. I was feeling bad because I hadn't taken my horses off the highline to feed them that morning. Heck, the poor horses hadn't had a good chance to eat since we had arrived two days ago. I would try and get this buck harvested as soon as possible and get back and take care of the horses. I finally reached the last patch of trees. I glassed up the mountain and spotted the large buck again, pretty close to the same area that I had seen him earlier that morning. I couldn't believe that he was still there and that I was now about 500 yards from him. I would need to walk in the open for about 100 yards to get back into some cover. This would be the hard part. If I could pull this off, I would have adequate cover to close the deal and get a shot within 300 yards. But only if he didn't run off between now and then.

I glassed the entire area and didn't see any deer in sight. I slowly started hiking up the mountain in the open sage brush to get to the next patch of timber. If I made it that far, I would have a good chance of harvesting this trophy buck. As I headed out across the open sage brush, something happened to me that I was not expecting. My stomach began to churn and rumble. I had drunk my morning sheepherder's coffee without taking my morning ritual. I felt like if I took one more step I would take my morning ritual in my shorts. This was a horrible feeling and I could not stop it. I was standing out in the open sage brush, fearing for my life that if I took one more step it was going to be a wilderness mess. I looked up into the sky and said to myself, *Dear Lord, I can't believe you have finally put a trophy buck into my sights and now I'm about to shit my pants! I should not have eaten the entire can of beans last night.*

I took one more step and that's exactly what happened. The worst feeling of my life just occurred on that mountainside on that beautiful morning. (For those that hunt, I know you have been there at least once in your life.) This was also not my first rodeo. I dropped my pants and cut my soiled shorts off with my hunting knife. While doing so, I heard a doe snort about fifty yards away. She could definitely smell me and bolted up the mountain towards the large buck, snorting like a curious antelope. My pants were around my legs as I watched the trophy buck of a lifetime stand up from his bed and disappear into the heavy timber. My hunt was now over, the deer were all gone. I had the buck in my scope for a split second and decided not to take the running shot while my pants were wrapped around my ankles. I will never forget that hopeless moment. I headed back to camp to take care of the horses.

I arrived at camp and the horses were still buzzed up on the highline. I felt like if I tried to hobble them to feed, they would take off again. My fun meter was pegged. I spent one day chasing horses on a racehorse, had wolves in my camp, had a grizzly bear charge me, got bucked off twice, and now I shit my pants and my horses were acting like assholes! I was mad at Lana that she didn't pack me in and drop me off so that I wouldn't have to deal with horses or leave my patrol truck at the trailhead for the illegal outfitter to find out about or see for himself. I decided it was time to pack up and make a mile. I had had enough!

I tied Trooper to a lone pine tree to pack him. My lash rope was extra-long because I had used it to pack a draft horse several weeks earlier. I damn sure hadn't perfected the Tennessee box hitch and didn't give a pinch of shit about ever trying to learn it again. If I had bungee cords, I would have used them! I loaded Trooper up and threw the lash rope over the top of him to the other side. He spooked when the rope hit the ground and took off circling the small pine tree as fast as he could. Pretty quick he had tied himself tight up against the pine tree and all the lash rope had wrapped around all four of his legs. It was a damn mess, but he couldn't go anywhere.

I tied a quick Swerbe hitch and away we went. For those of you who don't know, a Swerbe knot is a knot that is not known to any other human being in the world and is impossible to ever untie; you must cut it with a sharp knife. Over the years many game wardens have accused me of tying a Swerbe knot. I tried to learn the Bowlin knot but it was way too complicated for Swerb. Something about a rabbit runs into the hole and back out of the hole and around the bush, hell, I can't remember how it goes. Trooper was packed and we were headed for home. We would have to go back through the heavy timber and back up the steep mountainside by Jake's camp to return home. We made it to Jake's camp and there was not a single person or horse around. The entire camp was cleaned up and gone. This seemed weird to me because he told me that he was taking some friends hunting in a few days. I bet he had ridden down to the trailhead to pick up his hunters from Texas and they told him the story about the game warden that they had helped pack his wild horse several days earlier.

At this point I was feeling like a worthless game warden and hunter. As I rode down the mountain on the dusty and rough trail, the country was absolutely beautiful. The high snow-capped mountains in the background seemed to whisper beauty and danger all at once. It was a beautiful blue-sky day, and the patches of aspen trees along the high mountain lakes were in full fall colors. I rode through a beautiful patch of aspen trees; the red, yellow, and orange leaves fell slowly through the air and gently landed on the trail in front of me. The horses' metal shoes were in rhythm as they worked their way down the rocky trail ahead. I noticed fresh grizzly bear tracks in the trail ahead of me. This reminded me just how wild and dangerous this country can be. I thought about the wolves that had circled me in the night by my campfire and how scary the loud howl of the wolves was, especially when all alone. I smiled and felt blessed that I just got to experience all of that alone. I think these are the moments in your life that you really get to know yourself, and those moments make you a better and stronger man.

I was within one mile of my patrol truck. I could barely see it hidden in the tall pine trees off in the distance. I was relieved that me and ol' Trooper hadn't had any mishaps and it was going to be a successful and safe pack out. I rode up to a small winding creek with tall willows growing on each side of the creek. I was hoping that we wouldn't encounter any moose along the creek. This moment also reminded me of the time that a bull moose tried to mount poor ol' Spook, my black pack horse, in the Upper Green River.

Champ was hesitant to cross the small creek for some reason. He stood there and splashed water with his nose and pawed the ground in front of him. I knew from experience that I had better grab the saddle horn with both hands and hold on tight because Champ was about to launch both of us over the small creek. And that he did. This caused my lead rope to tighten up with Trooper, as Champ was in the air. Trooper pulled back hard and then lunged forward even harder. Trooper tried to run past us and the pannier hit Champ in the ass just as his feet hit the ground. This spooked Champ and he started bucking to relieve me as the rider. I held on tight for several jumps but couldn't stay in the saddle. Champ sent me on an undisturbed launch into the earth's atmosphere and then into the small babbling brook, face first. As I lay face down in the creek, I could hear sounds of metal shoes hitting rocks and horses farting. I looked up and both horses were headed home without their faithful owner. I stayed still for a moment in the creek, making sure none of my bones were broken. I thought, *You sonsabitches, I feed you all year long and this is how I'm rewarded!*

I would end up walking the next mile to my truck. I was not hurt, but a little humbled and embarrassed. I was hoping that the Texas hunters were not in camp to see the high-country ranger walking back to camp, soaking wet, dragging a leg, with the one of the most despicable hitches tied on a pack horse that anyone has ever seen before. Luckily the horses were waiting at the trailer when I arrived. I looked around the campground and it was completely empty of campers. The Texas hunters had packed up and were gone. I think they were the hunters that were going to be illegally guided in the wilderness by Jake. Man, did I screw that whole investigation up. Maybe at the end of the day I just prevented it all from happening and Jake learned a lesson. A lesson that you never know when you might run into an undercover game warden with a Tennessee box hitch.

The horses and I had not had a very good trip. We were all ready to get home where we could sleep and eat peacefully without worrying about grizzly bears and wolves joining us for a meal or having us as their meal. I unpacked and loaded the horses up and headed for Daniel. I had lost track of the days and wasn't sure what day of the week it was, even though I hadn't been gone that long. As I came up and over the hill, headed south towards Daniel Junction, I could see flashing amber lights ahead. I had forgotten that one of our biologists was going to have a check station set up over the weekend. I realized it was Sunday and the biologist was working alone. From a distance I could see a line of horse trailers backed up. The biologist was very busy checking dead elk and deer. I was soaking wet and very dirty from being bucked off into the creek. I just wanted to drive by the check station and go home and shower. But I could see that he needed help so I pulled in alongside of the line of trucks and horse trailers. The biologist looked up and saw me and nodded his head and smiled as if to say thank you for your help. He was pulling lymph nodes from a dead cow elk to test for Chronic Wasting Disease (CWD.)

I had just started to open the door on my truck and help the biologist, when a very scary-looking man approached my truck. I decided to stay in the truck and roll my window down to talk to the man. The man was dressed in rawhide, with a very greasy Australian-looking down under cowboy hat. He had a beard and was missing most of his teeth. His face and hands were black in color from not bathing in probably several months. I had seen this man before in different bars and occasionally walking up and down the highway near Daniel. He had a .44 mag in his holster on his right hip and a large bowie knife on his left hip. He also had a greasy-looking bald eagle feather in his hat band, which was illegal for him to possess.

My truck window was about halfway down when he began pounding on it with both hands and yelling at me. I didn't know what was going on and was tempted to draw my pistol. I finally got my window down and said, "What can I help you with today, sir?" The dirty man got right in my face and yelled, "YOU WANT TO CATCH SOME F------ POACHERS? GET YOUR ASS UP TO SHOAL CREEK RIGHT NOW! I JUST OBSERVED SOME NON-RESIDENT SON OF A BITCH SHOOT THREE COW ELK. HE'S PROBABLY ASSOCCIATED WITH THAT DAMN OUTFITTER'S CAMP UP THERE. YOU CAN'T CATCH ANY F------- POACHERS DOWN HERE SITTING IN YOUR DAMN TRUCK ALL DAY!"

Chapter 5

SHOAL CREEK

I finally got the dirty-looking mountain man to calm down a bit and asked him some questions. I had heard from others in the small community that this man was a poacher and hated game wardens. If that were true, why was he reporting a violation to me? He was so upset and angry that he couldn't quit yelling at me. He wasn't able to give me much information other than he had observed a man dressed in full camo early that morning shoot three cow elk down in a canyon near Shoal Creek. He told me that the man was standing on an isolated rock outcropping by himself. Shoal Creek was in the same area that I had just come from. This was in Hubba's warden district and I didn't know that area at all. I was tired and wet and just wanted to go home.

I jumped out of my truck and informed the biologist that I couldn't help him, as I needed to respond to a poaching report up at Shoal Creek. I didn't know if I should take my horses home or just take them with me. I didn't even know what the terrain would be like in this area. I did know that it was near an elk feed ground that I use to manage and that there was some private property and locked gates to get to the outfitter camp that I had never been to before. How would I get through the locked gates? Would I need my horses? Could I even pull a horse trailer up the steep mountain that I'd need to climb to get to the outfitter's camp?

With all those questions racing through my mind I tried to call game warden Hubba Healy and pass the information along to him, as this was his warden district and he knew way more about the area than I did. The phone call went right to his voicemail, indicating that Hubba was out of service. It was getting later in the day and this all happened early that morning. Would these guys even still be in the area? Wet, tired, and dirty, I decided to run my horses home quick and unhook my horse trailer. I could always come back and get them, if need be, but I needed to get headed that direction right now if I was ever going to catch them in the area. One thing about killing three elk in a canyon, it's going to take them a while to get them all packed out. But I didn't even know if these hunters were locals or non-residents hunting with an outfitter.

After unloading my horses and putting them in the pasture, the drive to this area would be about one hour. I turned on my tiny red and blue lights that were mounted to my grill guard and hauled ass to the area of Shoal Creek. My sirens still didn't work, as I had not had any time to take my truck into the radio technician and have the problem fixed. I would simply get behind a car, and if they didn't pull over I would honk my horn until they heard me. This generally resulted in me scaring the shit out of the driver in front of me and having them pull over abruptly right in front of me, nearly causing an accident. I would zip by them and wave; they would generally flip me off and shout obscenities as I passed by.

I was near the area and turned off onto the Little Jenny Road. I observed a man getting out of his truck to open a locked gate up a two-track road to the north of me. I decided to go up and talk to the man to see if he knew where the outfitter camp was located. The man was just locking the paddle lock on the chain around the gate when I approached.

The man looked up and said, "Oh, do you need in here? I will leave the gate unlocked if you do."

I didn't know the man and replied, "Do you know where the outfitter camp is located?"

The man replied, "Just stay on this road all the way up and over the mountain and this road will take you right to the camp."

I thanked the man and told him that I needed to go to the outfitter's camp.

He responded, "Oh, okay, well if you need to get to the camp there is another locked gate up the road about one mile and I can unlock that gate for you as well."

I thanked the man and told him that I would be sure and lock both gates on my way back out. I didn't know who this guy was. I never even asked him for his name. Hell, it could have been the guy who shot and killed three elk for all I knew. He must have been a landowner or someone associated with the outfitter camp to have a key for both gates. I didn't want to tell him why I was in the area and he didn't ask. He was very friendly and drove off. I looked in my rearview mirror as I drove off through the gate and I thought to myself, *Man, that was a blessing to run into a guy with a key to the gate, tell me where the hunting camp was located, and open the gates for me.* I had found through my career that oftentimes animals were poached behind locked gates because game wardens never had access to catch them.

The road was narrow and the mountain was steep. I put my truck in four low and inched my way up the mountain. Once halfway up the mountain I noticed something shiny at the top of the mountain. I stopped and got my shitty department spotting scope out and mounted it to my driver's side window. Once it came into focus, I noticed a newer model four-door Ford truck parked off the side of the road near an open meadow of grass. The bright sun was deflecting off the chrome mirror on the truck. If it wasn't for this, I would have never spotted the truck. I zoomed my spotting scope in as much as it would zoom and discovered four men walking around in the open meadow. It appeared to me that they were all talking on their cell phones. Maybe this was the only spot in the area with cell service?

The only information that I had received from the mountain man down at the check station was that he had observed one man dressed in full camo shoot three cow elk near Shoal Creek. That is the only information that I had! These kinds of cases can be very tough to solve because people lie and lie and then lie some more to game wardens. If you don't witness these kinds of cases, they are very difficult to prove. Generally, it will require the game warden to find a bullet in each dead elk and match the hunter's rifle to the bullet or bullets collected. Oftentimes bullets go clean through an animal and the game warden has no evidence. Even if the game warden finds bullets, they are sometimes incomplete to match to a rifle. Once a bullet is found, then the warden needs a suspect with a rifle. The warden then needs enough probable cause to seize the hunter's rifle and send to our forensics laboratory for testing. This process can take weeks and sometimes months to get results back. A chain of custody has to be completed by the warden documenting the caliber, serial number, and owner of the rifle. The rifle has to be stored safely and secure from the time it is seized until it arrives to the laboratory. Anytime the rifle changes hands it needs to be documented in the chain of custody. Many good game warden cases have been lost over the years due to a prosecuting attorney finding error in the chain of custody.

I sat and watched the four men for several minutes. It appeared that one of the men was wearing full camo and none of the other men were wearing any camo clothing. Could this be the man that I was looking for?

I headed up the road, trying to figure out in my head how I was going to interview these guys to make this case. I couldn't give them a chance to lie to me. Once someone tells a lie it is very difficult to get them back out of a lie and back on track with the truth. As I pulled up next to the brand new four-door Ford all the men were still walking around the small meadow, talking on their phones. I was tired and not in the mood for any bullshit. The license plate on the truck was from California. It was very possible that these guys were being guided by the outfitter whose camp was a short distance away down in the trees.

I stepped out of my truck and headed for the man wearing camo clothing. As I approached him, I said, "Sir, please hang up the phone. I need to visit with you about a few things."

The man gave me a surprised look and replied, "Okay, honey, I need to let you go as I have someone who needs to talk to me. Okay, love you too, goodbye."

I looked the man directly in his eyes and said, "Sir, I'm a Wyoming game warden and I need to visit with you about a few things. Could you please step into my truck for some privacy?"

The man replied, "What is going on? Is there a problem?"

I replied, "Yes, we have a huge problem, please get in the truck." The man stepped into my truck and shut the door. I could tell he was very nervous. I knew I had only one shot at this before the man would sit there and lie to me for hours. I also noticed fresh blood stains on the man's camo pants and blood underneath his fingernails.

So, I gambled and said, "I have been trying to catch up with you all day. Do you know it's illegal for you to shoot elk for your buddies? Do you know that you can only kill one elk yourself?

The man replied, "I'm confused here; I only shot one elk this morning."

I replied, "That's a damn lie. I watched you shoot three elk this morning down in the canyon at first light. You were on a rock outcropping all by yourself and took down three cow elk."

I had lied to the man, telling him that I had observed the whole event take place. I didn't like doing this and I didn't know if I even had the right guy. But I figured that if I had just accused someone of doing something wrong that they didn't do, they would become very angry and maybe even take a swing at me. But that wasn't the case. I had the right guy.

He dropped his head down towards his knees and placed his hands over his face. He rubbed his face for a few seconds and looked at me and said, "You're right, I killed three elk this morning and I apologize for that. It's been tough hunting and we are paying a lot of money for this hunt. I had the opportunity to fill everyone's license this morning and I did it. I'm very sorry. Write me a ticket and do whatever you need to do."

I asked the man if he had a guide with him and if the guide knew what had happened.

The man responded, "We had a guide but he was not with me when I shot the elk, and he thinks that we all legally shot our own elk."

My guess was that they didn't have a guide with them or none of this would have happened. Either that or the guide knew what happened and he was protecting the guide. I didn't really care, as he admitted to shooting the elk and I was thankful for his honesty. I actually couldn't believe how easy it was to make the case, considering I was not there and had very little information to work with. I was proud of myself for solving the case even though I was feeling pretty worthless after my trip into Rock Creek with the illegal outfitter and that outcome.

I asked the man if the elk were packed out and where the meat was hanging. He replied, "Yes, all the meat is packed out and hanging in a tree at the outfitter's camp." I requested for the man to gather his hunting buddies and lead me to the outfitter's camp. I followed them a short distance over the top of the mountain and soon arrived at the outfitter's camp that was tucked back into the trees. I looked around and there were elk quarters hanging everywhere. I met with the guide in a large wall tent. The wall tent had couches and recliners set up in it. They even had a large screen TV set up and huge wood stove. This was probably the most luxurious wall tent that I had ever seen. The guide apologized and claimed that he had set the men out on a rock outcropping to look for elk while he rode down into the canyon, looking for elk sign. He claimed that he hadn't been gone but a few minutes and heard three shots, then he turned around and rode back to find that the hunters had all killed their elk. He was excited for them and began packing all the elk back to base camp. It is illegal for the guide to not be with the hunters and at their side while hunting, but I didn't pursue that one.

I told the hunters to load all the elk quarters into my truck, as I was confiscating all their meat and licenses. They all pitched in and helped load the quarters while I issued the California man a citation for taking an over-limit of elk. Everyone was very cooperative and I appreciated that. At the end of the day, it probably didn't matter who killed the elk as long as they were all tagged and no meat was left to waste. But in Wyoming it is illegal to kill someone else's elk and use their license to tag it. It was my job as a Wyoming game warden to enforce the law. I thanked all the men for their honesty and cooperation and shook their hands. I looked over at my patrol truck to see twelve quarters of elk rising above the bed of my truck. This was a shit load of elk meat, and I would end up donating it all to needy people in the community.

As I was getting ready to leave the guide asked me if I could step into the wall tent again and visit with him about something that had been bothering him. I stepped into the large wall tent again to hear what the man had to say. He claimed that he knew of two Kansas hunters who had been camped near him for over ten years and had been hunting in the wilderness without a guide all these years. He said it didn't really bother him, but yesterday they became lost and the Search and Rescue had to rescue them down in a deep canyon. His wife was on the Search and Rescue and reported the information to him. Apparently both men nearly died of hypothermia and were rescued at the last minute of their lives. The men were flown out of the mountains to the hospital in Pinedale and were currently recovering in a motel room in Pinedale.

The man was very upset and said, "This is exactly why non-residents need to have a guide in these mountains. These men nearly died, and that wouldn't have happened if they had a guide or outfitter with them. That is the reason we have this regulation." The guide told me that if I didn't cite them for the violation that he would take it up the chain with my administration. He also told me the name of the motel where the men were staying in Pinedale. I thanked the guide for the information and told him that I would meet with the Kansas hunters and deal with the violation. I didn't personally agree with this regulation, but it was the law. and I'm a Wyoming game warden that took an oath to enforce the laws and regulations of Wyoming. You can literally do anything you want in the wilderness as a non-resident except hunt big or trophy game animals without a resident guide or outfitter. I thought this law was a racket for the industry.

For example, if I were a Wyoming game warden for thirty years and knew the mountains better than anyone in the world. Let's say I retire and move to Arizona and lose my Wyoming residency and want to come back and hunt in the wilderness. I would need to hire an outfitter or have a resident guide accompany me in the wilderness. My guide may be some guy from Pennsylvania that passed the guide's test and has never stepped foot into the wilderness where I have spent my whole life. The outfitters may argue that this regulation allows for fewer non-residents in the wilderness and a more quality hunt for residents. This may have some merit, but I still don't agree with the regulation.

I left the outfitter's camp with my patrol truck heaped with elk quarters. I would need to take them to Pinedale and hang them in the Quonset hut at the regional office. This was turning into another very long day as a Wyoming game warden. Once the meat was hung and properly cared for, I would need to go visit with the Kansas hunters in their motel room. that nearly died on their elk hunt and had to be rescued.

As I was leaving the outfitters camp bouncing down the rough road with a truck full of elk meat, a thought came to my mind. I left my pack trip early for a number of reasons. Why did I show up at the check station at the exact moment that the mountain man showed up to report the violation? Why was the mountain man in the area where these elk were killed at daylight? Why did the mountain man drive all the way to the check station to report the violation when he is a poacher himself and doesn't care for game wardens? Why did I meet a guy at the locked gates with a key to let me in and tell me where the outfitters camp was located? Why did I observe the glare of the truck's mirror to get my attention to then get my spotting scope out to observe a man dressed in camo? Why did the hunter immediately confess to the violation? This just all seemed to me that it was meant to be, and something much deeper was happening.

In my experience as a Wyoming game warden, you can poach for many years and get away with it. But when your number is up you will be caught, and it may be unexplainable as to how you finally got caught. In my opinion the guide knew exactly who killed all three elk and was right at his side. The mountain man observed this and didn't like the guide or outfitter, so it was reported. There is always more to the story than what meets the eye. And sometimes you probably don't want to even know the whole story.

I hung all the meat up in the Quonset hut. Twelve quarters of elk meat took up most of the room in the Quonset hut. Hubba would be pissed at me that I made a good case in his district. I didn't care and was proud of myself for solving the case as quickly as I did. Now it was time to go find the Kansas hunters in their motel room.

It was approximately 8:00 p.m. when I arrived at the Lodge of Pinedale motel. I met with the front office manager and asked her what room the Kansas hunters were staying in. She quickly gave me their room number. They were on the first floor, a short distance from the front office. I approached the door with their room number and knocked on the door kind of loudly. I stood there uncomfortably for several minutes and nobody answered the door. I banged again and waited. Again, nobody came to the door. I was actually relieved that I didn't have to deal with the situation and turned and walked away down the long hallway. I just wanted to go home and sleep in my own bed and tell Lana about my pack trip. As I was about twenty yards from their door, I heard a faint voice say, "Can I help you with something?"

I turned back to see a man sticking his head out the door. His hair was standing on end and it looked like he might be naked. I turned around and approached the man standing in the open door. I introduced myself and shook his hand. He was naked and very pale in color. He invited me into their room. Once in the room I observed the man's brother in bed with the covers pulled over his head. He was shaking and recovering from hypothermia. I quickly explained to both men who I was and why I was there. I didn't want to be there and it was very uncomfortable for me to be there with both men recovering from hypothermia.

I told the men that they had been reported for hunting in the wilderness without a guide or outfitter and that I was there to document the violation with a citation. This is not what the men wanted to hear at all in their condition. I didn't want to interrupt them any more than need be so I got right down to business. I asked the men if they had a driver's license or an elk license.

One man replied, "We got lost and our wallets are still in our hunting camp; we have no identification with us."

I replied, "Okay, no problem; I will just ask you a few questions and get these citations filled out."

Both men were still shaking and their voices were very weak and hard to understand. I could hardly hear either man talk and I didn't have my reading glasses with me to issue the citation. I was really struggling with hearing and seeing what I was writing. After struggling to hear what they were saying for several minutes, I handed my citation book to one man and said, "Here, just fill this out; it's all pretty straightforward personal information with your name and address, etc." I handed my citation booklet to the man who was sitting on the edge of the bed naked. He grabbed my pen and wrote out his own citation. Once he was done the other man crawled out of bed and was sitting on the edge of his bed naked writing out his citation. I stood there uncomfortably for about twenty minutes watching each of them write out their own citation. Once they were completed, they handed me the citation and my pen back. I said, "Oh, you both need to sign the citation" and handed my pen back to them. They both signed and out the door I went.

I felt absolutely horrible about having to issue these two men citations while they were recovering from hypothermia. And I didn't even agree with the regulation that I was hired to enforce. I jumped into my truck and turned on the dome light to look at the citations to make sure they were properly filled out. I couldn't even read a single word that one of the men had written. He didn't have good handwriting to begin with and was shaking with poor penmanship due to hypothermia. I would have to look up the guy in our system and rewrite the citation before turning it in to the courthouse. I would later turn in the citations to my boss. He reviewed them and called me into his office. He said, "Swerb, I noticed you wrote a few citations to a couple of non-residents for hunting the wilderness without a guide or outfitter. How come these citations are not in your handwriting?" I explained the whole story to my boss about the naked men writing out their own citations. He just laughed and said, "Only Swerb would do something like this." One thing for sure, I'll bet those Kansas guys never violated that law again and I'll bet they never will forget writing out their own citations while freezing nearly half to death that evening in a motel room in Pinedale.

On the drive home I thought about my whole day. I had started the day stalking a buck deer bigger than I had ever seen in my life. I shit my pants, got bucked off a horse, and solved an over-limit case that was given to me by a crazy, poaching, mountain man. I had two non-residents issue themselves a citation while sitting naked in a motel room after nearly freezing to death. It was just another day as a Wyoming Game Warden. It was time to go home, pour a whiskey, tell Lana about my entire pack trip, and crawl into my warm bed and not worry about something eating me in my sleep.

I arrived home late at night. I poured a whiskey and told Lana all about my pack trip and my crazy day. I also told her that tomorrow was the last day of deer season and that I was going to go out early in the morning to shoot the first buck deer that I saw. I was done trophy hunting and wanted to put some deer meat in the freezer for the family. I had hunted harder for a trophy mule deer buck that year than I had ever in my entire life. I awoke at 5:00AM, jumped into my jeep, and headed out to Warren Bridge just north of my house. This was an area that many mule deer migrated through to get to their winter ranges. I got back on a two-track road about three miles from the main highway and parked my jeep, waiting for daylight to come.

Once daylight arrived, I noticed the white-colored butt of a mule deer standing on top of a tall hill about three hundred yards away. The deer was on the very top of the hill with his head down, feeding away from me. All I could see was the white rump of the deer. Finally, the deer picked his head up and I could plainly see that it was a yearling two-point buck. I thought, *Perfect, this will be a good tasting piece of meat to put in the freezer. You are all mine, buddy.* I slowly exited the jeep and crawled through the sage brush for about thirty yards to get a clean shot at the small buck. I had the buck in my crosshairs and was slowly squeezing the trigger when I noticed something flash to my left. I swung the rifle scope to my left and observed a trophy buck mule deer approximately 250 yards away in some tall sagebrush. The buck had frost on his antlers and the morning sun made them glisten when he moved his head to look at me. This was the only reason that I noticed the buck just prior to shooting the younger buck.

The large buck deer had been watching me stalk the younger deer. He was lying down, looking straight back over his body at me. The deer looked wide-eyed, like he was ready to bolt at any second. If he jumped up and ran away from me he would be gone in seconds, as he was bedded down right on the edge of a steep hill. I placed my crosshairs in the center of the deer's neck. My heart started to pound and I began to shake. Was I getting buck fever? I had never had this happen before. I knew that I would only maybe get one shot at this buck and he would be gone in a second if he decided to jump up and run away. I decided to try and shoot him in the neck at about 250 yards away. This would be a difficult shot, especially since I was shaking. I got my crosshairs in the center of his neck and slowly squeezed the trigger. The gun went BOOM. The deer jumped straight up in the air and disappeared over the hill in about two seconds. As the deer was bounding high in the air jumping over tall sagebrush, his rack looked absolutely huge running away from me.

The deer was gone. I was sick to my stomach. I had just missed the trophy of a lifetime. I jumped up and ran over to the area where he had disappeared over the hill. I glassed the huge sagebrush bowl and did not see him running anywhere. He was flat gone. I had missed this buck and was sick to my stomach. I kept glassing and glassing, then I noticed a deer standing right below me under a tall sagebrush plant. The sagebrush must have been six feet tall. As I focused my binoculars in on the deer. This was him. He was standing in the dark shadow of the tall sagebrush plant. His head was hung down and I could see fresh blood coming out of neck near his throat. I was so excited. The buck was not dead, but at least he was hit and I had him spotted at about 150 yards straight below me. I laid down and got a good rest. I put the crosshairs right behind his shoulder and squeezed the trigger. BOOM went the rifle. The deer jumped straight in the air and headed away from me, running very fast. I heard the sound of the bullet hitting him. It made a WHAP sound. I even observed hair fly from his shoulder area. I knew I had hit the buck hard, but he was not slowing down.

The deer ran out another hundred yards or so and stopped broadside. I was breathing hard and shaking by now. I put the crosshairs of my scope right behind his shoulder again and squeezed the trigger. BOOM went the rifle again. I heard the impact of the bullet hitting the deer again, WHAP! The deer turned and continued to run away from me. I jacked in my fourth shell and found the running deer in my crosshairs again. I took a deep breath and was getting ready to pull the trigger, when the deer stopped suddenly. The deer stood up on his hind legs and ran backwards for about ten yards. He fell to the ground, dead. I couldn't believe that I had just killed the biggest deer of my life a short drive from my house! The deer was right off the main road in the area. Anyone could have killed this deer on that morning.

I walked down to the deer and took pictures and dressed him out. This was the biggest mule deer that I had ever harvested. How would I get this deer back up the hill and loaded into my jeep by myself? About that time, I looked up to see a man walking towards me. As he approached the deer, he said, "Man, you sure got a dandy there. If I would have been ten minutes earlier this morning, this buck would be mine." The man sounded kind of mad at me. But he congratulated me and took a picture of me with the buck. He also helped me drag and load the deer into my jeep. I went home with a smile on my face that day. I couldn't wait to show Lana my last-day deer. Heck, I was going to shoot a two-point. This deer would end up scoring 190 Boone and Crocket points. Sometimes hunting is not all about skill, it's about being in the right place at the right time.

Warren Bridge Deer

Chapter 6

BINKY THE CAT

Both of our kids, Wesley and Wendy (Rusty and Audrey), were now full-blown teenagers. If you haven't had the opportunity to raise teenagers, you haven't truly experienced all that life has to offer. Lana was still working up at the Antelope Run Ranch. This would be her fourth year at the Ranch. She loved this job and was gone pretty much seven days a week from daylight until dark. I had become good friends with her boss. I had even hired him to feed elk at the Jewett feed ground a few years back when I was still the Feed Ground Manager. Now, he and Lana would feed the elk each morning together. Lana always loved working with the draft horses and feeding elk. My job kept me very busy as well. I don't know how we did so much and raised two kids. It seemed like Lana and I were doing fewer fun things like hunting and fishing together. It seemed that we were no longer doing much of anything together and slowly getting further apart. But she loved her job and I loved my job, and we both supported one another with our busy careers.

I was never so happy than when Wes got his learner's permit. I would end up purchasing him a used Dodge pickup. The truck was maroon in color and had low mileage. What a relief it was that Wes could now drive himself and his sister into town for school and sporting events or whatever they had going on in town. It seemed like Lana and I were driving the kids into town for something almost every day. This was about a thirty-mile roundtrip and often during the evening hours on slick roads. Wes was motivated to go to school each morning. He excelled at school and sports. Wendy on the other hand was not a morning person and didn't give a rat's ass about going to school each morning. Wes was now driving Wendy to school every morning instead of riding the school bus, Cheese Wagon as Wendy called it. They hated riding the Cheese Wagon.

Each morning, I would wake up to the sound of Wes yelling at Wendy to get out of bed. He would literally drag her out of bed and help her get dressed so that he wouldn't be late for school. This led to fighting and screaming from both parties nearly every morning. I used to sit back and chuckle; it was good to see them both learning some responsibility. I learned a valuable lesson that year. Never buy your kid their first vehicle. At least make them come up with half the cost so that they have some ownership and pride in what they are driving. Wes was a great kid, but failed to wash it or change the oil in his truck. Most of the time you couldn't even get a passenger in the truck with all the dirty clothes, tennis shoes, helmets, shoulder pads, and food wrappers on the passenger floorboard and seat. The inside of his truck smelled like a sweaty body with a rotten catfish under the seat or something. I'm sure once he found a girlfriend he might tidy things up a bit. Both kids were playing basketball and excelling at the sport. Wendy discovered boys and her grades started to drop. I could get online and look up her missing assignments. Thank God my parents weren't able to do this when I was young. Most of the time she was missing math assignments.

I would try to help her with her missing assignments each night. This would generally turn into a fight because I was doing the math wrong. You are not supposed to carry numbers and show your work. If you do, you will fail. This was the dumbest thing that I had ever heard. Wendy would yell and scream at me that I was doing it the wrong way. I would yell back, "I DON'T GIVE A CRAP WHAT YOUR TEACHER THINKS, THIS IS HOW YOU DO MATH!" At the end of the night, I would just do all of Wendy's homework to get her caught up. All she had to do was sign her name on the paper and turn it in. I would check online each week and see that her homework assignments were still missing. I would ask her why she didn't turn them in and she would respond, "Dad, I lost my backpack with all my assignments."

One day I was completely out in the middle of nowhere, checking antelope hunters. My bag phone rang and it was Wendy's principal, Mr. V.

I answered the phone, "Hello?"

Mr. V. replied, "Hello, Mr. Werbelow, this is Mr. V., Wendy's principal here at the middle school in Pinedale. How are you doing today, sir?"

I responded, "I'm doing pretty well, just out in the hills checking antelope hunters on the opening day of hunting season."

Mr. V. responded, "Well good; I will keep this short. I have suspended your daughter and her best friend today for disrupting class. She will be suspended for the next three days and I need you to come into town and pick her up right now."

I was furious and responded, "So you suspended my daughter and her best friend today for three days for disrupting class? Now you want me to drive to town on opening day of antelope season to pick up my daughter and take her home where she and her best friend will call each other and play grab ass over the phone for the next three days! My daughter is missing many different assignments; I suggest you keep her in your office while she completes all her missing homework assignments and give her some real discipline."

Mr. V. responded, "With all due respect, sir, I don't think I can stand to be around your daughter in my office for the next three days."

I laughed to myself and replied, "I understand, sir; I will be there shortly to pick her up."

About one week later, I returned home from work. Wendy met me at the front door all excited and said, "Dad, Dad, I found a cat today. Can I have him, Dad? Can I please have him?"

I responded, "Hell no, we aren't getting no damn cat! We have enough pets to feed already. Besides, you won't feed it or take care of it."

Wendy replied, "Dad, please, please. I found this beautiful calico cat down on the Green River. Some old man has a bunch of cats and wants to give me one. Dad, he has hundreds of cats to pick from and I found the most beautiful cat of all of them. I have already named her Binky."

I asked Wendy a few more questions of where this man lived and how she had heard about the cats. She told me that he was an old man living in a trailer house by the river and that a friend had taken her out to look at the cats. I knew exactly who she was talking about because we had done a search warrant on this man's trailer a few years back. This was one of the most disgusting things that I had ever seen. This man had over three hundred cats living in his trailer house. The cats had been pooping and peeing all over the place for years! Many of the cats had distemper and had green snot coming out of their eyes and nose.

I told Wendy, "Absolutely, not! These cats have distemper and we are not bringing one of them home."

Wendy started to cry and grabbed my leg and said, "Please, Dad, I want to save one of these cats."

This broke my heart. Wendy was such a kind girl who loved animals and was only trying to save one cat out of the hundreds available. I didn't give in right away. I was hoping that she would forget about it over time. Three weeks later she was still begging me to help her save Binky. I finally told her that she could have the cat but she would have to figure out how to get it home, as I was not going back out there to get it. I'm sure the man didn't want to see me again after searching his home previously for hunting violations. A few days later Wendy showed up with the calico cat. I have to admit it was a beautiful cat. I'm not a cat lover, but it was a pretty and sweet little kitty that appeared to be healthy.

A few weeks later I noticed that the cat had green snot coming out of its nose. The cat would walk around the house and blow snot on every piece of furniture in the house. Including our brand-new projection big screen television that I had just paid nearly $2000 for. We took Binky to the vet for all of her shots including distemper for about $200. This didn't include the large bag of cat food, cat feeder, and odorless cat box that we came home with. Over the next two weeks Binky continued to blow green snot on every piece of furniture in the house. I was pretty much over Binky the green snot flinger.

One morning at about 6:30 I overheard Wes and Wendy fighting about something upstairs.

I overheard Wes, yell, "WENDY, YOUR CAT SHIT IN MY BEDROOM. GET IN HERE AND CLEAN UP AFTER YOUR CAT!"

The fight was on because Wendy didn't want to get out of bed let alone clean up cat poop in her brother's room. I was getting ready to leave for work as the fight continued.

I yelled up the stairs, "WENDY, CLEAN UP AFTER YOUR DAMN CAT RIGHT NOW!"

I heard more yelling and screaming as I left the house for work. Several days later Lana asked me if I would grill steaks for dinner. I couldn't cook anything but I was the master at grilling steaks. I stepped out on the front deck and turned the grill on high. I always liked to get the grill up to about 500 degrees before putting the steaks on the grill. This high heat would sear the meat and keep the tasty juices in. I went back in the house to properly prepare the marinated meat for grilling.

After being in the kitchen for a few minutes I heard Lana yell, "HONEY, YOU ARE BURNING THE DAMN HOUSE DOWN!"

I looked out the porch window to see large flames shooting out the sides and top of my barbecue grill. The smoke was black like tires burning. I quickly rushed outside with a pitcher of water and slowly opened the lid of the grill. What I discovered next, I will never forget. Lying on top of the grill was a plastic Walmart bag full of cat shit. Yup, you heard me right, cat shit on my grill!

I yelled, "WENDY, GET YOUR BUTT DOWN HERE RIGHT NOW!"

Wendy stepped out on the deck and said, "What, Dad?"

I replied, "Why in the heck did you throw a plastic bag of cat poop on the grill?"

Wendy replied with a soft voice, "Because I was too lazy to put my shoes on and carry it out to the burn barrels. I was going to do it the next time that I was out of the house but I forgot. Sorry, Dad."

I absolutely had no words for this one. To this day, I peek under the lid of my grill before I fire it up to make sure there is not a bag of cat shit on my grill. You have got to love teenagers!

The snot blowing went on for several more weeks. Binky was not responding to the distemper shots. I returned home from work early one day to find Binky blowing snot all over the couch. I decided that I had had enough. It was time for Binky to find a new home. I gently caught the cat and hauled it out to my patrol truck. We were about to perform a relocation of a domestic cat. There was a neighbor friend who lived about three to four miles away. She was in the country and had several cats running around her house. I figured that I would drive down the road a short distance and relocate Binky to a nice home with a huge barn.

So, there was Swerb with a calico cat stuck with all four paws hanging on the back of the passenger seat in the Game and Fish patrol truck headed down Horse Creek Road. The cat was yowling like a mountain lion in heat. It was the damnedest noise that I had ever heard. I got near the farm house and stopped in the middle of the highway to quickly release Binky to her new home. I reached over and opened the passenger door and tried to throw Binky out of the truck really quick. Binky would have nothing to do with this. She buried at least twenty claws into the back of the passenger seat and would not let go. I grabbed her by the scruff of the neck and pulled until her claws came free from the seat. Every time that I would try to throw her out the door, her claws would catch on something like Velcro and she would stick to it. After several failed attempts to release the cat from the truck, I exited the vehicle and walked over to the passenger side door.

I grabbed the cat with both hands and hurled it into the barrow pit next to the truck. The cat landed on its feet and quickly ran underneath my patrol truck and up into the engine compartment of my truck. This sent a wave of panic through my body, as my truck was still running and I didn't want the cat to get tangled up in the fan and chopped up into pieces. I ran around to the driver's side of my truck and quickly shut the engine off and popped the hood. About that time another truck pulled up behind me as I was looking into the engine compartment.

An older man who looked like a rancher walked up and said, "Are you having engine problems?"

I was embarrassed and replied, "No, sir, but I had a damn cat try to cross the road in front of me. I slowed down to a stop to keep from running over it and it ran up into my engine compartment. So I'm just trying to get the cat out."

The cat was now growling and hissing at both of us as it clung to the inside of the radiator. The rancher said, "It must be someone's pet; looks like it's wearing a collar."

Shit, I thought to myself. I had forgotten to take the damn collar off the cat before relocating it. The two of us finally got the cat pried out of the engine compartment and released into the wild. Wendy came home from school day after day looking for her cat. I did not tell a word to anyone including Lana about the cat's whereabouts. Finally, Wendy came home crying one evening. She had been playing at a friend's house near the area where I had released Binky the snot blowing cat.

Wendy approached me while she was sobbing and said, "Dad, somebody shot my cat. I found it dead today while playing back in the willows at Miranda's house."

I didn't know what to say so I replied, "Are you sure it's your cat, Wendy? And how did it get all the way over to Miranda's house?"

Wendy cried even harder and said, "Yes, I'm sure it's my cat, Dad, it still has the collar on it. Miranda's dad doesn't like cats and shot it in their back yard."

I felt absolutely horrible and didn't have the heart to tell Wendy about the cat relocation program. I gave her a hug and told her that I was sorry. It took me nearly twenty years to tell Wendy the truth about relocating Binky the snot blowing cat. This was also the time that Wendy opened up and told me stories about her teenage years and all the stunts that she pulled that I never would have dreamed of. I don't know how many times she had snuck out of the house in the middle of the night and I never knew a thing about it. She even told me about the night that she and her best friend snuck over to my poker cabin and drank an entire bottle of Crown Royal whiskey straight from the bottle. They both ended up puking all over the yard and passing out behind the poker cabin. She told me that they both woke up in the early morning hours, nearly froze to death. They crawled back to the house and went directly to bed and faked having the stomach flu for two days. It's a wonder that they didn't freeze to death or end up with alcohol poisoning. Heck, maybe they did and nobody ever even knew about it.

Chapter 7

NEW SOUTH PINEDALE GAME WARDEN

South Pinedale game warden Dennis Almquist had retired over a year ago. His replacement would be Brian R. Nesvik, who had just returned from a year and a half tour of duty in Iraq. Brian worked for the Wyoming National Guard and led a brigade of troops while in Iraq. I had never met Brian before but had heard a great deal about him over the years. It sounded like he was a hell of a game warden while previously stationed in Elk Mountain. I had overheard other wardens state that Brian was the luckiest game warden that they had ever seen, as he always seemed to be in the right place at the right time to catch the bad guys.

Brian arrived at the Pinedale office on May 15, 2005. He was a few years younger than me. However, his head was nearly bald and he wore glasses most of the time. He had a great personality and a very strong work ethic. Brian was already good friends with North Pinedale game warden Hubba Healy. They had worked together when Hubba was the Mountain View game warden before coming to Pinedale. I was excited to work with both of them and Big Piney game warden Brad Hovinga. I truly felt like I was supervising the best team of game wardens in the entire state right out of the Pinedale office.

I hadn't spent any time working in the field with Brian and really didn't know much about him. He called me one day just after lunch and said, "Hey, Swerb, I'm headed out south of Pinedale in the oil field to deal with a couple buck antelope that have their horns locked together; would you like to ride along?"

I was very excited to finally have an opportunity to work with Brian in the field and responded, "Heck yeah, come pick me up at the office."

Brian picked me up a few minutes later and we headed south. Brian explained to me that a supervisor in the oil field had called him to report that two antelope had been fighting and they got their horns locked together near an oil rig. It sounded like one antelope was down on the ground and the other antelope was standing up looking over the antelope on the ground. As we headed south, we told stories and laughed about many different topics. We rounded a corner out in the oil field, Brian was laughing so hard about something that I had just said that he had tears streaming down his cheeks. I looked up to see about twenty oil field workers standing beside the road ahead of us. I told Brian to stop the truck right now. Brian hit the brakes and the truck came sliding to a stop on the gravel road. He looked over at me and said, "Why do you want me to stop right here?"

I responded, "Brian, we have an audience just ahead of us to deal with. This means you are going to have to act very professionally for once in your life in front of all these workers. Do you have everything we need to do our job professionally to release these antelope?"

Brian responded, still laughing, and said, "Yes, sir, I have a lariat rope, a bone saw, and a couple orange hats to put over their faces to calm them down while we release them."

I replied, "Perfect, now do you think you can do this without f----g something up in front of all of these spectators?"

Brian responded, "Yes, sir, I think I got this handled."

We pulled the truck forward and parked next to the workers. Brian introduced us to the supervisor of the rig.

Brian said, "Damn, you didn't tell me that you were going to shut the whole rig down and babysit these antelope until we arrived."

The supervisor replied, "We were just concerned about these antelope and wanted to do everything possible to save their lives. We couldn't get them unhooked, as the horn from the live antelope is stuck in the side of the head from the dead antelope."

This is when I realized that the antelope on the ground was already dead. I grabbed the lariat from Brian and put the loop around both hind legs of the live antelope. I then pulled the rope tight and brought the live antelope down to the ground and stretched him out. Brian grabbed a florescent orange hat and put it over the antelope's nose and eyes. When a wild animal can't see it tends to calm them down. Brian grabbed the bone saw and had to cut the horn off the live antelope. This was the only option to get them released. Once the horn was completely sawed off, I looked at Brian and said, "Once I release the antelope's hind legs from the lariat, grab the orange hat simultaneously and pull it off his face.

I didn't figure that the antelope had much energy left after fighting with this buck and being hooked up for over an hour. Just as soon as I released his legs from the lariat the buck jumped up and ran over the top of Brian. Brian grabbed for the orange hat and missed it. The antelope took off running at nearly fifty mph in the opposite direction with the orange hat securely placed over both of his eyes. The buck antelope was actually headed right towards another group of antelope that were located about five hundred yards away. The other antelope looked up to see the buck with a florescent orange hat on headed towards them. They all took off running in four different directions to get away from the crazy antelope with the bright orange hat. This buck antelope ran right through the large herd and scattered them everywhere. This was the craziest thing that I had ever seen. All the oil workers started laughing uncontrollably.

I looked down at the dead antelope on the ground. He was covered in blood and had hair missing in spots. He also still had a horn stuck in the side of his face from the live antelope. I was trying to figure out what we were going to do with the dead antelope. I jokingly said to one of the workers, "Do any of you want to eat this antelope?"

One worker wearing a blue hard hat replied, "Hell, yeah! We have a grill up at the rig and we will eat every part of that antelope tonight."

I couldn't imagine that this antelope was going to taste very good at all considering what he had been through before dying. But it would save us from having to haul him off and go to good use. I told the men that they were free to dress him out and consume him. We shook hands and thanked the supervisor for calling us. Brian and I jumped into his truck and drove off. I looked at Brian and said, "You, kind of f------d that one up, Brian. Now we have a one horned antelope running around with a damn florescent orange hat on during hunting season. No does will breed him and hunters will surely report this to us."

Brian responded, "Sorry, boss, my bad."

I replied, "I'm just giving you a hard time. Good work; that hat will surely fall off soon and he will be just fine."

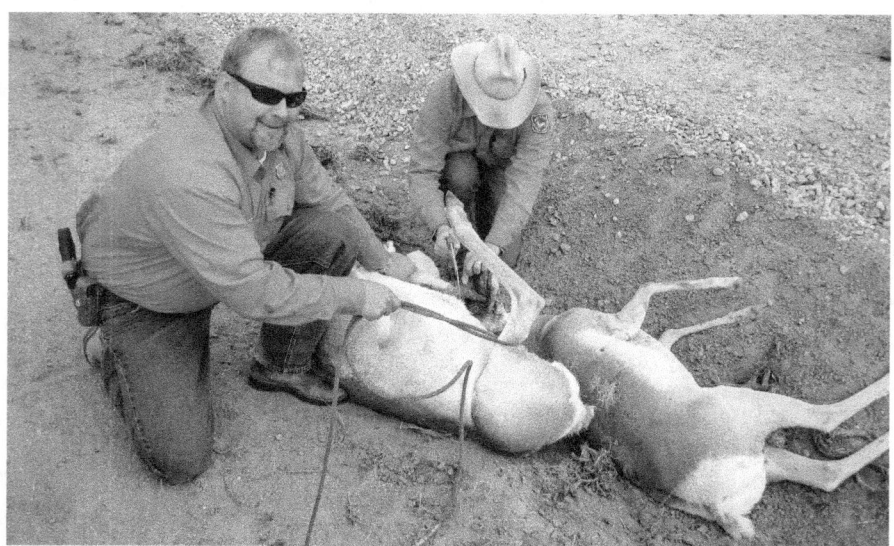

Buck antelope with horns locked together

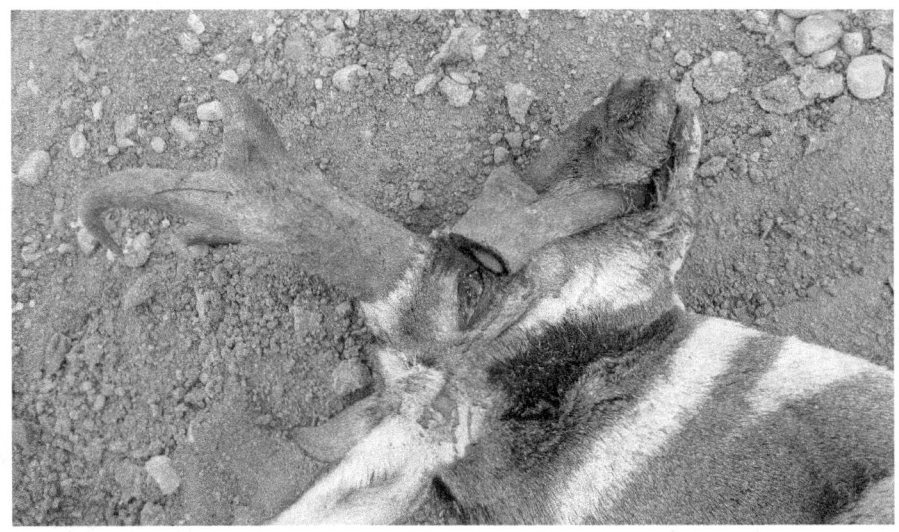

Horn stuck in the side of dead antelope's head)

About one week later a hunter stopped by the office to report that he had observed an antelope running around the Jonah field wearing a florescent orange hat. I explained to the man that I knew that antelope and was directly responsible. The man just laughed as he left the office. About another week later a different hunter stopped by the office to report that he stalked a buck antelope with his bow and arrow out in the Jonah field. He thought he was stalking a freak antelope with only one horn. But as he got within about twenty yards of the antelope, he determined that it wasn't a freak antelope but that someone had sawed his damn horn off. I looked at the hunter and responded, "Who in their right mind would ever do something like that?" We laughed and I said, "Actually, that buck killed another buck so we cut one of his horns off to prevent him from killing any other antelope." The guy looked at me with a funny look on his face and replied, "Well, I guess if he's out being aggressive and acting like an asshole that was probably the right thing to do." I was going to tell the guy that I was only kidding, but decided to leave the story just like it was. I never heard about that antelope again.

Brian and I hit it off really well. He was fun to work with and be around. He had a great attitude, a strong work ethic, and a great personality. He was very intelligent and all about catching the bad guys.

At this point in time, we were dealing with more and more grizzly bears in the Upper Green River that were depredating on cattle and sheep. Wardens would get the call from livestock producers that they had grizzly or even black bears killing their sheep or cattle. Wardens would then have to travel up into the rough high country and confirm their losses in order for the producers to get compensated. Once confirmed the warden would try and trap whatever was responsible for killing livestock. This job got so busy for wardens that the department hired trophy game conflict personnel to assist the wardens with investigating and trapping large carnivores responsible for killing livestock. Most game wardens appreciated the extra help but some game wardens didn't appreciate the extra help, as they felt this was part of their job and they didn't need any help doing their job. Many game wardens were also very efficient at catching problem grizzly bears, black bears, and wolves, and they didn't want help. They also enjoyed this aspect of their job.

Hubba Healy was very proficient at catching problem bears. He didn't want help in his district and he didn't need help. He didn't agree with hiring extra trophy game conflict personnel, and they were not welcome in his warden district. For that matter, nobody was welcome to work in his district. If caught working in Hubba's district without prior permission, you were considered trespassing or poaching and would be issued a citation.

I ended up riding with Hubba one day to travel up to Union Pass in the Upper Green River and help work a grizzly bear that had been snared by the front foot. Large carnivore personnel had caught the cattle-killing bear the night before. I had very little experience dealing with conflict grizzly bears and was looking forward to assisting with this bear. The conflict biologist loaded up a tranquilizer dart and let me shoot the large grizzly bear. They told me that it was best to shoot them in the hind quarter if possible. I approached the bear in a patrol vehicle and shot it in the rump at about twenty yards away. We were told to avoid setting a leghold snare in an area that you can't drive your patrol vehicle to. Ideally, you want to be in your patrol truck for safety in case the bear gets out of the snare and charges. Sometimes the bear may only be caught by a couple of toes and pull free from the trap. Other times the bear may lie there in the night and chew on the quarter-inch steel cable and nearly break through it. If the bear charges, the cable may break. Many things can go wrong with a large grizzly bear in a trap. It's just safer to be in your patrol vehicle for cover if things go wrong.

At the time of writing this, the Wyoming Game and Fish Department has no authority over the management of grizzly bears. Wardens and other large carnivore biologists investigate kills to livestock and even sometimes human beings. If livestock is confirmed killed by any trophy game animal, the department reimburses the landowner for their losses. Once a grizzly bear is captured the work begins. If the captured bear already has an ear tag, collar, or tattoo on the inside of its gums, the bear has been caught before. If the bear has been caught before it will have a history (rap sheet) of how old it is, where it was caught, where it was relocated, and what kind of problems it was causing. So, if a grizzly bear was caught killing cattle in Pinedale one summer and had no other history of killing livestock it would be relocated in, say, a place like Cody, Wyoming. If this bear is caught killing livestock in Cody or anywhere else at a later date, it will be euthanized. The department must receive authorization from the Feds to remove any grizzly bears from the population, and with good cause.

The problem with all of this is that once a grizzly bear is captured in a leg snare or culvert trap, they get very trap-smart. This can make them very difficult to catch a second time. So bears continue to

115

kill livestock while the game and fish continues to try and trap bears and pay for livestock losses. Obviously, a livestock producer is not able to find every dead cow or sheep on the landscape, and dead carcasses disappear quickly with other predators eating the carcasses before personnel can confirm cause of death. Due to some scientific research on this subject coming from the Green River Cattleman's Association, the department is liable to pay 7 to 1 for each confirmed wolf loss to a domestic calf and 3.5 to 1 for every confirmed domestic calf killed by a grizzly bear. This information has been captured over the years with producers knowing how many cattle or sheep entered the grazing allotment and how many cattle or sheep left the allotment at the end of the grazing season. This data has been tracked closely before wolves and grizzly bears were in this area and after their presence, showing differences in numbers. So, as you can see, these numbers add up very quickly and are very costly to the department. It is in the department's best interest to remove these depredating bears and wolves as soon as possible. It is also a very time-consuming and dangerous part of the job.

I made a nice shot in the rump of the large grizzly bear in the leg snare. This was my first grizzly bear that I got to actually dart. I helped the large carnivore crew work the bear and learned as much as I could about dealing with problem grizzly bears. Once the bear was worked it was loaded into a culvert trap with tires to transport out of the area. This particular bear had not been caught before and was released back into the wild north of Cody, Wyoming. We have learned over the years that sometimes these bears cover hundreds of miles back to where they were originally caught within two-weeks' time. This involves crossing rugged mountain ranges even at times when snow levels are still very deep in the high country. They are truly an amazing animal with a high fidelity to their home ranges.

I jumped back into the truck with Hubba and left the area. While traveling down the rough road to head back home, I heard

Damage Technician Dave Hyde talking on the radio. Someone was trying to call him and he responded by saying, "Can I call you right back? I'm having a bit of a situation right now." Apparently, Dave had just released the grizzly bear from a culvert trap that I had darted earlier that morning. The angry bear ran underneath Dave's truck and bit his rear tire, causing the tire to go flat.

Hubba and I rounded the corner to discover a Peruvian sheep herder riding his horse down the rough two-track road ahead of us. He flagged us down and tried to explain something to us, except he couldn't speak a word of English. We listened to him for several minutes and looked at each other, like what in the hell did he just say? He wanted us to follow him on his horse up into the mountains to show us something. So, we parked the truck and followed his horse while on foot up the steep terrain. Hubba understood more Spanish than I and thought he was trying to show us where a black bear had killed a sheep. The sheepherder kept saying, "Oso Negro." Meaning black bear. After nearly a mile, the sheepherder got off his horse and pointed at the ground. I could see drag marks in the tall grass with some blood spots here and there. The man was rambling along in Spanish and pointing at the ground and then up towards a patch of aspens at the top of the mountain. It appeared he was trying to tell us that he had observed a black bear kill a sheep and drag it up the mountain towards the patch of timber above.

We followed the drag marks up to a small patch of aspen trees. Inside the trees we discovered what looked like an ewe sheep that had been buried under leaves, dirt, and branches. We call this a cache. Hubba looked at me and said, "It appears that a black bear has killed this ewe and dragged it into the trees out of sight to come back and eat later. I have a leg-hold snare in my truck that we can set right now and hopefully we can catch this black bear tonight." Hubba did not want to turn this over to the large carnivore team, as we were there right now and could catch the depredating bear hopefully that night to avoid more sheep losses. The only problem was that the truck was a longways away and there were no roads in the area to the cache site. So, we hiked back down to Hubba's truck and got all the supplies that we needed and hiked back up the mountain to make a set. I watched Hubba set the leg-hold snare. It appeared that he knew what he was doing and had done this before. He placed stepping sticks in the ground so that the bear would step in the center of the leg-hold snare. Stepping sticks are sharp stick that protrude out of the ground. Animals don't like stepping on sharp sticks, so they place their foot in the area that doesn't have anything sharp protruding out of the ground. The snare was made out of quarter- inch metal cable and was approximately eight feet long. Hubba buried the snare in the dirt and anchored the other end of the cable around a large aspen tree with heavy duty cable clamps. The tree was about eight inches in diameter. This was the largest aspen tree in the area and should hold a black bear with no problems. We made the set right at dark and hiked back to the truck in the dark. Hubba and I agreed to meet at the same location of where the truck was parked at 6:30 the next morning. It was a long rough ride out of the mountains that night and it had been another long day.

The next morning, Hubba, Brian, and I met at the same location to check the leg-hold snare. We had our trucks shut off and the morning sun was just starting to rise over the mountains to the east. It was a chilly morning as the steam rolled off our coffee cups as we sipped. We had been waiting for it to get daylight to walk into the area of the set snare. This is when I heard a noise that made the hair stand up on my neck and back. I heard the loudest roar that I had ever heard before. Whatever it was kept roaring loudly in the direction that we had set the leg-hold snare. I looked at Hubba and said, "I think you caught something big, Hubba."

We snuck up through the trees and looked across a grassy meadow towards the area where we had set the snare. What I saw next, I will never forget. We had caught one of the largest grizzly bears that I had ever seen. The bear was standing on his hind feet like a human. It would pant hard, roar, and charge hard right towards us. You could see steam coming out of the bear's mouth and nostrils as he roared. Every time that he charged the small aspen tree that the snare was anchored to would bend over as if it was going to break in half. After a closer look, we realized the bear was caught by his hind foot in the snare. This allowed the bear to back up and charge hard towards us, nearly breaking the tree in half each time.

I looked at Hubba and said, "Oh shit, we caught a large grizzly bear not a black bear. We need to pioneer your truck up here and dart the bear from the truck. I'm certainly not walking out in the open to dart this bear at close range without the protection of a truck." Hubba agreed and we made our way back down to our trucks. The Forest Service would not have been proud of us if they knew what we drove through to get Hubba's truck close enough to the bear to dart it. Let's just say that it got a little "Western." I loaded a tranquilizer dart while Hubba drove through the thick timber and over the downfall dead trees. He drove me within twenty yards of the large growling bear. I felt way too close to this bear even though we had the protection of our truck. I was afraid that the bear may break the cable or snap the tree in half and attack our truck.

I was now a trained professional at darting bears, as I had just darted my first bear the previous day. I waited patiently for the bear to turn broadside so that I could place the dart in its rump. This is generally the best place to dart them because of the large muscle mass in their hind quarters. The bear would not give me a broadside shot and kept charging and growling. Hubba yelled at me, "SHOOT THE DAMN THING IN THE CHEST BEFORE HE BREAKS FREE!" I took careful aim and shot the dart right in the center of the bear's chest, as he was standing on his hind legs facing us. The bear dropped down to all four legs on the ground and ate the dart. That's right, he pulled the dart out of his chest and swallowed the damn thing. He then stood back up on his hind feet and started growling again. I started to load another dart and noticed the bear start to wobble back and forth. The bear was going to sleep. I was happy that the dart had worked perfectly.

Once the bear was down, we cautiously approached him on the ground. I noticed that the tree that the bear was anchored to was nearly bit in half. The bear had also climbed up the tree and bit the top of the tree off about twelve feet from the ground. He also had dug a huge hole all the way around the base of the aspen tree about two feet deep. This bear would weigh well over 500 lbs.

I had brought up a culvert-style bear trap that was hooked to my patrol vehicle down below. I was glad that I had brought the trap with me and didn't have to rattle all the way back to Pinedale on the rough road. It was going to be a challenge to get the trap into the bear's location with all the downfall and timber between it and my truck. I told Brian and Hubba to start working the bear while I hiked back down to get my truck.

I was able to drive and get the truck and bear trap right next to the drugged bear. By this time, the Peruvian sheep herder had ridden his horse up and was standing next to the bear, talking to Brian and Hubba. I exited my patrol truck to overhear Brian, trying to teach the sheepherder how to say 'F------g grizzly bears, F------g grizzly bears'. We ended up dragging the dead weight of the grizzly bear into the culvert trap. For those of you who have not done this before it's not very fun, as one person has to crawl into the culvert trap and pull the bear towards the front while several other people push the rear of the bear. Keep in mind there are usually some maggots and something very stinky still in the front of the culvert trap from a previous setting. And there is not much room to crawl over the live bear while exiting the trap, so you end up getting really close and personal with a stinking grizzly bear.

Nesvik with large grizzly bear

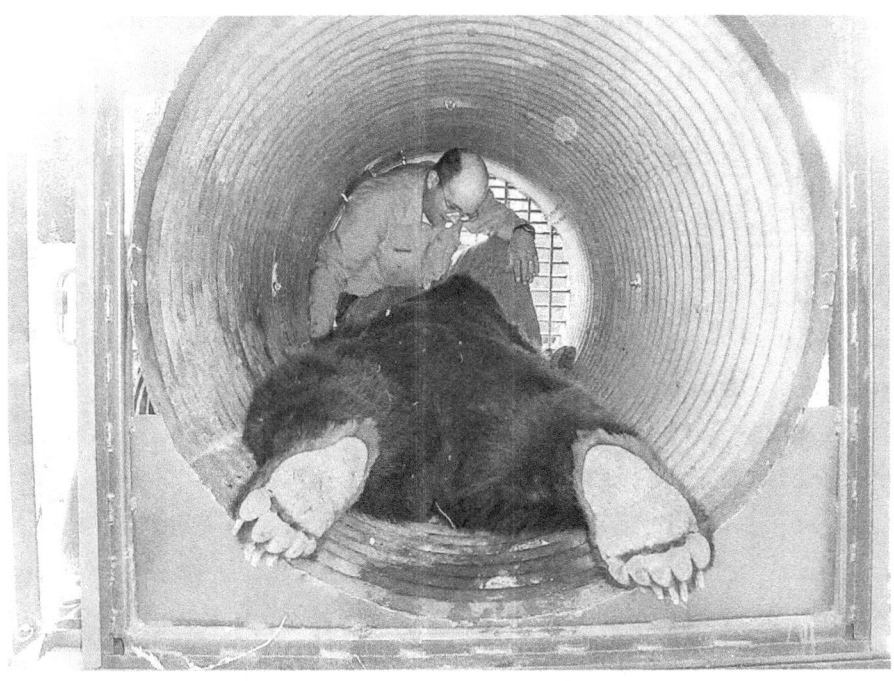

Nesvik in culvert trap with drugged grizzly bear

I was not impressed with Brian, and by the time we left the area the sheepherder rode off into the trees yelling "F--------G GRIZZLY BEARS, F------G GRIZZLY BEARS!" I swear these were the only words of English that the sheepherder could speak. Brian jumped into my truck, looked at me, and said, "Sorry, boss; that probably wasn't one of my most professional moments back there." All I could do was laugh because I knew that sheep herder was going to tell everyone he knew about them F------G GRIZZLY BEARS.

I was happy that we had caught the grizzly bear and had him loaded up in the trap and headed back down the road. Except, the sheepherder had told us that he observed a black bear dragging the dead sheep and not a grizzly bear. I wondered if we had even caught the right bear. Once we had cell phone service, we would need to contact the Feds and other Game and Fish personnel to see if this bear had a track record to determine if it would be put down or relocated away from the area. We had trapped this bear before, as we discovered a tattooed number on the inside of the bear's gum line. This number would tell us when the bear was caught and if he had been in trouble for killing livestock previously. The drive out of there was going to be very slow and rough, pulling the culvert trap.

I eased down a steep hill completely covered in large boulders. I was doing about five miles per hour when my truck came to a sudden stop. I stopped so hard and fast that my head hit the steering wheel. I looked up to see one of the tires of the bear trap rolling down the rough road ahead of me. SHIT, I had just broken the axle on the bear trap and lost a tire. I looked into my passenger mirror and could see that the frame of the bear trap was resting on the ground between two large boulders. Mind you, this was probably about a 1960s bear trap that had probably never had its bearings packed in the past thirty years or any other maintenance done to it. Everyone else had gone ahead of me. I told them that I would be fine and take my time down the rough road. The damn tire rolled and bounced all the way down the mountain side. I couldn't even tell where it was or how far it had rolled. I guess I really didn't need it anyways, as the axle on the trailer was busted in half.

I was now in a bit of a predicament. My truck and trailer were broken down in the middle of the road on a Saturday. It would be just a matter of time before someone else came up or down the road and there was not any room to get around me, with large boulders and trees on each side of the road. I stepped out of my truck to assess the situation. The passenger side of the bear trap was lying on the ground, hung up between two large boulders. The bear was panting so hard that the trap was shaking on the ground. This concerned me because it's important to keep animals sternal and cool while they are drugged. If they aren't kept sternal their lungs can aspirate and they can die from it. If they get too hot, they can become dehydrated. The bear was starting to wake up. I could hear him moaning and growling as the trap shook back and forth on the ground from his heavy panting. It was late morning and starting to get very warm out. I got on my radio and tried to call anyone that would listen. I finally got a hold of our new bear guy in Pinedale and explained that I needed another trap to transport this bear. The bear guy was not impressed because Hubba and I had trapped this bear without his knowledge and this was his job to trap the bear, not ours. Nevertheless, he said he would bring another trap but it might be about two hours before he could get to my location. I told him to bring some more drugs, as we would have to dart the bear again to move it to the new culvert trap. I didn't know where in the hell Brian and Hubba went. They were probably having a cheeseburger at The Place, just down the road. The Place was the actual name of a restaurant in the Upper Green River. They served awesome food and had pool tables and a bar. Hell, they were probably in the bar, drinking beer and shooting pool in their red shirts while they celebrated the capture of the large grizzly bear.

The bear was now up and trying to get out of the trap. He charged and bit the heavy metal screen on the front of the trap. He was roaring so loudly that it was scary to even listen to him. I didn't even want to be near the trap. What if he was actually able to break out of the trap? I walked over to the front of the trap to take a quick picture. He roared so loud that it scared me as he charged and bit the metal openings on the front of the trap. I noticed that he had broken off at least two of his canines from biting the metal. This bear was pissed, and wanted out of that damn trap. I knew in two-hours' time that the bear would get too hot. I didn't have any shade where I was broken down. Luckily, I had a plastic tarp in my large metal toolbox. I pulled the tarp out and covered the entire bear trap. You couldn't see the bear, but you could darn sure hear him roar and the entire trap would shake due to his heavy panting. I sat down on a large boulder a short distance away. As I was sitting there, I could hear the sound of ATVs coming up the road. *Great,* I thought, *now I have company coming.*

Culvert bear trap with broken axle

Pretty soon a family of four pulled up on their ATVs. It was a mother and father and their two young children. The father pulled up next to me and yelled over the sound of his ATV, "WHAT YOU GOT HIDDEN UNDER THE BLUE TARP?"

I replied, "Just a little ol' bear, waiting for another trap. You guys go on around and head on up the road."

Grizzly bear in culvert trap

As the family drove right next to the trap, the bear let out the loudest roar that I had ever heard. They almost wrecked their four-wheelers trying to get out of the way. I'm sure they thought, *yeah right, just a little ol' bear!* Help finally arrived. We had to dart the poor bear in the trap and wait for him to go back to sleep. I don't know how the two of us got that bear from one trap to the other, but we did. I thanked our new bear guy Zach and headed for Cody to relocate the bear. Just before South Pass, my bag phone rang. It was one of our bear guys. He called to tell me to turn around and come back to Pinedale, as the bear would be euthanized. Apparently, the bear had been captured two years earlier for killing cattle in the Upper Green River. He had been transported and relocated north of Cody and made his way back to killing cattle again. Sometimes our jobs are not always fun and glamorous. This really pulled on my heart strings to have to put this beautiful animal down. Especially after everything that we had been through together that morning.

Chapter 8

TEXAS HOLD 'EM AND PROBLEM BEARS

Summer was flying by fast. I had spent a great deal of time meeting with the man from Idaho who had received the bid to build the large elk trap that would be put to the test sometime in January and February on the Muddy Creek elk feed ground. I also spent a great deal of time attending the Governor's Brucellosis Coordination Team Meetings (GBCTM). These meetings were strategically placed all over the state of Wyoming to reach different audiences. There were over twenty members assigned to the team. Many of the members had PhDs in various studies. I was one of the few members on the team that did not have a doctorate degree. I never dreamed that I would be giving Power Point presentations in front of the Governor and all these highly educated people. I just wanted to be a game warden, so how did I get myself into this position?

The Governor knew that everyone on the team was extremely busy with their professional lives and careers and didn't have much extra time to attend various meetings across the state. So, he decided to fly all the members of the team to the meetings in his personal jet. I felt pretty darn important flying around the state in the Governor's jet to attend all these meetings. I also felt pretty important sitting at the table with all the agency directors and leadership of Wyoming.

We left the Pinedale airport for a meeting in Riverton early one morning. The flight only took eleven minutes to go over the Wind River Mountain range. This would have taken me over two hours driving time in my patrol truck. The Governor's jet saved everyone hours of time driving. I later got to know the pilot and he would even find a place for my golf clubs on the plane so that I could go golfing with my brother, Wade, in Riverton during the evenings after our meetings. My brother would pick me up at the airport with my golf clubs and just shake his head and say "You Big Dumbass!" I told him, "Excuse me, but that's Mr. Dumbass to you sir!"

I returned to Pinedale on a Friday afternoon after several days of long meetings. I jumped into my patrol truck and noticed that I was about 5,000 miles over my last oil change. I decided to stop at a service station in Pinedale and get my oil changed really quick before I headed home for the day. The man that owned the service station was a good friend of mine, named Steve. He would always get me in immediately to change my oil or repair a flat tire. I pulled up to the station at about 3:30PM. Steve told me that they were swamped but I could leave my truck there and they would try and get it done by 5:00PM. I told Steve that if he didn't get it done by 5:00 that I would leave it over the weekend and he could do it first thing Monday morning. I also told Steve to be sure and lock the truck if it were to sit out over the weekend, as I had many firearms in the truck. Steve replied, "Yes, sir, I will lock it up tight over the weekend and call you when it's done." Lana met me at the service station and gave me a ride home. I was pretty sure Steve was not going to get to my truck done until Monday morning.

I took the entire weekend off and felt relieved to finally have some rest. I was pretty much worthless anyways if I didn't have my game and fish truck to take calls. We practically lived out of our trucks 24/7. Our trucks were equipped to handle just about any call, from catchpoles to metal detectors and everything in between. I'm certain I stored over 2000 rounds of ammunition in my truck between my pistol, shotgun, and rifle. If my truck were to ever catch on fire, you better run like hell because it would be one of the most spectacular firework displays ever seen.

Monday morning Lana gave me a ride back to Pinedale to pick up my truck. We pulled up to the service station but I didn't see my truck anywhere. I thought, *Steve must have my truck inside the shop working on it.* I told Lana to just drop me off, as Steve would have my truck done in a few minutes. I walked into the shop and said, "Good morning, Steve."

Steve replied, "Good morning Swerb, how was the poker game Friday night? Sorry I didn't make it out to your game. I ended up driving over to the casino in Riverton and got scalped by the natives. Damn, they sent me home with my tail between my legs!"

"Yeah, they will do that from time to time. I have been there myself."

"If you have a few minutes, come over to the front counter and play me a few hands of Texas Hold 'Em for ten bucks a hand," Steve said with a cigarette hanging out of the corner of his mouth.

I followed Steve over to the front counter in his shop. I slapped ten dollars on the counter and said, "Deal them out, buddy."

About that time a couple guys from the public came in to get a tractor tire repaired. Steve told them that he was busy but if they wanted to hang around and play a few hands of Texas Hold'em that he would have his helper repair the tire while they waited. The next thing I knew, Swerb was in a serious game of Texas Hold 'Em with three men that I had never met before, wearing my department red-shirt and pistol and gambling in the public. Good cards were running me over and it seemed like I couldn't lose even when I thought I had bad cards. I won a couple hundred dollars in about twenty minutes. One guy looked up and said, "Damn, that was an expensive tractor tire repair!" I laughed and looked at Steve and said, "I stopped by to pick up my game and fish truck; where is it?"

Steve looked at me kind of funny and replied, "I don't know. I thought you stopped by and picked it up on Friday."

"No, I left it parked here over the weekend."

"Shit, I don't know. We finished it Friday and I parked the truck right where you had left it. I didn't see it here this morning and thought you had already picked it up."

"No, I never picked it up on Friday. Did you lock it before you left for the weekend?"

Steve looked at me kind of funny as he took a puff off his unfiltered cigarette and replied, "I think we did."

SHIT, SOMEONE HAS STOLEN MY DAMN PATROL TRUCK OVER THE WEEKEND! I thought to myself. Steve went into a panic and started asking his employees questions about the missing game and fish truck. Nobody seemed to know anything. I started to panic as I looked all around the parking lot. About that time my cell phone rang. It was my office manager Des Brunette.

"Swerb, hey, this is Des. Do you know where your Game and Fish truck is at?"

I responded, "Hell no, I just noticed that it was gone!"

"I just got a phone call from a concerned citizen that there is a game and fish truck smashed into a large pine tree behind the Stockman's bar."

"Thanks for the heads up, Des, that's probably my truck. I will look into it."

The Stockman's bar was located right across the street from the service station. I told Steve that I had a lead on the whereabouts of my truck and that I needed to run. And run I did, right across Main Street with a pocket full of Texas Hold 'Em cash. As I walked around the backside of the bar, I discovered a large metal trash dumpster that had been tipped over onto its side. I then noticed the rear end of my green patrol truck sticking out from underneath a huge pine tree with low hanging branches. On the rear right of the bumper was a decal that read GF-14. Yup, that was definitely my truck. Dammit!

I crawled under the low hanging branches to assess the damage. Believe it or not, there was no damage to the front end of my truck. I had a push bar on the front of my truck that was embedded about two inches into the large tree. I panicked and thought, *oh shit, what about all the firearms and ammunition in my truck?* I forced the driver's side door open against the tree branches and crawled up into the truck. The keys were still in the ignition. The inside of the truck smelled like skunky beer. I noticed an open can of Budweiser in the cup holder. The beer can was half full. I frantically went through the entire cab of my truck and noticed that none of my firearms or ammunition were missing. I thought, *THANK YOU GOD!*

I stepped back out of my truck and did a preliminary investigation of the entire crime scene. From the tire tracks in the gravel parking lot, it appeared that someone had been spinning doughnuts in the parking lot with my game and fish truck. After several nice doughnuts the truck went out of control and smashed into a large trash dumpster, knocking it over, and then had an undisturbed launch into the large pine tree. I did not file a police report. I discarded the half drunken can of Budweiser into the tipped over dumpster and slowly backed my truck out of the tree branches and got the hell out of there. I drove the truck back over to Steve to tell him the story and finally get my oil changed. This led to some laughs and apologies for not locking my truck over the weekend. It also led to a few more hands of cards. I thought, *Heck, I should have just finished that half can of warm skunky Budweiser over a few hands of Texas Hold 'Em in the tire shop.* I'm sure if any of my friends observed my patrol truck parked into a tree behind the bar they would have laughed and said, "Looks like ol' Swerb had a long night at the Stockman's bar again!" Truth be known, it was probably one of my drunk jackass friends that took my patrol truck for a joy ride after the bar closed on Friday or Saturday night. I have no idea how long it was parked under that tree or how many people saw it there, but it was a bit embarrassing to say the least. I was always going to tell my boss Bernie about this story but I forgot to.

I left the shop with a fully serviced truck that smelled like a brewery and unfiltered cigarettes. As I was headed out of Pinedale, I received a call of a black bear that had broken into a cabin in the Upper Green River. The cabin belonged to one of the day riders who worked for the Green River Cattleman's Association. It had been a horrible year for bear conflicts. All of the wardens and Trophy Game Conflict personnel were busy with other calls. I decided to head up to the cow camp cabin and see what I could do to help with the bear situation. The Game and Fish Department also had a patrol cabin in the area that department personnel could stay in while working. This was a very small but fully functional cabin located in a very remote area. This cabin's location would save personnel hundreds of miles of travel time to and from Pinedale while dealing with problem bears or checking hunters in the fall. The cabin was named Two Bears Cabin. Years ago, there was an old-time game warden that observed two bears mating in front of this cabin and so the cabin was named. Near this cabin was also a Forest Service cabin that generally housed temporary employees during the summer and fall months. I had heard rumor that there was an older couple from Florida living in the cabin. Their names were Robert and Maria Seidler. I also heard rumor that Robert was a retired investigator/game warden from Florida. I was looking forward to meeting the two of them.

I rattled my truck into the cow camp cabin and met with an old-time cowboy named Bobby who was living in the cabin at the time. Bobby was in his early seventies. He wore a dirty cowboy hat with a stampede string. His pants were tucked into his handmade cowboy boots that came all the way up to his knees. He wore round brim glasses and had a long mustache. He spoke with an accent like he may be from Michigan. Bobby was pretty wound up about the bear visit that he had just encountered. He claimed that the bear went through the front door of the cabin, jumped on his bed while he was sleeping, and smashed through the window glass above his bed as it exited the cabin. I walked outside of the cabin to see shattered glass on the outside of the cabin and black bear tracks in the dirt. I told Bobby that I would get someone up soon to set a trap for the bear and transport it out of the area. Bobby thanked me and asked if I knew of anyone that had a good poker game from time to time. He told me that he would be out of the mountains during the winter months and really enjoyed a good game of poker. I told him that I had a poker game every Friday night in a little cabin behind my house. His eyes lit up and he giggled as he said, "That sounds like fun, I will give you my number and hope for an invite sometime." I shook the man's callused and arthritic hand. His fingers were long and tightly wrapped around my large hand. His knuckles were swollen and red. This man was a gentleman. I could tell by his hand shake and weathered hands that this man had worked hard his entire life. He had probably milked his share of dairy cows over the years. You can tell a lot by the look of a man's hands. Just look at a banker's hands someday compared to a cowboy's hands. Back in college I shot a lot of pool for money, sometimes big money, and nearly got killed one night. My partner was a Native American that shot very well and could clear the table most of the time. He told me one day, "Scott, look at a man's hands before you bet with them. You will know by their hands if they can shoot pool or not." I never fully understood what to look for in a man's hands to make them a better pool shot. However, most of the people that beat me over the years didn't have smooth banker hands. They were generally dirty and rough, with dirty finger nails. Probably meant they had grown up working hard for their money their entire life and they weren't going to lose it in no damn pool game.

I left Bobby's cabin and headed up towards Two Bears cabin to meet Robert and Maria from Florida. As I was driving down a rough two-track road near the cabin I noticed an older man riding a big quarter horse near the road. The man was wearing a western cowboy hat with a stampede string. He had a gray beard and also wore round wire frame glasses. The man came riding up to me as I neared the Forest Service cabin. I stopped the truck and rolled down the window.

The man said loudly with a strong Southern accent, "Well, all be damned, I don't know if there are more bears in this country or game wardens. In the past few days that's all that I have seen up here in the mountains."

I jumped out of my truck and introduced myself to the man while he was seated on his horse. He told me his name was Robert Siedler and that he was a retired game warden out of Florida. I told him that it was my pleasure to meet him.

He said, "Well hell, are you hungry or do you need a cup of coffee or a shot of whiskey? Pull that damn truck up to my cabin over there; I would like you to meet my wife, Maria. She just loves Wyoming Game Wardens and would really enjoy meeting you."

I had never seen a man so excited to meet a Wyoming game warden before. I was excited to meet Maria and get to know both of them better. Robert rode his horse up to the cabin and tied it to a nearby tree.

He yelled, "HEY, MARIA, GET OUT HERE! I WANT YOU TO MEET A FINE WYOMING GAME WARDEN. HURRY UP!"

Maria came out the front door of the cabin. She was a beautiful Hispanic lady with a smile a mile wide. Her eyes lit up as she approached me. I went to shake her hand and she said, "I don't want to shake no hands with a Wyoming game warden, I want a big ol' hug." Maria gave me a hug like my wife had never given me.

She said, "Please come into the cabin and have a fresh piece of pie that I just baked." I followed them both into the cabin and could smell the fresh aroma of apple pie. Maria said, "Please sit down. We don't have no ice cream up here but please try some of this pie."

Robert was busy making a pot of coffee. I don't think I have ever had better tasting apple pie before. These two people were the most gracious people that I had ever met. Complete strangers and they welcomed me into their cabin. They told me that I was welcome to stay there any time and for any reason.

Robert said, "You show up here late at night, tired and cold, and you need a place to sleep, just come on in. There is always whiskey in this cabinet if you ever need to warm up. I don't know if you drink whiskey or not but I like an occasional shot myself." I told Robert that I had been known to try a little taste of whiskey every now and again. He said, "Hell yeah, well it's right here in the cabinet if you ever need a snort."

I sat and visited with them for nearly two hours. They were so excited to hear about my job and share stories about themselves with me. Robert had been hired as a seasonal ranger for the Forest Service to patrol closed roads and trails during the summer and fall months. This was a perfect retirement job for Robert, and both of them absolutely loved riding their horses in the mountains of Wyoming.

After I finished my pie and coffee, Robert said, "Yeah, we know the game warden in this area, ol' Hubba Healy and the new bear guy Zach Turnbull. They are great people and we just love it when they stop by to visit about all their different bear stories. Man, those guys have been busy trapping bears up here all summer long. As matter of fact, we just had a black bear try to break into our cabin last week. They have set several culvert traps up here trying to catch that damn black bear, but unsuccessfully."

I told Robert and Maria about the bear that had just broken into Bobby's cabin. They thought it might be the same bear that tried to break into their cabin. I insured them both that Hubba and Zach were top hands and would get rid of their problem bear soon. I shook Robert's hand and gave Maria a hug goodbye. I told them that I would keep in touch. Maria told me that they had a mobile radio in the cabin and could call their dispatch if they needed anything or had any emergencies. As I was leaving, I noticed a bear trap that was set in the trees near their cabin. The strange thing was the trap was completely covered in bouquets of beautiful mountain wild flowers. This must be the trap that Hubba and Zach had set to try and catch the problem black bear. I didn't notice if the trap was set or not but assumed Hubba and Zach were on top of their game. I'm not sure the reason for all the wild flowers; maybe they were trying to make the trap look more natural in the beautiful mountain setting.

It was getting late in the day. I drove up the rode a short distance to the Two Bears patrol cabin to spend the night. I was hoping the key was still attached to a piece of wire on the beam above the front door. It seemed like anytime someone really needed to use the cabin the key was always missing. The key was bright silver and may have been an attractant for squirrels or pack rats to haul off. I just never could figure out how they got the key off the piece of wire that it was tied to.

Luckily, the key was there and I was able to open the door and get a nice warm fire started in the old-time cook stove. I just loved staying in a rustic cabin in the mountains. I thought, *I may have to invite Robert and his bottle of whiskey up to enjoy the beautiful sunset off the tiny little deck attached to the front of the cabin.* I hadn't packed any food with me and the apple pie was starting to wear off. I dug through the cupboards of the cabin and found the usual. Ramen noodles, granola bars, canned beans, stale saltine crackers covered in tiny mouse turds, etc. I opened the last cupboard and noticed something with a golden halo shining over it. It was a half bottle of Crown Royal. I would get me some ice-cold creek water and sip a drink out on the deck as the sun went down behind the beautiful mountains. I dug through the cupboards and found a tiny metal coffee cup full of mouse shit. This would need a good washing in the creek out front but would be perfect.

As I left the cabin to wash my cup, I noticed another culvert bear trap set right behind the cabin. The door was closed on the trap. I also noticed that both tires were flat on the trap and the license plate was lying on the ground in front of the trap, all chewed up. After further observation I noticed two huge canine bite marks in the metal license plate. I also noticed that both tires had been punctured by a bear. The trap smelled horrible and had flies buzzing around it. I peeked my head inside the trap and noticed the hind quarter of a deer covered in maggots hanging in the trap. Apparently, the bear guys had left the trap at the cabin to set for a later date. A grizzly bear had smelled the rotten meat and visited the trap, probably last night sometime. The door was closed on the trap and the bear couldn't get the food reward so he punctured both tires and ripped the license plate off. I also noticed fresh bear tracks in the mud by the creek. This appeared to be a large male grizzly bear. At that moment the thoughts of me enjoying a whiskey on the deck of the cabin with a stinky bear trap nearby dampened. My thoughts of staying in the cabin that night sounded less appealing. I couldn't even move the bear trap because both tires were flat. I suppose I could have dragged the trap out of the area on the rims but I didn't want to damage them.

I awoke at daylight the next morning with no bear issues during the night. I stepped out the front door to watch the sun rise over the beautiful mountains. Just below the cabin, standing in a small pond surrounded by willows, was a giant bull moose. The moose had frost on his large beautiful antlers. The night had been cold and I could see steam coming out of his nostrils with every breath. The bright morning sunshine glared off of his large antlers and illuminated every breath that he took. This was truly an amazing thing to witness. I started up my patrol truck and turned the heater on high to let it warm while I packed up my supplies. I decided that I would go back down the road and check on Bobby and see if he had any new bear visitors in the night.

I arrived back at Bobby's cow camp cabin. He had just finished saddling his horse and had it tied to a tree next to the cabin.

"Well good morning, young man," Bobby said with a smile. "I was just getting ready to eat some breakfast if you would like to join me."

This sounded really good to me, as I hadn't packed anything for breakfast that morning.

I replied, "Good morning, Bobby! It looks like another beautiful blue-sky day in God's country. Any bear problems last night?"

"Nope, they left me alone last night," Bobby replied as he opened the cabin door for me to step inside. "I'm fixing to cook up some sourdough pancakes, bacon, and eggs if you would like to join me for breakfast."

I stepped into the old rustic cabin and smelled the aroma of bacon and eggs already frying in a pan full of grease on the top of the wood stove. There was a thin layer of blue smoke that filled the cabin as the morning sun shined through the windows. There was steam coming out of the top of the coffee pot as it sat percolating on top of the stove. This moment reminded me of growing up as a kid, my stepfather Martin cooking me breakfast in our tiny homestead cabin in the Bighorn Mountains during hunting season. If someone killed an elk Martin would always fry up the heart and liver mixed with onions and scrambled eggs for breakfast. I know you don't think this sounds good, but it was actually pretty tasty. For some reason, I just felt like I was right at home that morning in Bobby's little cabin.

Bobby pulled out a chair from beneath the table and said, "Sit down, young man, while I get you a plate." Bobby opened the oven door and pulled out a large plate stacked high with sourdough pancakes. He then loaded my plate full with everything that he had cooked and placed it in front of me.

"Let me get you something to drink with your breakfast," Bobby said.

Bobby opened a cooler next to the front door and pulled out two bottles of Corona beer. He placed the beer top on the edge of the wooden table and smacked it with his hand. The metal beer top went flying up in the air and landed on the floor. He then did the same with his beer and sat down next to me.

"Oh man, this looks good," Bobby said with a smile as he took a bite of bacon.

I looked at Bobby and held up my bottle of Corona to toast him for such a wonderful meal.

I told Bobby, "Man, this is great, and I honestly can tell you, Bobby, this is the first beer that I have ever had for breakfast in my entire life."

Bobby laughed and replied, "Well, it probably won't be your last one once you discover how good it tastes with your sourdough pancakes."

That may have very well been the best breakfast that I had ever eaten. After breakfast I was full as a tick and just wanted to take a nap. I thanked Bobby for breakfast and told him that I would have the bear guys come up and try and capture his problem black bear soon. Bobby thanked me for stopping by as he mounted his horse for the day. As he rode off, he stopped and looked back at me and said, "Don't forget to invite me down for a poker game sometime this winter."

I replied, "Will do, Bobby, and thanks again for a wonderful breakfast."

I jumped back into my patrol truck and headed down the road. A short distance later I could hear some chatter on my mobile radio. It was coming through on a Forest Service channel and it sounded like a woman. I rarely ever listened to this channel but decided to turn up the volume because the conversation just didn't sound very professional. As I turned up the radio, I heard a female voice say "Hello, hello, can anyone hear me? This is Maria up at the cow camp. I have just captured a problem black bear in a culvert trap and need assistance moving it out of the area." She sounded very excited that she had just caught this problem bear. Heck, this was probably the bear that Hubba and Zach could never catch.

Someone finally answered her on the radio and responded, "This is FS-3219, confirming you have caught a black bear in a culvert trap at the Forest Service guard station, over."

Maria responded, "YES, YES, I caught the problem bear using pepperoni pizza for bait last night!"

I nearly ran off the road and blew coffee through my nose when I heard this traffic. Maria was the hero and had caught the problem bear herself. She was so proud of herself.

"FS-3219 confirming that you caught a problem black bear utilizing pepperoni pizza for bait. I will pass the information on to Game and Fish personnel and get someone up to assist very soon."

Maria responded, "Thank you, 10-4, over and out."

I could hear her giggling in the background, as she still had the mic keyed for a few seconds after the conversation. About that time, I heard Zach come on the radio and respond, "This is GF-211, I copy your traffic and I will be 10-76 to the area. My ETA is approximately one hour."

I couldn't wait to give Hubba and Zach a hard time about Maria catching the problem bear with pepperoni pizza. I also couldn't wait to give Maria a hug and congratulate her on a job well done. I later found out that she was the one who'd decorated the trap with bouquets of wild mountain flowers to help the trap blend into the landscape so that a bear would actually enter the trap.

I really got to know Robert and Maria well that summer. They were great people and became life-long friends. Later that fall my poker buddies and I decided that we should change our venue for the Friday night poker game and have a game up at Robert and Maria's cabin in the mountains. I ran the idea by both of them and they were so excited to host a poker game.

Robert said, "Hell, yeah, you guys come up anytime and I will grill you a steak dinner before your game."

So, one Friday afternoon the guys loaded up two vehicles and headed up to their cabin. This would be about a two-hour drive on a rough road. That particular day it just happened to be snowing huge wet snowflakes the entire drive up the mountain. I actually was a little concerned that we may get snowed in during the night and not have a place for all of us to stay in Robert and Maria's small cabin. Hubba had asked me if I would help him run a deer decoy early Saturday morning. I agreed and drove up to the cabin alone in my patrol truck. I knew that I would need my patrol truck in the morning to assist Hubba with the decoy operation.

So here it was Friday evening. We all met at the cabin and Robert and Maria were absolutely delighted to have us there and cooked us a steak dinner. We finished cleaning up after a wonderful meal and broke out the cards and poker chips. Bobby was even invited to attend his first official poker game in the mountains. Most everyone would start the evening out buying in for one hundred dollars. It was dealer's choice and no carnival games or wild cards were allowed. We mostly played Texas Hold 'Em, Omaha, and five card draw high low split pot. As the night went on the whiskey went down smooth. It was a beautiful evening with huge white snowflakes floating down from heaven like soft feathers dancing in the sky.

Robert and Maria finally went to bed sometime after midnight. The snow piled up and the cards kept flying all night long. We were having so much fun that we all lost track of time. Robert entered the poker room sometime around 5:00AM. We were still playing cards.

Robert said, "Damn, I never seen such a thing in my life! You guys keep playing and I will fix you all some breakfast while you play." Maria woke up and joined the room. She actually took each of our orders of what we wanted for breakfast. She walked around the poker table like a waitress with her little note pad and wrote down our orders. They served us one at time and the game went on. Soon, it was daylight. I heard the sound of a vehicle pull up next to the cabin. Pretty quick I heard a knock at the door. Robert opened the door and snowflakes and Hubba Healy entered the warm room. Hubba was dressed heavy for the cold. He poked his head into the cabin to see us all still playing poker at about 6:00AM.

He looked right at me and said without a smile, "Swerb, are you ready to go to work or are you going to play poker all damn day?" He then slammed the door shut. I don't think he was very impressed with his boss that morning.

I replied, "Just been waiting all morning for you to show up, Hubba. Let's get it!"

I looked at the boys at the poker table and said, "I guess it's time for Swerb to go to work."

Robert said, "Finish your damn breakfast while they cash you out."

I was still wearing my red shirt and pistol. I grabbed my winnings, threw on my green work coat and hat, and thanked everyone for their hospitality. I had to start a cold truck with snow piled high on the hood and windshield and attempt to try and find Hubba as he headed off into the fog. I couldn't find my ice scraper so I used my company credit card to clear the heavy layer of frost off my windshield. Hubba was now out of sight, so I would need to track his vehicle in the snow to find what direction he had gone.

I finally came across Hubba and his patrol truck parked at a main intersection in the road. He was carrying a life size four-point buck mule deer decoy over his head and out across an open meadow. He carried the deer approximately 200 yards from his patrol truck and stood it up in front of a patch of lodgepole pine trees. I grabbed my binoculars and looked at the deer as Hubba walked back to his truck. The deer looked awesome standing out in the snow with its dark antlers. It definitely looked like a real deer. This deer even had a remote control that you could use to move its head back and forth and raise its tail up and down.

Hubba made it back to the truck, approached me, and said, "This deer is standing in a closed area for hunting; my goal is to target shooting from a public road and hunting in a closed area. You need to hide your truck somewhere far away and hide in the trees where you can see someone if they decide to shoot the decoy. Do you have a portable radio that works?"

I replied, "Yes, I do, do you think I'm a trainee or something?"

Hubba jumped into his truck and said, "I will hide my truck up the road a mile or so. Call me if you have a shooter and I will come down and write the citations."

Hubba jumped into his truck, revved the engine and spun his tires as he took off for cover. I hid my truck down the road and hiked back to the location of the deer decoy and hid in some nearby trees. I sat there underneath a large pine tree for nearly an hour when I heard the sound of a vehicle approaching. A man and his wife stopped their truck right in the middle of the public road about twenty yards from my hiding spot. I was so close to them that I could hear every word that they were saying.

The man told his wife, "Lean over the hood and get a good rest and shoot that buck over there next to the trees."

BOOM went the rifle. The deer never moved. The husband whispered to his wife, "Just relax, honey, and take a steady rest; I think you shot right over his back."

Of course, I had to try out the remote control to see if it worked. I raised the buck's head and shook his tail a few times. Everything worked perfect; the deer looked and acted just like a real deer.

BOOM went the rifle again. The deer just stood there looking towards them.

I grabbed my portable radio and whispered as I called Hubba, "GF-24, GF-14, we have a female shooter, no florescent orange, shooting at a deer in a closed area from a public road."

Hubba responded, "GF-14, GF-24, copy 10-76."

A few minutes later Hubba came roaring up and parked right behind the husband's vehicle. The lady had just shot at the deer for the third time. Hubba approached the husband as his wife was still leaning over the hood. The husband looked up at Hubba as he approached and held his finger in front of his lips and said "SHHH, my wife is trying to kill this deer."

Hubba responded, "I'm a game warden with the Wyoming Game and Fish Department. Your wife is shooting from a public road at a deer in a closed area and with no florescent orange on." The man's eyes got large as he looked at Hubba. His wife shot again, BOOM!

The husband turned around and yelled at his wife, "Quit shooting, it's a damn fake."

The wife replied, It's not fake. I seen it move its head and tail several times. BOOM, she shot again. Hubba then walked up to her and tapped her on the shoulder as she was still aiming at the decoy with her rifle.

Hubba yelled, "Madam, please put the gun down, you are shooting at a decoy."

The lady finally put the gun down and was issued several citations by Hubba. Both of them were pissed at Hubba and chewed his ass for using a decoy to catch them violating the law. I was just happy that I was hiding in the trees and didn't have to deal with them. I would end up hiding under that damn tree all day in the cold snow with a massive headache from not getting any sleep from playing poker with the boys all night.

I was taking a little cat nap when I heard the sound of vehicles approaching again. This time there were two trucks stopped in the road, looking at the deer. The driver of the first truck stopped and exited the vehicle. He was standing in the road, pointing towards the deer. I over heard him say, "Look over there, Dad, that's a hell of a nice buck."

Dad replied, "It's not real, it's a damn decoy, and pretty quick the Game and Fish is going to pull up and tell us to get the f---k out of the road."

About that time, I grabbed the remote and moved the deer's head slowly in one direction and raised his tail up and down. The man saw this movement and replied to his son, "Shit, you are right, son. That is a real deer, and a damn nice buck."

The man jumped up into the back of his truck and was digging through his toolbox, looking for something. I thought maybe he was looking for a rifle to shoot the deer. He grabbed something and put it in the pocket of his coat. I couldn't tell what it was due to the distance that he was away from me. The man started sneaking through the trees to get closer to the deer. Pretty quick he was crawling on his belly in the deep snow about twenty yards from the deer. Now, he was lying in the snow behind a large log. He would peek up slowly over the log to look at the deer. Every time he would peek over the top of the log I would move the deer's head to look right at him. He would then quickly duck back down under the log and hide again. I finally realized that the man was trying to take a picture of the deer. This went on for quite some time. Finally, the man peeked over the log and I grabbed my remote control and moved the deer's head back and forth as fast as I could. It looked like the deer was shaking his head at the man. Like 'leave me alone and go away'. The man then realized it was a decoy. He stood up and looked around everywhere and yelled, "F--k YOU, GAME AND FISH!"

I just sat under my tree and chuckled. We finally called it a day. We had a total of six people try and shoot that deer in a closed area that day. One thing about decoys, they put the wildlife, the game warden, and the would-be violators in the same spot at the same time. One thing about decoys, you never know who may try and shoot one illegally. I have caught a school principal, town cop, and several prominent businessmen shooting decoys. It's always a very humbling experience when the shooter is approached by a game warden after shooting a decoy. To this day, Robert and Maria can't believe that I played poker all night until the sun came up and went straight to work the next day without missing a beat.

Chapter 9

WINTER RANGE POACHING

Winter range poaching was becoming a real problem in the Pinedale area. Wardens were detecting an average of about twelve headless mule deer each winter. In my opinion this was one of the most gregarious of wildlife crimes. These large mule deer bucks were very vulnerable from November through January. They were only trying to breed does and survive some very tough winters. Some of these mule deer migrated over 200 air miles to get to their crucial winter ranges south of Pinedale. These cases were very difficult to solve with often very little evidence to go off of. In a typical winter range, poaching wardens would locate a headless mule deer usually several days after it had been shot. Ravens, magpies, and eagles seen feeding on dead carcasses would generally show wardens the location of a dead deer. I called these birds deputy game wardens. Because without them we would probably never find the dead deer. The carcass would usually be almost completely consumed by predators and birds, leaving very little evidence. The best evidence a warden could hope for was a tire impression in the snow or mud and maybe a spent shell casing and a human boot print. It was rare to have all three. Even when you have a tire track, boot print, and spent shell casing your case will still be very difficult to solve. When you have a homicide you have people, friends, and associates to interview. You also generally have a motive to why someone killed another person. With a headless mule deer, you have no one to talk to and interview, only a rotten carcass lying out in a remote area. If you are lucky, you might even recover the bullet that killed the deer to be able to determine the caliber of rifle used to poach the animal.

In 1998 wardens in the Jackson/Pinedale area started a mule deer winter range task force to patrol the crucial winter ranges in the Pinedale/Big Piney areas. Wardens would patrol winter ranges 24/7 from November through January. Wardens would volunteer from all over the state to spend one week in the Pinedale area patrolling for poachers. This was a pretty good duty because you got to look at a lot of trophy buck deer. During these patrols wardens would look for poaching activity and detect any deer that had been poached. When I became Game Warden Supervisor in April of 2004, wardens had not yet caught anyone poaching deer on the winter ranges. And we were still detecting nearly a dozen poached deer each winter. This told me that the people that we were contacting on the winter ranges were doing the poaching but we were not catching them. I made it a personal goal to figure out how to catch these scumbags. I wasn't sure how to do it, but I was determined to figure something different out.

We had an internal meeting with all the Jackson/Pinedale wardens. We decided that we would create a log book. If a warden contacted anyone driving around on the winter range, they would document who it was, their location, their vehicle description, and any firearms that they had in their vehicle. The firearms' caliber and serial number would be documented in the log. Over time this log would show us everyone contacted on the winter range. It would also show us their location and what firearms they had in their vehicles. If we detected a headless deer in a given area we could go back and look at the log and determine who was in that area. If we recovered a bullet from the carcass, we could look at the log and see if anyone had that particular firearm in their vehicle.

148

Keep in mind, it was still legal for the public to be out photographing deer, hunting coyotes or rabbits or mountain lions. Many of these people were doing nothing wrong but made our jobs that much more difficult. We really needed "No Human Presence Closures" in these areas to protect the deer. But that would become very difficult to achieve because people want to recreate and hunt during the winter months.

We gathered a huge amount of intel over the years but still were not catching any poachers. We were able to determine that the same non-residents returned year after year to photograph large mule deer bucks and the areas that they spent the most time in. We were still documenting poached deer every year and catching no one. Trail cameras had just been invented. We considered putting trail cameras on power poles and fences in the areas with high concentrations of deer, especially large bucks. If wardens observed a buck with an antler spread over thirty inches, it was considered a "High Risk Buck" and we would spend additional time babysitting those large bucks. We had investigated several poached deer that we had absolutely no evidence on. I believe there were times when someone would shoot a large buck and drop it in a remote location. This person would not even get out of their truck or pull off the road to leave any tire tracks or foot prints in the snow. They would leave the poached buck until the spring of the year and then act like they found a winter killed buck and bring the head into a regional office to get it tagged with a Wyoming Interstate Game Tag. Some of these deer we would investigate but generally never found much evidence after the deer had been left to decompose all winter long. Sometimes the bullet would pass clean through the deer and we were unable to recover the bullet that killed the deer.

Over the years I have decided that if you want to take Thanksgiving and Christmas Day off, you should probably not become a game warden. It seems like these are the more popular days for people to poach. Maybe they think the game warden is more likely to be home taking the day off with his/her family and they have a better chance of getting away with poaching. Generally, most people have Thanksgiving Day off and the large bucks are in full rut. This makes them very vulnerable and stupid. They only have one thing on their mind and that's breeding does. A large buck may walk right in front of your truck and never even look at you parked in the road.

So, at 4:00AM on November 27, 2005, Warden Hubba Healy was notified by a highway patrolman that someone was found at a gas station in Pinedale with a large mule deer buck dead in the back of their truck. The man was arrested on other charges and was currently sitting in the Sublette County jail. We knew this man had more than likely poached a large mule deer buck, but we didn't have any other details to go off. The man's vehicle was confiscated and towed to the game and fish office, where it would sit until a search warrant was issued by the local judge. Wardens Healy and Nesvik went down to the jail to identify and interview the suspect. Meanwhile, around 9:00AM I received information from a local guy in Pinedale that he had found where two different deer had been poached up by Burnt Lake. It sounded like there were vehicle tracks off road in the snow everywhere and evidence of at least two deer that had been poached.

After interviewing the man in jail, the suspect was identified as Michael Acuna. Acuna was a tall and very fit Native American in his mid-thirties. Acuna lied to wardens and told them that he had harvested the buck deer in the Sheridan area where whitetail season was still open. Once he learned that it was only open for white tail's he changed his story to the deer being harvested in the South Pass area. This area was also closed to deer hunting. Wardens then decided to drive up to Burnt Lake and investigate the earlier report of two deer being poached in that area. Wardens found that the tire prints in the snow matched the tire tread on Acuna's truck. What they also found didn't make much sense. They found the hide and guts from two different deer that didn't match the deer in the back of Acuna's truck. This man had poached at least three deer that night. But where were the antlers from the other two bucks? Wardens Healy and Nesvik returned to Pinedale and met with the highway patrolman who had arrested Acuna at 3:00AM that day to gather more information. What they learned will blow your mind.

Acuna was evidently observed in the Corral Bar the night that he poached the deer. It was reported that he became so intoxicated that he passed out in the bar. Someone dragged him out of the bar and placed him on a park bench in front of the bar around midnight. Acuna awoke at some point after midnight and jumped into his truck in a rage. Apparently, he had just broken up with his girlfriend from Jackson Hole. He headed up the Burnt Lake Road and decided to take his rage out on wildlife instead of people. He claimed that he was seeing red and needed to harm something before he killed someone. Acuna had a spotlight and a borrowed 30.06 rifle that belonged to a friend. He shot a buck mule deer in his spotlight and completely skinned and gutted it. A few miles down the road he found another buck that was larger than the first so he shot that one as well. He discarded the first buck and completely skinned and gutted the second larger buck. He then ended up on the Mesa south of Pinedale, where he found even a larger buck than the first two. He killed this buck and discarded the second buck. He then found even a larger buck than the three previous bucks and shot and killed a fourth deer. This buck was in the back of his truck, gutted and skinned. It was also discovered that Acuna was a convicted felon and was not to be in possession of a firearm.

So, the story continues. After poaching the fourth buck Acuna drove back to Pinedale and entered some lady's house to sleep on her coach at about 3:00AM. He did not know this person at all. The lady heard a noise in her living room and found Acuna asleep on her couch. She called the Sheriff's Office and told the man to leave her house immediately. Acuna jumped into his truck and headed for the gas station to get gas. This is when the highway patrolman checked out the truck and called Warden Healy. The truck matched the description that the lady had given to the Sheriff's Office.

I don't know about you, but I have never been drunk enough to pass out! I can't imagine being that intoxicated and having the energy to poach and completely process four buck deer in a span of three hours by yourself. There must have been some other drugs involved. This was a man who, if we had received a report of someone spotlighting that night, would have more than likely killed whoever approached him in cold blooded murder. He was seeing red and was in a rage when he poached these deer. Thank God no one saw him spotlighting that night and reported it. It may have resulted in a horrible situation for one of our wardens or other law enforcement personnel.

We gathered as much information as we could and decided we needed to go back to the jail and interview Mr. Acuna. Heck, for all we knew there may be even more poached deer out there on the landscape than we knew about. From my experience interviewing poachers, you never stop with one animal. Generally speaking, you are only scratching the surface when someone is caught poaching. There is almost always more than one animal involved. And sometimes you learn that someone has been poaching for years and has killed many, many animals illegally over their lifetime.

Hubba and I went back to the jail to reinterview Acuna. I had not yet met him. I was actually kind of excited to meet such a killer for some reason. When someone does something like this you always want to see what they look like and what made them do something so horrible. Hubba told me that the man would lie and probably not tell us anything, based on his first interview. I told Hubba that maybe we should try playing good cop/bad cop with this guy. Hubba agreed as we entered the interview room.

Acuna was over six feet tall, and standing in a bright orange pumpkin suit with his hands cuffed to a belt around his waistband. Hubba introduced me to Acuna. I shook his hand even though it was difficult with handcuffs on. The man looked scary to me. He had deep dark black eyes that seemed to pierce right through your soul when you looked him in the eyes. He had a stone-cold face with no expression and a long scar that ran down the length of his right cheek. It looked like he had been cut with knife or something very sharp. His fingers and arms had tattoos on them. I also noticed fresh blood underneath his fingernails from his night out poaching deer.

Hubba read the man his rights and started in with more questioning. The man glared at Hubba and would not say a word. Hubba moved his face within two inches of Acuna's face and said in very firm words, "If you don't start talking, I will see to it that you spend the rest of your f-----g life in jail." He then jabbed Acuna's chest with his finger as he stared into Acuna's deep black eyes. I couldn't believe that Hubba had just done this; we are usually pretty nice when interviewing suspects. I jumped over and pushed Hubba out of Acuna's face and yelled, "Get the hell out of here right now. I will talk to this man one on one."

Hubba pushed me back and exited the door, slamming it shut. I felt a little nervous being in an interview room alone with Acuna. I don't know what happened to me, but I looked over at Acuna and put my hand on his shoulder and said, "I'm sorry about that; he is hot headed and doesn't like you at all. I will try and keep you guys separated."

Acuna responded, "Thank you, I appreciate that."

I told Acuna that for some reason I really liked him and just felt that he poached some animals because he was upset with his girlfriend and maybe a little intoxicated. I told him that he was not a hardened criminal for what he had done, but we needed to figure out why he did it so that we could get him some counseling and get him out of jail. Meanwhile, Hubba kept pacing back and forth in his red shirt by the window that had half open Venetian blinds. He had a pissed off look on his face.

I looked at Acuna and said, "Shit, here comes Hubba and he is pissed. Just tell me exactly what happened last night and where all the deer carcasses are located so that we can get you out of jail before Hubba comes back." I couldn't believe my ears. Acuna told me all the details as quick as he could. He started to tell me the details of where the last deer and all the antlers were stashed. He couldn't think clearly and didn't know the area. He was trying to explain the location but he didn't know what any of the roads were named in the area.

I said, "Hurry up, Hubba is coming back!"

Acuna replied, "Hurry, give me a piece of paper and I will draw you a map of where everything is located."

I quickly gave him a pen and piece of paper and he drew me the most detailed map that you have ever seen. Hubba was now pounding on the door, wanting us to let him in. I told Acuna to keep drawing and I would keep Hubba out of the room. I went over to the door and acted like I was holding it shut, preventing Hubba from entering the room. I thanked Acuna for the detailed map and wished him well before I left the room. I stepped out of the interview room and handed Hubba the detailed map. Hubba looked it over and said, "How in the hell did you get him to draw you a damn map?" I responded with a smile, "Good Cop/Bad Cop." We would end up piecing all of the puzzle together once we had the map.

At the end of the day Acuna was held in the Sublette County jail until the end of December, when his girlfriend posted a $25,000 bond. He was fined over $17,000 in fines and restitution and lost his hunting, fishing, and trapping privileges for 20 years. On April 6th he was sentenced to spend two to three years in the Wyoming State Penitentiary for committing a crime with a firearm as a felon. Acuna had just spent nearly four years in the state penitentiary for aggravated assault.

We did not catch Acuna, he caught himself. Ironically, on Thanksgiving Eve, Wardens Nesvik, Healy, and Hovinga also caught two men poaching two deer near Fremont Lake. Both men were from out of state and worked in the gas field. They were all on standby in the early morning hours waiting for these suspects to arrive at home when the Acuna call came in. We had an awesome county attorney back then named Ralf Boynton who worked hard over the Thanksgiving holiday weekend to draw up search and arrest warrants and provide wardens with any guidance that they needed to put the bad guys in jail. Ralf assisted us with many great cases over the years. Ralf was recognized by the Wyoming Game Wardens Association the next spring. He received a very nice plaque for the Wyoming Game Warden Support Person of the Year. Finally, we were starting to catch some of these hard-core poachers. I hadn't had much of a chance to work hand in hand with investigations with Game Wardens Nesvik, Healy, and Hovinga but I was really looking forward to it. These guys were top notch game wardens and I was proud to have the opportunity to supervise them.

Chapter 10

TEST AND SLAUGHTER

I was busy attending meetings all over the state with the Governor's Brucellosis Coordination Team. The team eventually came up with eighteen recommendations to the Governor to reduce the prevalence and spread of brucellosis from elk to cattle. Of course, there was a push from other members of the team to eliminate elk feed grounds altogether. The team also discussed building huge elk fences around private property to keep elk out of cattle producer's feed lines and cattle.

If you could think of a way to keep elk and cattle separated, it was discussed. If you could think of a way to reduce the prevalence of brucellosis in the area elk herds, it was discussed. The top recommendation from the task force was to try a five-year pilot program to perform test and slaughter of elk on three different feed grounds. This effort would be an experiment to eradicate or greatly reduce the prevalence of brucellosis in elk. There was a great deal of politics that influenced this decision. A local rancher had to depopulate his entire cattle herd because brucellosis was detected in the herd. This ranch was located near one of the elk feed grounds that was proposed for test and slaughter. A federal agency attempted to gain control over wildlife management as it pertained to disease management. Meaning, if they got control, the agency could kill elk if they were commingling with cattle or a threat to cattle. Our director, Terry Cleveland, also served on the Governor's team and felt a great deal of pressure to do something out of the box to show that the department was very serious about eradicating brucellosis in elk.

Shortly after the recommendations were reviewed by the Governor, I received notification from Director Cleveland that he would like feed ground supervisor Ron Dean and me to meet with him at Cheyenne headquarters. Ron and I nervously carpooled to Cheyenne, wondering what Director Cleveland wanted to discuss with us. When we arrived at headquarters, an office manager escorted Ron and me to Mr. Cleveland's office. Mr. Cleveland opened his office door, greeted us, and invited us to come in and sit down. His office was very large and organized, with several comfortable leather chairs to sit in. I was nervous to be in the Director's office. This meant something big was about to come down the pike. Director Cleveland didn't waste any time on small talk. He explained the recommendations of the Governor's Brucellosis Coordination Team to us. He also explained that we needed to catch as many elk as possible on three feed grounds over the next five years in an effort to eradicate or greatly reduce the prevalence of brucellosis in the Pinedale elk herd.

Mr. Cleveland looked both of us in the eye with his hands folded in front of him. He had a very serious look on his face as he peered over his reading glasses. He asked with a very slow and stern voice, "Can you guys design an elk trap large enough to catch over five hundred elk at once?"

Ron and I looked at each other, waiting for the other to respond to Mr. Cleveland's question. I folded my hands and looked at Director Cleveland and replied, "I think if we have adequate funding and resources to work with, we will figure something out."

Mr. Cleveland replied, "Don't worry about the funding, it will be there, and I will allocate whatever resources that you guys deem necessary to make this a successful pilot project. But hear me closely, this pilot project needs to be done very professionally and it's imperative that we are successful. There are a lot of people watching and following this project and we need to be successful."

Ron and I assured Mr. Cleveland that we would look into this and keep him updated. Mr. Cleveland thanked us and shook our hands and said, "I look forward to hearing back from you very soon. We need to get the ball rolling on this."

Ron and I had a very interesting conversation on the way back to Pinedale. We discussed many logistics of this five-year test and slaughter pilot program. Some questions that we had were: Could we actually capture all the elk on three separate feed grounds in five years? Could we design a trap large enough with working chutes and alleyways to handle that many elk? What would we build the trap out of and how much would all this cost? We would have to open all the roads into each feed ground and keep them open all winter. This was a huge and expensive job in itself. My question was, was this all political or could we actually eradicate or greatly reduce the prevalence of brucellosis in this elk herd? My final question was, why in the hell was I in charge of this operation as the newly appointed game warden supervisor? It was probably because of my feed ground manager experience and my role on the Governor's Brucellosis Coordination Team. I thought, *the only thing wrong with this picture is I'm in it!*

I lost many nights of sleep wondering how to best design this trap and how big to make it. I completely wore out a notebook scribbling drawings of this trap. Keep in mind I'm not an artist. I was curious if anyone had ever attempted to catch this many elk before, and if anyone had already designed a trap somewhere else in the world. This was also before the advent of Google Search on your iPhone.

Later that week I ended up meeting with the supervisor of the BFH (Brucellosis, Feed Grounds, Habitat) program. He told me that he was going to research if anyone had ever built a trap of this magnitude before. I told him that was a good idea and we shouldn't try to reinvent the wheel if it had been done somewhere else before. One week later we met again. Low and behold he found a man in Idaho who had designed a similar trap to capture elk. I looked at the blueprints and it looked huge and complicated to me, not to mention very expensive. There were pictures of the trap in its final form, all set up. I started to get very excited about purchasing and constructing three of these traps over the next few years.

One problem that we faced was that state government would have to put the construction of this trap out for bid to at least two other vendors. We didn't have two other vendors in the whole world who built such a trap. We would also need to design our own trap and our own blueprints to put out for bid. If we used the blueprints from the guy in Idaho we would be stealing his patent on the design of the trap. This trap was exactly what we needed. I didn't want to take the time to re-design the trap and hire an engineer to re-design the trap when we had exactly what we needed with the vendor in Idaho.

After several phone conversations and trips to Jackson Hole to meet with the trap designer from Idaho we became very interested. We had the designer of the trap give us a bid for one trap. The bid came in at almost $500,000. I thought to myself, *the state is never going to agree with the cost of this trap, let alone three of them!* I nervously phoned Director Cleveland to let him know what we had found out. I explained the whole situation to him of having to get three quotes from different vendors and the cost and time to design our own traps.

Director Cleveland responded, "That sounds exactly what we are looking for. We will sole- source this trap since no one else makes one and we don't want to steal the patent from this design. I will contact our Fiscal Chief today and get the ball rolling to contract with the man from Idaho. Great work, you guys, let's get this project rolling."

I couldn't believe what I had just heard. I had purchased thousands of tons of hay for the feed ground program over the years and it was always difficult to get anything done with all the red tape involved. I guess when the Director wants something, much of the red tape goes away! We spent the next several weeks dealing with paperwork and contracts. Ultimately the trap would be built that summer and delivered in the fall. We would only build one trap for Muddy Creek feed ground for the upcoming winter. We wanted to see how well it worked before we committed to the other two traps.

I honestly couldn't believe the day when they arrived. Two semi-trucks pulled up to the Muddy Creek feed ground, loaded to the gills with panel after panel of pieces of the elk trap. The man who designed and built the trap was also there with a crew to help us set the trap up. All I had ever done was look at blueprints. I couldn't believe how large this trap was on the landscape. It was absolutely huge and very well-designed and built. The trap had several large holding pens with alleyways and working chutes built into it. It was a really nice state-of-the art elk trap. I was very proud of everyone involved with making this happen. The question remained, could we catch a large number of elk and successfully work them in this trap without any casualties? Would we have to separate the bulls from the cows to keep the bulls from goring the cows to death? How would we do this? I still had lots of questions racing through my mind.

Once the trap was set up and completed, I was asked by the Assistant Division Chief Scott Talbott how many people we would need to man the trap and take care of all the logistics from start to finish. This was overwhelming to even think about. We would need personnel to work the elk and get them into twelve different holding chutes. We would need people to draw blood and collar each captured elk. We would need daytime and nighttime security to protect the elk while they were in holding pens awaiting blood test results. We would need people to transport blood samples to our lab in Laramie. We would also need people to transport brucellosis-infected elk via horse trailer to an approved slaughter facility located in Rigby, Idaho. I was asked to put together a very comprehensive working plan to show what positions we needed and how many people would need to be involved.

The final number was 42 people. These people would be game and fish biologists and wardens from all over the state of Wyoming. Most of them would be on per diem and be required to stay in motel rooms for at least one week while trapping elk.

After a great deal of planning, the big day finally came. The whole team showed up at the regional office in Pinedale for a briefing meeting. Each employee was given his or her assignment and told that they would remain on this team with the assignment for a period of five years. A handful of people would plan on going into Muddy Creek feed ground at daylight the next morning and attempt to trap as many elk as possible. The rest of the team would remain on standby at a chosen location near the feed ground. Once elk were caught, I would radio the entire team to move into the trap area and perform their job. This was going to be very interesting because nobody had ever attempted to capture and handle this many elk at one time, ever!

The date was January 28, 2006. Our plans soon changed with a huge blizzard that night that left temperatures at 30 to 40 degrees below zero. The road into the feed ground was completely drifted shut and we had over forty people ready to go to work that morning. I contacted Sublette County Road and Bridge and they agreed to bring their heavy equipment in that morning and open the road into Muddy Creek feed ground at no cost to the department. This was a huge relief to me and a huge undertaking for them. It took the entire day, but they eventually made it all the way into the feed ground. The road was finally opened! After this incident, the Sublette County Road and Bridge agreed to be on standby to assist with road plowing the entire winter. What a blessing and huge saving this was for us.

The next morning was -32 degrees. My plan was to go in early with elk feeder Frosty Hittle and our very own videographer Ray Hageman. Ray was the famous voice on the radio for the Wyoming Game and Fish Department. We wanted to capture this first-time event on film. Our plan was to bait the trap with fresh alfalfa and sit up in a haystack located about fifty yards from the elk. We had designed a remote-control trap trigger to release the large gate and close it automatically once the trap was full of elk. The elk were very hungry due to the fact that they didn't get fed the day before, due to the road being drifted shut. Hungry elk and fresh alfalfa should do the trick to entice them to come into the large trap. Frosty fed a line of hay with his tractor and hay sled up to the trap and baited the trap. He then left the area in his pick-up just as he always does. Ray and I snuck up and found a spot to sit on top of the large stack of hay that was underneath a large metal hayshed. We wanted everything to look normal to the elk so that they wouldn't be spooked and run off. Frosty had actually been feeding the elk in the trap for several weeks prior to trapping to acclimate the elk to the new trap. He claimed that they had been going into the trap very well and cleaning up all the hay each day. That morning there were approximately 500 elk on the feed ground. It was so cold that you could see the breath of each elk as they walked across the feed ground to eat on the feed line. With the morning sun coming up and all the steam in the air from the elk breathing, it was quite a sight. A moment that I will never forget as I sat motionless with Ray on top of the nearby haystack at -32 degrees.

The rest of the team was waiting in a plowed-out parking lot approximately three miles away. I was hoping that the batteries in my portable mobile radio would hold up with the cold weather. If the radio didn't work, we would not be able to communicate with the team. Ray and I sat motionless in the haystack, watching the herd of elk slowly work their way towards the trap gate. I was very excited to see if elk would enter the trap and how many we could get in the trap prior to releasing the gate. Ray whispered to me that his feet were frozen and he couldn't feel them at all. I looked over at Ray and will never forget what I saw. Ray had two icicles of snot hanging out of his nostrils about four inches long. His face was starting to turn blue and I'm sure his nose was frost- bitten. We were going to have to catch some elk pretty quick and get Ray to a truck heater somewhere soon.

The elk started to enter the trap very cautiously one at a time. I was very excited to finally see this happen for the first time. The wind started to blow a bit and it was really getting cold, especially when we couldn't move in fear of spooking the elk off. The trap would get nearly full of elk and then something would spook one elk and the trap would empty in about five seconds. Then we would wait again for the trap to fill up as it got colder and colder.

By now the trap was nearly out of hay, and there was no feed available to encourage more elk to enter the trap. I estimated that we had about 300 elk in the trap. This was going to be the most elk that we were going to capture for the day, and Ray was nearly frozen to death. I slowly reached over and grabbed the remote control to release the large gate and capture approximately 300 elk. Ray looked over at me with the icicles hanging out of his nose and nodded his head yes, as if he was in total agreement to trigger the trap. I slowly took my glove off my right hand and placed my frozen finger on the button to release the trap. About that time, a magpie flew over the elk in the trap and spooked them. The entire trap emptied in about five seconds. We were done trapping elk for the day. If I had had a shotgun, I would have shot that damn magpie dead! Ray looked over at me and tried to smile, but his face was frozen and he was unable to. I just saw his eyes kind of light up. I grabbed my portable radio and called my contact at the parking lot. My message was, "Send everyone home for the day. We were unsuccessful due to a magpie flying over and spooking all of the elk out of the trap."

I helped Ray and his frozen little body out of the haystack. I have to admit I was pretty frozen myself, but had spent many years in very cold weather and was probably just a little more acclimated to the elements. Ray and I were both very happy to finally get to the truck and soak up some heater time. We returned to Pinedale to the motel where everyone assigned to the team was staying. Everyone essentially had the day off now that we were unsuccessful in trapping the elk. Nobody on the team wanted anything to do with the capture and slaughter of elk. We all took our jobs because we had a passion for managing and protecting wildlife, not trapping and killing them. This was very hard for many employees to even be involved with. The only positive thing that was coming out of all of this was the camaraderie of everyone getting together and spending time telling stories and working with others from across the state.

After my debriefing meeting I was soon challenged to an arm-wrestling match by Rawlins' game warden, Benge Brown. This did not work out so good for Benge. This led to other arm-wrestling matches, copious amounts of alcohol being consumed, and a late-night poker game in the lobby of the motel. I stayed up way too late and probably shouldn't have partied on a school night. I drove home and crawled into my cold bed and snuggled up with my warm wife. She was not impressed that she hadn't heard from me all day as I reached over and set my alarm again for 4:00AM.

My alarm sounded way too early. I did not want to get out of my warm bed and drive an hour away to crawl back up and sit in a cold haystack all morning again. I wasn't sure if Ray was willing to repeat another frost-bitten moment in the haystack. He probably still didn't have any feeling in his feet, but hopefully the icicles had melted out of his nostrils by now. We all met at the regional office for a briefing meeting (Game Plan.) Ray agreed to ride with me again, but was dressed with another layer or two.

We soon arrived back at Muddy Creek feed ground and repeated our daily exercise of feeding the elk and baiting the trap. It was still -30 degrees and would be another cold morning for us. Ray and I found our little spot in the haystack and stacked bales of hay all the way around us to block the wind the best that we could. The trap was nearly full of elk again. We had more elk in the trap than we had ever had before. I reached over to trigger the trap and I think that same damn magpie flew into the trap and landed on the head of a cow elk. The cow jumped and again the trap drained of elk in a matter of seconds. We tried several more times to get the elk in the trap that morning, but they were done playing for the day again. I radioed back to the group to abort mission for the day and go back to the motel. This was later followed by another night of story-telling, drinking too much, and playing poker until the wee hours of the morning. Lana was really not impressed with me by now as I crawled into bed and set my alarm again for 4:00AM.

Day four. Ray and I were back in the haystack with elk trickling back into the trap. I was determined to catch elk this day and not let a damn magpie screw up the whole event. There were about 300 elk in the trap and no magpie in sight. I reached over and quickly pushed the magic button to close the gate on the trap. The door didn't swing shut as fast as I had hoped it would, and some elk blasted out of the door just before it latched. Nevertheless, we had just successfully trapped approximately 300 elk in one catch. I'm pretty sure this was the first time that this has ever happened in the history of elk feed grounds in Wyoming. We had finally done it. Now what did we do with that many elk in the trap? I radioed for the team to head into the feed ground. I think everyone was excited that we finally caught some elk and the team had a job to do.

If you haven't ever stepped into a round pen with 300 free-ranging elk running around in circles you truly haven't lived your life to its fullest extent. My job was to haze the elk to run along the outside rounded wall and into an alleyway. Except the alleyway would only hold about 50 elk at a time. If you allowed too many elk in the alleyway, they would blow the walls apart on both sides and there would be elk running everywhere. Don't ask me how I know this. So, to accomplish this mission I would need to close a twelve-foot-wide gate as

166

300 elk were trying to enter the alleyway at a high rate of speed. It didn't matter which side of the gate I was on, I was going to get my ass kicked. And that I did, but I was successful in closing the gate. This was a moment I will never forget. I was standing behind the gate next to the outside wall watching 300 elk run into the alleyway right next to me at about 30MPH. I then had to push the gate through the middle of the running elk herd and cut them off.

Bull elk in trap

Everyone showed up to their assigned areas and began working elk. This was the smoothest elk working moment that I had ever witnessed. It was safe for everyone, including the elk. I sat there for a moment and watched everyone working the elk. It looked like they had all done this before. The whole operation went off very organized and professional. At the end of the day, the team worked over 300 elk in about two-hours' time. Every adult cow got bled and received a collar with a number on it. The adult cow elk were held in a large holding pen overnight to allow for the test results to come back from our lab in Laramie. We had personnel assigned to transport the blood to

Laramie after each trap event. Our folks in the lab would spin and test the blood samples overnight, and send us a printout of which elk were seropositive for brucellosis. We would have these results before midnight each time. The next morning, personnel would arrive back at the feed ground and run all the tested elk through a sorting chute. If they were tested as positive, they were hauled to Rigby, Idaho to be slaughtered. All the meat from these elk would be processed and donated to needy people across the state of Wyoming. They didn't even have to pay for the processing. The negative elk would simply be released back into the wild with an ear tag number that matched their collar number. This really helped us over the years to gain a better understanding of where these elk traveled, which feed grounds they visited each year, and if they tested negative for brucellosis one year and maybe tested positive the next.

This team stayed together for all five years, trapping elk on three different feed grounds each winter. We literally became experts in trapping and handling elk. We learned something different every time we trapped elk to make us more efficient and better at our job. We had nasty blizzards each year that drifted roads closed into feed grounds and closed roads to Laramie. One winter, all the roads were closed to get the blood samples to Laramie. We contacted the Wyoming highway patrol and they gave us a police escort through the drifting, blowing snow all the way to our lab, so that elk wouldn't have to stay in the holding pen any longer than necessary before being released back to the wild. We learned that bull elk will gore cows when caught in captivity. We designed a bull excluder gate that would only allow cows to walk into the trap through narrow metal windows. Of course, this all took time to acclimate the cow elk to the new gates to get the courage to walk through them again. We also learned that the bull elk will learn how to fit their large antlers through the bull excluder and join the cows back in the trap and gore them to death if they are not removed. When this happened, we would simply dart all the bulls the second that the trap was door was closed. The bulls would go down and personnel would enter the trap and drag the bulls out one at a time. If you have never walked alongside a drugged bull elk, leading him through the gate by his antlers, you still haven't truly lived life.

At the end of the day, we learned a great deal from this pilot test and slaughter five-year program. On Muddy feed ground, the prevalence of brucellosis was about 56% the first year that we tested. On the fifth year, it was down around 6-7%. We greatly reduced the prevalence of brucellosis on all three feed grounds over five years. What we did learn is that we were never going to catch all the elk on all three feed grounds, and that some years elk winter out in different areas. Some years not even on an elk feed ground. We also learned that it would not be logistically possible to try and catch every elk on Wyoming's 22 elk feed grounds which feed an average of about 17,000 elk per year.

Escorting bull elk out of the trap

Elk in alley way

Elk running into alley way

After five years of test and slaughter, we hauled nearly 300 seropositive elk to the FDA approved-slaughter facility in Rigby,

Idaho. After these elk were slaughtered, culture tissues were sent to our lab where it was determined that only about 50% of these elk actually had brucellosis. I almost cried every time that I watched a horse trailer full of elk head for Idaho. This was not why I signed up to be a wildlife manager. A great deal was learned from this project and it all came with a big price tag. Was it all political? Maybe so, but we did learn a bunch at the end of the day. To this day we still use these traps on Muddy, Fall, and Scab Creek feed grounds to trap elk to gain more information about brucellosis surveillance in that elk herd. The department continues to receive pressure from other entities to perform test and slaughter again, and on all feed grounds. This simply is not logistically possible, extremely expensive, and will only lower the prevalence of brucellosis in Western Wyoming and never completely eradicate it. Now that CWD (Chronic Wasting Disease) has reared its ugly head, you rarely hear much about brucellosis and elk feed grounds in Western Wyoming. My guess is that CWD will eventually show up on elk feed grounds and may be devastating to elk populations in the future. If the prions actually do live in the environment for years on end, this will be an unmanageable disease to ever control.

What I do know for sure is the employees who served on that test and slaughter team for five years still talk about it to this day. It was not something that any one of them wanted to do or agreed with. But they built lasting relationships and memories working with other department employees doing work that nobody had ever tried to accomplish before, and they did it very well. This five-year event gained a great deal of media attention and people against test and slaughter. It got to the point where we felt it necessary to appoint security people to stay with the elk in the holding pens overnight with locks and chains on all the gates. We also sent extra security with the horse trailers headed to Rigby, Idaho with chains and locks on the horse trailer doors. Each truck had a game warden driving with all their department-issued firearms, mostly in case the trucks were to wreck and the elk were to escape into Idaho and need to be put down. Can you just imagine the headline news: "Wyoming game warden wrecks truck and trailer loaded with brucellosis-positive elk in Idaho! Wild, infected elk on the run near herd of domestic cattle!" For the record, we only wrecked one truck and trailer during the transport of elk to Rigby, and no elk escaped.

Elk held in holding pen awaiting blood test results

I made one trip to Rigby to see how the elk were handled at the slaughter facility. After seeing this, I chose to never go back again. It was probably one of the saddest moments of my entire career. Elk were unloaded out of horse trailers and herded down narrow domestic cattle alleyways. They would slip on the icy cement surface and fall down and slide on their sides until able to regain their feet. Once back on their feet they would be missing hair and bleeding in spots from sliding on rough concrete. The eyes of the elk were bulged out and nostrils flared as they entered the dark building with a low-hanging roof. The elk were separated into individual holding pens. Each pen had a single light bulb hanging over the pen for light. Elk were immediately put down and dragged to another room where they were gutted and skinned. This room was the most disgusting thing that I had ever seen. It smelled of death and had rivers of blood running across the cement floor into a drain system. The poor elk had no idea what they were in for from the time they entered the horse trailer to the time they were shot. A sad memory that will never leave me.

On March 28, 2006 we donated all the processed meat to the public at the Pinedale regional office starting at 8:00AM. We ended up dividing all the processed meat out equally across all eight regional offices. Pinedale would end up with sixteen forty-pound boxes of elk meat. People from the public showed up as early as 5:00AM to be first in line. I remember waiting on an attractive, young pregnant lady who was standing first in line with a young child in each arm. It was very cold outside and I could see that she was so cold that she and her kids were shaking. I felt sorry for them so I invited them to come into the heated shop early. I asked the lady why she had arrived so early to stand in line for elk meat. She responded, "My husband dropped me off at 5:00AM and told me to get my ass in line for a guaranteed free elk. He also told me that I had gotten my ass out of bed on many cold mornings to go hunting and came home with nothing. This is your chance to come home with a guaranteed elk." I couldn't help but laugh, her husband had a good point.

8:00AM finally came, and I bet there were nearly 100 people standing in line. The line of people ran nearly a block long. I realized that we were not going to have enough elk meat for everyone. I started opening boxes of meat and handing packages of meat to people standing in line. The next thing I noticed was that people were fighting over the best cuts of meat and wanting to trade others for different cuts of meat. One guy stomped off mad because all he received were a couple elk rump roasts. He wanted some hamburger and tenderloins.

The department felt that none of the meat should go to waste and that it should all go back to the public. We would later get criticized by others for donating brucellosis-infected meat to the public. Sometimes you just can't win.

Chapter 11

DECOY OPERATIONS

We had received some funding from Bowhunters of Wyoming (B.O.W.) to purchase some new decoys. We ended up with a really nice-looking bull elk and buck mule deer. The old decoys were so shot up over the years that they didn't even look real anymore. However, I have noticed over the years that they can be the ugliest decoy in the world and people still shoot them illegally. I swear you could hang an old antelope hide over a piece of plywood and someone would still shoot it. Hubba had called me and asked me if I would assist him with an elk decoy operation in the Upper Green River over the weekend. We had been getting reports of hunters shooting from a public road and killing elk in a closed area. The main road up in that area was the boundary between two different hunt areas. So, it was legal to hunt elk on one side of the road and illegal to shoot an elk on the other side of the road.

Hubba and I met at the Pinedale office at about 5:00 that morning to load up our brand-new elk decoy that we had named "OH SHIT" because that's usually what the hunters would say after realizing that they had just shot a decoy. The decoy was a life-sized elk that stood up very tall and was very heavy to try and carry alone. It generally took two people to carry the decoy to set it up. The elk was designed to have detachable legs from the hocks down. The legs also had steel rods stuck in the bottom of each foot so that you could essentially plant the elk in the ground to keep it from falling over. However, this was difficult to do if the ground was frozen.

We had left Pinedale early that morning hoping to have the elk decoy set up before daylight near the Green River Lakes feed ground. We were running late and arrived at the location just after daylight. Since it was already daylight, I told Hubba to find his hiding place and that I would run out and set up the decoy alone. I would need to carry the large decoy over my head for about two hundred yards and place it next to a patch of timber along the main public road. Our goal would be to catch hunters shooting from the public road and hunting in a closed area. I didn't want any hunters to observe me carrying the bull elk out across an open sage brush flat. So, I ran as fast as I could with the elk hanging over my shoulders. This was harder than I had imagined. The elk was awkward and heavy and I really didn't want a hunter to shoot me while I was carrying the elk out across the open meadow.

I hurried and had just got the elk set up, when I heard the sound of a truck coming down the main gravel road. I thought, *Oh shit, I need to run back across this meadow very quick before some hunter sees me standing next to an elk out in the middle of nowhere.* Well, I wasn't fast enough. I was standing right in the middle of the open meadow next to an old two-track road when the vehicle came racing around the corner. The truck came to a sudden stop. The hunter was either looking at me or the elk or both of us. I was only about fifty yards from the elk decoy and now walking towards a patch of trees to hide with Hubba. The truck turned on the two-track road and came racing right towards me. I was wearing my green coat with the Game and Fish emblem displayed on my left shoulder. I figured whoever was driving the truck probably had figured out what was going on and just wanted to talk to me. So, I quit walking and waited for the truck to approach. The truck came to an abrupt stop right next to me. Once the dust cleared, I noticed a bearded man wearing a florescent orange hat driving the truck. He quickly rolled down his window and whispered, "Hey, are you going to shoot that bull elk standing over there?" as he pointed in the direction of the elk.

Brand new never been shot elk decoy

I replied in a whisper, "No, I wasn't planning on it."

"Well, if you aren't going to shoot him, I'll damn sure take him."

The man jumped out of his truck, grabbed his rifle, and leaned over the hood of his truck. BOOM went the rifle. I couldn't believe that this dumb bastard had just shot at this bull elk in a closed area right in front of the game warden. Did he not realize that I didn't have any orange hunting clothing on? Did he not realize that I wasn't even carrying a rifle? Did he not see my green Game and Fish coat with the bright patch on my shoulder? Did he not wonder why someone was just out walking around in the middle of nowhere within fifty yards of this elk? Did he not wonder where my vehicle might be parked?

The man quickly jacked in another round and was taking careful aim, thinking that he had missed the first shot. Before he could blow the shit out of our brand-new decoy, I yelled, "Stop shooting, it's a damn decoy." The man turned around and looked at me in disbelief and said, "You have got to be shitting me right now. And are you a game warden?"

I replied, "Yes, sir. And you just attempted to kill that elk in a closed area."

The man was completely embarrassed and apologized profusely. I told him to drive his truck up to the game and fish patrol cabin and that he would be met by another warden for the paperwork part of all of this. I just wanted both of us out of the area before another vehicle showed up to see us that close to the elk decoy. As soon as the man left, I decided to run towards the main gravel road and hide somewhere that I could have a closer view of the decoy and the next possible shooters.

As I was crossing the main Green River Lakes Road, I could hear the sound of another vehicle coming towards me. I started to panic, as I was standing out in the open with no good hiding place. I needed to do something quick or the occupants of the vehicle would spot me as a game warden. I observed a culvert sticking out of the bank right next to me. The culvert was about 36" in diameter. It would be a tight fit but I would only be in it long enough for the vehicle to pass on by. I shoved myself into the culvert feet first and pushed my body back until I was completely hidden. The only problem was I couldn't see the decoy or anyone if they tried to shoot at it. I expected the vehicle to go racing by, but it didn't. Instead, I heard the tires of the vehicle sliding in the gravel above my head, coming to a quick stop. I called this sound the modified stop. This meant that the occupants of the vehicle had spotted the decoy off in the distance while traveling at a high rate of speed. This sound comes from the driver mashing on the brakes to get stopped as fast as possible to more than likely shoot at the decoy. If you have not heard the modified stop before, just take your truck out on a gravel road and mash on the brakes at a high rate of speed. You will then understand the sound that I'm trying to describe.

Shit, I thought to myself. *You have really done it now, Swerb. You have yourself shoved in a culvert backwards with the shooters right above your head and you can't see anything to report to Hubba.* Hopefully Hubba was done issuing citations to the first shooter of the day. I lay there motionless in the culvert, trying to listen for sounds of anything. Pretty quick I heard a door slam and a man's voice say, "Man, I got to piss!" The man walked over to the edge of the road and pissed right over my head in front of the culvert pipe. I had a stream of yellow pee hitting the rock in front of my face and splashing back into my eyes. I covered my face with both hands and said to myself, *Oh dear God, I can't believe this is happening right now.*

I heard another man's voice say, "Oh, shit, there is a nice bull elk standing right over there next to the trees. Get your rifle out and shoot that sumbitch!"

The other man responded, "What? You have got to be shitting me right now!", as his final yellow drips splattered in my face.

Now all I could hear was the sounds of both men loading their rifles. A rifle makes a very distinct sound when you slide the bolt back and then forward to load the bullet into the barrel. This action is generally done very fast, especially when someone is trying to get a quick shot at an elk decoy before someone else comes down the road.

Before I knew it, I heard the sound of a rifle go off. BOOM! It was the loudest sound that I had ever heard before. I didn't know it at the time but one man had laid down in the road and his gun barrel was right above the culvert on the other side of the road. This loud recoil echoed through the culvert into my ears. It nearly blew my hearing drums plumb out of my head. I couldn't take another shot to my hearing so I slowly crawled out of the culvert and snuck up behind both men as they were shooting. One man was now leaning over the hood of the pick-up truck. BOOM, BOOM went both rifles. I observed both men shoot at the decoy from the public road and hunting in a closed area.

I yelled at the men, "Cease fire, it's a damn decoy!" I startled both men as they were getting ready to shoot again. You should have seen the look on both of their faces when they turned around to see a game warden standing there with pee on his face.

One guy turned around and said, "You are kidding me, right? That's a fake elk decoy?"

I replied, "Yes, sir, it is, and both of you are in violation of shooting from a public road and hunting elk in a closed area.

I grabbed my portable radio and called Hubba. "GF-24, GF-14, I've got two male subjects shooting from a public road and hunting in a closed area."

Hubba responded, "10-4, send them to my location; I just got done with the first shooter."

I explained the regulations to both men and checked to make sure that they both had hunting licenses valid for that area. Thankfully both men had the proper license to be hunting elk in this area. I told the men to drive up to the Green River lakes cabin to meet with Hubba for their citations. I also made sure that I properly identified each hunter before releasing them in case they decided to haul ass out of the area and not meet with Hubba. Don't ask me how I learned this trick the hard way.

I scrambled to find a good hiding place before the next vehicle came along. The morning had started off crazy with three shooters in a row. Sometimes you may sit on a decoy all day and never have a single shooter. But that was rare. Generally speaking, there was always some level of entertainment by the end of the day. I would end up finding a great hiding place behind a rock out-cropping located about two-hundred yards from the decoy and about one-hundred yards from the public road. I would now be able to see everything in plain sight and not worry about getting peed on again.

I had only been hiding and watching for about twenty minutes when I observed one of the craziest things that I had ever seen before. A modified school bus was coming down the rough road towards me at a high rate of speed. The school bus (Cheese Wagon) had been modified with a six-inch lift kit and was four-wheel drive. The bus was traveling so fast that it left a screen of dust behind it for about a half-mile. I dug out my spotting scope and zeroed in on the license plate. The school bus looked like it had Michigan license plates on it. It was hard to tell from a distance but I was pretty sure it had Michigan plates and was loaded with hunters. I could see numerous orange hats and vests on several occupants sitting in the bus. I decided that they were traveling too fast to even see the decoy. The bus was now past the decoy and I was actually relieved that they hadn't seen it. But I was wrong. All of a sudden, the bus did the modified stop on the gravel road. I bet they slid in the gravel for at least twenty yards before coming to a complete stop. I had never seen so many pumpkin heads and orange vests come out of a bus that quick in all my life.

Within seconds there were six hunters standing shoulder to shoulder, shooting off hand at the decoy while standing on the public road behind the school bus. They shot so many times that they knocked the damn decoy plumb over. The seventh person came out of the bus with her rifle in hand. She looked like an elderly lady to me from a distance.

One guy yelled to all of the hunters, "QUIT SHOOTING! THE ELK IS DOWN!"

I looked over at the elderly lady and she was kneeling down on one knee and banging the butt of her rifle on the ground. She did this several times and then aimed to fire. It looked like her rifle had jammed or something.

The man ran up to her and yelled, "THE ELK IS DOWN! QUIT SHOOTING."

BOOM went the elderly lady's rifle. She banged the butt of the rifle on the ground again and took aim. BOOM went the rifle again. About that time another hunter exited the bus and aimed his rifle in the direction of the downed elk decoy.

The man started screaming, "EVERYONE QUIT SHOOTING RIGHT NOW! THE DAMN ELK IS DEAD!"

I knew that I was in over my head with six shooters. I radioed Hubba and requested that he meet me down on the road, as we had a school bus with six shooters. Hubba soon showed up and met with all the hunters. I gave up my hiding place and walked down to the road to assist Hubba. As I showed up Hubba was arguing with the elderly lady. I looked at the lady and she had blood coming down both of her cheeks and her forehead was split wide open. I also noticed that the lady had a bloody hand with a large gash on her right hand between her thumb and forefinger.

Hubba looked up at me and said, "Swerb, you deal with the elderly lady. I will take care of the rest of them."

I wasn't sure what was going on or what had been said. The hunters were not convinced that they had shot a decoy. One guy yelled, "THE HELL? IT'S A DECOY! I SHOT THE DAMN THING AND WATCHED IT GO DOWN!"

Hubba responded very calmly, "If you look out there with your binoculars you will see all four of the elk's legs still stuck in the ground. You guys shot it so many times that you knocked it over."

I walked over to the elderly lady and looked over her bleeding face and hand. It appeared to me that she had cut herself with the scope of her rifle. The rifle's recoil had planted the rim of her scope firmly into her forehead. It also looked like her rifle had jammed and when she was banging it on the road the action opened and slit the web of her right hand.

I approached the lady, who was yelling, "I KILLED THE BULL ELK! MY LAST SHOT KILLED THAT ELK! I SAW IT GO DOWN!"

I replied, "Madam, you take your hunting pretty seriously, don't you? You scoped yourself and cut your hand while shooting and the decoy was already down when you shot twice."

The lady apologized and said, "I guess I get a little excited at times when I'm hunting."

We ended up issuing seven citations out of eight hunters. The only guy who didn't get a citation was the last guy to jump out of the bus when the others had already knocked the decoy over. We sent them on their way and walked out to see how bad the decoy had been shot up. When we arrived, there were four legs stuck in the ground and the body of "Oh Shit" was lying on his side. We picked up the heavy decoy and placed it back on its legs. I then noticed something very interesting. When a bullet travels through a Styrofoam body the exit hole is filled with white Styrofoam. So, you could tell exactly where every hunter had hit the bull elk by looking at all the exit holes on the opposite side of the decoy. The bad side of the decoy now resembled an appaloosa horse with little white spots everywhere. We counted all the exit holes and determined that the Michigan hunters had hit the decoy at least sixteen times. "Oh Shit" was no longer a virgin decoy. He now had war wounds and was considered a veteran of his kind.

Hubba and I got a chuckle out of that one and resumed our hiding spots. Several hunters actually drove by the decoy, looked at it for a few minutes, and drove on down the road. It was starting to get kind of boring, when a lady stopped in the road driving a Subaru. She was not hunting. She had no orange clothing and no rifle. She stood by the edge of the road, looking towards the elk. She then took off walking towards the elk, carrying a roll of toilet paper. She walked within thirty yards of the elk and took a dump while watching the decoy. Of course, I got to watch the backside of the dump and not the front side. I was starting to worry about the lady being so close to the decoy. I certainly didn't want a crazed hunter showing up and shooting at the decoy while she was happily dumping next to it. I was about to yell at the lady, when I watched her get up and walk right up to the decoy. She leaned down and threw a few small rocks at the decoy, trying to get it to run off. Of course, it just stood there and glared at her the whole time. The lady almost touched the elk and then decided to go back to her car. I decided to walk down and talk to the lady and explain the situation to her. I came walking out of the trees right next to her car.

The lady looked at me and said, "Excuse me, are you a Conservation Officer?"

I replied, "Yes, ma'am."

She said, "Well, I don't know if you know it or not but you have a very sick elk standing over there by those trees."

I giggled and said, "Ma'am, that is not a sick elk, that is an elk decoy."

She replied, "No sir, believe me it's real. I just walked right up to it and it looks like it needs some penicillin or something. I was afraid to touch him because he is just not feeling well and does not need the added stress of my presence."

I thought to myself, *why do I need to try and explain this anymore to this lady? Does she think that the game warden is just out walking around in the mountains with no patrol truck in his redshirt?*

The lady was adamant that she had just walked up to a sick elk and not a fake elk. Rather than argue with her anymore, I told the sweet lady that I would give it a shot of penicillin and keep an eye on it for a few days. She gave me a huge hug and thanked me for taking such good care of Wyoming's treasured wildlife. I walked back to my hiding spot, shaking my head in disbelief. Another hour or so went by and nobody had driven by the decoy. I was just getting ready to call it

184

a day, when two different trucks came to a sliding stop right in front of me. One truck stopped in the middle of the road and the other truck backed up about one hundred yards and parked his truck in the middle of the road in a small grove of pine trees. Almost as if he was trying to hide his vehicle. I watched the first guy exit his truck and walk towards the decoy. He was wearing an orange hat but had no rifle. I thought, *this is interesting.*

The man headed right towards the decoy, waving his hands in the air and yelling at the elk. He was yelling, "GET OUT OF HERE, BULL ELK! GET OUT OF HERE NOW!"

The other man got out of his truck and was leaning over the hood of his truck with his rifle and no orange clothing. The truck was parked right in the middle of the road and the hunter was aiming his rifle right towards his buddy's truck who was also parked in the road ahead of him.

The man walked within twenty yards of the elk, yelling and screaming "GET OUT OF HERE! HURRY UP AND GET OUT OF HERE!" The man then picked up a large rock and threw it at the elk. The rock hit the elk firmly in the rib cage area. The elk just stood there and glared at the man. He finally came walking back to his truck as if he was in a rush. I decided to head down to the road and visit with the man.

I asked him what he was doing. He explained to me that his buddy had an elk license valid for the other side of the road and he was trying to heard the elk back across the road to his buddy.

I said, "Let me get this straight. You are trying to herd the elk across the road to your buddy. Yet your buddy is parked in the middle of the road, and if the elk crosses the road, he will be shooting right towards you and your truck. Not very smart, buddy. And he will still be shooting from a public road, which is a violation."

The man apologized and felt pretty stupid. I explained the regulations to his buddy and told him to get off the public road and make sure he has his florescent orange on before hunting in the future. Because neither man shot at the elk, there was no violation. I think both men learned something that day and would be more careful in the future. Or at least more sneaky next time.

It was getting late in the day. I went back to my hiding spot and sat another couple of hours with no more traffic. I radioed to Hubba to come down to my location and we would pack up the decoy for the day. As Hubba was driving down the road I looked up and observed another truck coming down the road behind Hubba. It was nearly dark out by now. I radioed to Hubba to keep driving down the road and hide his truck until this other vehicle had passed by the decoy. Hubba kept driving and disappeared over the hill just past the location of the decoy.

The truck slowed way down and stopped. Two men got out of the truck and leaned over the hood with both of their rifles. I grabbed my binoculars and could see a bull moose carcass in the back of the man's truck. Heck, they had already killed a large bull moose and now they were hunting bull elk? The two men watched the elk decoy for what seemed like forever. Finally, one man stepped back out into the middle of the road and looked around for a few seconds.

He yelled as loud as he could, "F---K YOU, GAME WARDEN!"

He then jumped into his truck and spun gravel as he roared out of the area. I radioed Hubba and told him that he had a truck coming his way with a dead bull moose in the back of it and they probably needed a little game warden attention. Hubba rolled in behind their vehicle and stopped them in a very remote area with his little red and blue lights mounted to his front grill guard. I could not see Hubba from my location and the radio had been quiet for quite some time. I was starting to worry about Hubba and tried to call him on my portable radio. No answer. I thought, *what if Hubba needs backup? My truck is parked over a mile away. Maybe I can just sneak through the trees to Hubba's location and assist him on foot if needed.*

About that time my radio went off, "GF-14, GF-24."

I grabbed my radio and quickly answered, "Go ahead, GF-24."

Hubba responded, "Good one, the driver killed a moose with no license. I have issued citations, confiscated the moose, and I'm clear of the suspect."

I couldn't believe it. This man had actually killed a trophy bull moose with no license. What balls he had to almost shoot at the elk decoy illegally and yell F---k YOU, GAME WARDEN. This would end up costing this man thousands of dollars and loss of hunting privileges for years. And the only reason he got caught was because we were up there running an elk decoy and he had a potty mouth towards game wardens.

I responded to Hubba on the radio, "Great case, I guess he should not have been yelling profanities about the local game warden up in the remote forest."

Well, it was another long but productive day on the job. Hubba and I walked out into the dark and loaded up "Oh Shit" the shot-up elk decoy. It would be another two-hour drive home on rough roads. I returned home tired and noticed the red blinking light flashing on my answering machine. Lana was in bed, snoring loudly. She must have had a long day as well. I leaned over the bed to kiss her goodnight. She looked at me through her squinted eyes and said, "Ew...you smell like piss." I had forgot about getting my face peed on earlier in the day. I headed to the bathroom and gave my face a good scrubbing. I heard Lana yell, "HOW COME YOU SMELL LIKE PISS, HONEY?"

I replied, "It's a long story, honey. I will tell you all about it in the morning over coffee."

I hesitated to push the play button on the answering machine and listen to all the messages that I had missed that day. I took my boots off, poured a whiskey, and sat down in my recliner before pushing the play button. I hit the play button and the answering machine yelled at me and said, "Hello, you have eight messages." I pushed the play button and listened to the first message.

"Hey, Swerb, this is Hall Sawyer. Hey, I was flying out in the Rye Grass area today locating mule deer collars and observed a headless mule deer on the north side of the Rye Grass Road about two miles west of the end of the pavement. You won't have any trouble finding it because the carcass is covered with ravens and magpies and it's only about thirty yards from the road. I tried to call Big Piney game warden Brad Hovinga but got no answer, so I wanted to tell you about it. Holler if you have any questions, but my guess is someone poached that deer and cut its head off."

After that message I didn't even play anymore messages. I took a sip of whiskey and sat back in my recliner. Those sonsabitches! I'd need to get a hold of Brad first thing in the morning and report this to him, as that was his warden district.

Chapter 12

CAPPUCCINO BUCK

My alarm went off way too quick at 5:00 the next morning. I jumped out of bed and put on a pot of coffee. I tried to call Big Piney game warden Brad Hovinga to report the headless deer to him. He didn't answer the phone so I left him a message to call me ASAP. I was hoping that he was home and would get my message, because I had a full day ahead of me after listening to the other messages on my answering machine. I grabbed a cup of coffee, my hat and my pistol, and headed out the door. I heard Lana yell from the bedroom, "HEY, YOU NEVER TOLD ME WHY YOU SMELLED LIKE PEE LAST NIGHT!"

I replied, "Sorry, honey, I will tell you all about it tonight when I get home. I have a big day ahead of me and a possible poached deer to look at."

I headed out the door and the damn house phone rang. I swung back through the door and answered the phone. "Hello?"

"Yeah, Scott, this is Loren over here at 518 Shelter Park. Hey, I just had two large bull moose fighting in my yard and it looks like one of the bulls has broken his front leg while fighting. He is down in my front yard and can't get up. It looks like the other bull is knocking the shit out of him right now. I'm guessing this injured bull needs to be put down sooner than later."

I replied, "Thanks for the call, Loren. I will head that direction and be there in about twenty minutes." I jumped into my patrol truck and hauled ass to Pinedale. I knew this Loren guy; I had met him shooting pool one night at the Stockman's Bar. He seemed like a pretty cool guy what little I got to know of him. As I slowed down to turn into his driveway a blue Jeep Cherokee cut right in front of me. It looked like an elderly lady was driving. She damn near ran into my truck as she slid sideways right in front of me. I followed the lady into Loren's driveway. This little old lady was dressed in a house robe and slippers and had her hair in rollers. She jumped out of her jeep and started running towards the injured moose. Her arms were straight up in the air as she ran right up to the injured moose and gave him a huge hug. I ran up behind the lady and said, Madam, please get back! That moose is injured and may hurt you."

She turned around and ran towards me crying and gave me a big hug. She said, crying, "OH MY GOD, THAT IS JOSH AND HE HAS BROKEN HIS FRONT LEG. WHAT ARE YOU GOING TO DO WITH HIM? LORD, PLEASE HELP JOSH, LORD PLEASE HELP JOSH.", as she looked up towards the heavens.

The lady then put both her arms high up in the air and starting praying for Josh. I replied, "I'm very sorry, Madam, Josh has a broken leg and will need to be put down. I will donate his meat to the needy. You may want to get in your jeep and go home now."

I then gave the lady a game warden hug and patted her on the back as she walked back to her jeep and left the area. Now I remembered this lady. She lived right across the street and she and her husband would feed all the moose and deer in the area. She was very protective of her moose. Once the lady was completely gone, I walked up to Josh to look at his injuries. His front right leg was completely broken in half above the knee joint. At this time in my career, I had never put down a large bull moose before. All I was packing was a 9mm Beretta. I looked at Loren and said, "I will need to put this moose

190

down, do you have a larger pistol that I could borrow? Like a .44 mag or something?"

Loren replied, "Yes, I have a .44 mag. I will run and get it quick."

Loren returned with his loaded .44 mag and handed it to me. I was a little embarrassed to borrow his pistol to put the moose down but I wanted this to be a very quick and clean kill. The moose was in town and right across the road from the lady that loved them so much. I wanted one shot to the head and a dead moose. I slowly approached the moose and decided to shoot him right in the back of the head. BOOM went the .44 mag. The moose never even flinched. He looked to his right and back to his left as if nothing had happened. The sound of the pistol was very loud in the neighborhood. I really didn't want to have to shoot it again. So, I waited a few minutes for the moose to die. After several minutes the moose still looked fine, so I decided to walk around in front of him and shoot him between the eyes. BOOM, right between the eyes and the moose didn't do a damn thing. He never even attempted to lay his head down or get up or anything. I was getting very frustrated and embarrassed because I'm supposed to be a trained professional at dealing with these sorts of things.

I walked around to the side of the moose and shot him right in the ear hole. BOOM went the .44 mag. Again, the moose didn't do anything, but a large stream of blood about as round as a garden hose came spewing out of his head every time the moose's heart would beat. I didn't want to shoot the moose again so I just stood there and watched him bleed out. Mind you, there was about three inches of snow in this man's yard and now it looked like I had slaughtered about twelve bison in his yard. I looked up and observed a lady riding a bicycle down the nearby street. She was wearing a Sony Walkman and just pedaling away. She looked up and saw the moose lying in the yard. She stopped and jumped off her bicycle and ran up to the moose and took a picture of him. She had no idea that he had been shot in the head three times and was dying. She looked at me and said with a smile, "Such a gorgeous animal, thanks for the picture." I couldn't believe that she didn't see the gallons of blood in the snow next to the moose. I then looked across the street and noticed that the little old lady was watching me from a second-floor window in her house. Now, I was really embarrassed. I looked at the moose and said, "Dear Lord, please die, Josh!"

The moose finally laid his head down to rest. He had nearly blead out and the yard was a mess with bright red blood in the bright white snow. I looked up at my patrol truck. I had forgotten about 'Oh Shit' the elk decoy still being in the back of my truck. All four legs were sticking straight in the air. Loren looked at me and said, "What the hell is that in the back of your truck? It looks like an appaloosa horse."

I replied, "It's supposed to be an elk decoy but some Michigan hunters shot the shit out of him."

I would need to load the dead moose up and get it out of Loren's yard, but I had no room in my truck with the decoy being there. I called one of our biologists and asked him to bring a flatbed trailer to the address of the dead moose. Except, the moose wasn't dead yet. The biologist soon arrived and jackknifed his trailer up to the moose. I then pulled my patrol truck up to the front of his trailer and ran my winch cable over to the moose and wrapped it around his neck. I grabbed my remote control and started the slow process of dragging the body of the moose up onto the trailer. The moose was finally loaded on the trailer with the winch cable wrapped around his neck. I was so relieved to just get me and the moose the heck out of there. About that time the moose decided he still wasn't dead and tried to stand up on the trailer. He nearly got to his feet then down he went, thank God. The moose had finally died. I shook Loren's hand and thanked him as I gave back his .44 mag. I later learned that the moose's brain is very small and is located right in the top of their head. All three of my shots had missed the brain. It's experiences like

192

this that make you a trained professional someday. I would now need to gut the dead moose out in the hills somewhere and donate the meat to people in need. I would also need to drop off the elk decoy at the office before investigating the headless deer on Rye Grass Road.

Poor Josh

As I was headed out in the hills to dress out the moose, my bag phone rang. It was south Pinedale Game Warden Brian Nesvik. Brian told me that he had received a report of a headless deer in Rye Grass and that he couldn't get a hold of Big Piney Game Warden Brad Hovinga. I told Brian that I had also received the same information and was headed out later in the morning to investigate the dead deer. Brian told me that he was planning on going out as well and wanted to know if I wanted to jump in with him and do the investigation together. I had never done an investigation with Brian before and was eager to work with him and see what I could learn from him.

One moose carcass donated, one elk decoy put back in storage, and Brian and I were on our way to investigate the headless deer. We had just left the end of the pavement on the Rye Grass Road. The deer carcass was supposed to be on the north side of the two-track dirt road that we were traveling on. I looked up and observed a bunch of ravens and magpies fly off in the distance.

Brian said, "Stop right here, it looks like the carcass is lying up ahead of us. Let's work this crime scene from the backside and work back towards the main road so that we don't destroy any evidence such as boot prints or tire tracks."

Brian grabbed his evidence kit and I grabbed my metal detector. We circled way around on the backside of the deer, thinking that once we reached the deer carcass, we would work any evidence back to the two-track road. As we approached the dead deer it appeared to be bloated up, with all four feet sticking straight up in the air. The body of the deer appeared to be large, indicating that it may have been a large buck deer. The head was completely missing. We looked over the body cavity very carefully and ran the metal detector over every square inch of the body cavity. It didn't appear that the deer had been shot anywhere in the body cavity. More than likely, it was shot in the head and we wouldn't be able to recover a bullet, making it even tougher to solve the case. Brian put on his blue plastic gloves and went over the entire deer very thoroughly. Brian said, "Oh, this is interesting." Then he carefully removed a down feather that was stuck between the front hooves of the mule deer. He placed the small feather in a small zip lock bag and wrote 'Exhibit #1' on the front of the bag with a sharpie marker.

Then he looked up and said, "This is very interesting. This feather didn't come from a raven or a magpie. It looks like it's a feather from someone's down vest or something." We then carefully skinned the entire deer out. We found no bullet holes and no hemorrhaging. Heck, maybe the deer hadn't even been shot and died of natural causes and someone came along and just cut its head off.

Brian said, "This is a very healthy-looking deer; healthy deer don't just die during a mild winter." Heck, it was only the end of October and winter hadn't even really started yet. We then started moving slowly towards the road where the deer may have been shot from.

We noticed a pretty good boot print in the dirt. Brian measured the track's width and length and took several pictures of the track. He then mixed up some Plaster of Paris in a large zip lock bag and poured the plaster over the boot track. He then pulled out a handful of blue and orange pin flags. He told me to place a blue pin flag in each boot impression that we found heading back towards the main road. He also told me to place an orange pin flag on every drop of blood that I observed on the ground.

I thought this was pretty cool. By the time we reached the road you could tell exactly where one person had left the road and walked out to the dead deer, cut its head off, and walked back to their truck. Each pin flag showed the exact path that was taken. The orange pin flags indicated drops of blood coming off the deer's head as it was being carried back to the main road. It appeared to me that there was only one person that walked out to the dead deer. It also looked like that person carried the deer head in his right hand as he headed back to the truck.

Once we reached the road I observed fresh tire tracks in the dirt. The tracks had been traveling west down the road and made a sharp turn to the right. The dead deer would have been lying right in the center of their headlights and about thirty yards off the road.

I told Brian, "Hey, look at these tracks in the road. It looks like someone spotted the deer on their right and made a sharp turn to place the deer in their headlights before they shot it." I then looked near the tire track on the passenger side of the vehicle. Thank God we had some evidence. I found two empty shell casings from a .17 caliber HMR. Both shell casings were lying right next to the passenger side tire track. I also found an empty box of .17 HMR shells on the ground.

Brian walked over and stood next to me and said, "Look right there, Swerb; we have some excellent evidence in that bush over there." And he pointed to my right.

Brian walked over and carefully picked up a small Styrofoam cup with his blue plastic gloves on. He examined it carefully and said, "This is good evidence; it's a cappuccino cup. Does anyone have a cappuccino hut in Pinedale anywhere?"

I responded, "Yes, there is a little hut on your right as you come into Pinedale."

Brian said, "Oh, this is good evidence; we are going to catch these guys. People who drink cappuccino have to have it every morning."

I looked confused at Brian and replied, "You may be right, but this cappuccino may have been purchased two weeks ago in Rock Springs or somewhere else, and may have been rolling around on their floor board for a couple weeks before falling out of their truck."

I personally didn't think it was good evidence at all. We continued looking over the scene and found another empty shell casing of a .17 HMR right next to the tire track on the driver's side. After measuring and casting tire and foot prints, we determined that the passenger of the vehicle had shot at the deer at least twice and the driver shot at the deer at least once. The driver exited the vehicle and walked out and cut the deer's head off. He/she then headed back to the truck, carrying the deer head in their right hand. You could even tell by the blood splatters on the ground that the driver's side door was open on the vehicle, as the blood splatters went out and around on the ground as if someone's door was open. The blood splatters also indicated that the driver of the truck also slung the deer head into the back of their truck with their right hand. Once all the pin flags were on the ground you could see exactly what had happened.

We then began to examine the tire prints in the dirt. It looked to me like the vehicle had gone up and down the road several times. I told Brian that I was confused because it appeared that the vehicle went back and forth before shooting the deer. Brian said, "It really doesn't matter, Swerb; we have the right tire track and that's all that matters."

I said, "I know that, but I'm just trying to figure out exactly what happened here. Did they drive by the deer and go down the road and turn around and come back and then shoot the deer? There are just too many damn tire tracks here to make sense of all of this."

Brian replied, "It doesn't matter. Let's get to Pinedale and talk to the owner of the cappuccino place before they close."

It was about 3:30 p.m. when we left the area. As we got back to the main highway, we met Big Piney Game Warden Brad Hovinga as he was turning off on the Rye Grass Road. We told Brad about all the evidence that we had collected and told him that we were headed to Pinedale to visit with the owner of the cappuccino hut. I think Brad was a little butt soar that Brian and I had just conducted an investigation on a headless deer in his warden district. Brad had been away from his warden station and had just got the message that I left him earlier that morning.

Brad said, "Thanks for all your help, guys, but I'm going to drive around and look for any more dead deer and any additional evidence that may be in the area." We thanked him and headed for town. About twenty minutes later Brad called on the radio to report that he had additional information/evidence. We pulled off the road and called Brad on his bag phone. Brad told us that he found a spot where the truck had turned around in the soft dirt. He said the truck was definitely a dually truck. That made sense to me now, because I couldn't figure out why all the same tire tracks were in the road. Brad also told us that he followed their tracks completely out of the area and back to the highway.

He said, "I think these guys are local because they took the long way back to the highway and had to make at least four different turns to get back to the highway. Someone new to the area would not have known how to find their way back to the highway at night. Last night was Halloween night. These guys may have partied it up at the Green River Bar (GRB) until closing time, got drunk, and went spotlighting on their way back home. With a dually truck they likely work in the oil field or live on a remote ranch somewhere nearby."

Now that we knew it was a dually truck this limited our search a whole bunch. We thanked Brad for the additional information and pulled into the cappuccino hut. I walked through the front door and noticed a dark haired and very attractive young women working behind the counter. I think this must be a requirement to work at a cappuccino place, as I have never seen nothing but pretty women working at one of these places. Brian and I took the small white Styrofoam cup up to her and asked her what she could tell us about the cup. The attractive lady looked it over very carefully and said, "Hmm, this is actually very rare. Looking at the residue in the bottom of the cup this appears to be a small coffee. Most everyone generally orders a large cappuccino in the mornings and not a small coffee."

We then asked the lady if she would help us look out for a dually pick-up truck with two possible male subjects in the truck. Especially if the passenger ordered a small coffee. We also told her that they may have a rifle between the two front seats of the truck. We gave her both of our phone numbers and she seemed eager to help us with our case.

I finally made it home after another long day. My wife had also had a long day and had just got home when I arrived. She reminded me that we needed to hurry and go back into town to watch our son Wes play in a basketball game. I took my red shirt off and threw it on the bed and quickly put on another shirt.

I said, "All right, let's go; where do you want to eat dinner?"

Lana replied, "I'll order a pizza and we can pick it up on our way through town."

It seemed like all we did was run our asses off between our careers and our kids. I guess that is what life is all about. It's a good thing we were young and just didn't know any better. We both got home late that night and Lana jumped into bed tired. She needed to get up early in the morning and go feed elk at Jewett feed ground and train horses on the Antelope Run Ranch. I poured a whiskey and sat down in my favorite thinking recliner. Heck, I didn't even get to tell my wife about my day or even the day before for that matter. I sipped my whiskey and contemplated how we were going to catch our deer poachers. I couldn't even sleep that night. I went through every imaginable thought that I could come up with on who was responsible for poaching that deer. It was always fun to try and figure out exactly what happened in your head, then catch the poachers and see if you were correct on anything. Most of the time it would turn out completely different than what you thought happened.

I didn't set my alarm but was woken up by my phone ringing at 6:15AM. Lana was just getting ready to leave the house and I was trying to say goodbye to her. I looked at her as she was walking out the door and said, "Sorry, honey, I better take this call; it might be important."

She smiled and replied, "See you tonight. And you still haven't told me why you smelled like pee the other night and why your pants were covered in blood last night when you got home."

I laughed and replied, "We will have a date night tonight and tell stories; now I better answer this phone call. Have a good day. I love you."

"Love you too!"

I picked up the phone and heard a woman's voice say, "Hello, is this Scott?"

"Yes, it is, how may I help you?"

"Hey, this is Heather down at the cappuccino place. I think I just found your suspects. They just came through a few minutes ago driving a gray Dodge dually pick-up. The passenger ordered a small coffee and the driver ordered a large cappuccino. You were right; they did have a rifle leaning on the seat between them. They are regulars here and come through every morning at about the same time. They are working on a job site west of town and I can tell you where that's at if you want."

I couldn't believe what I was hearing. Nesvik was exactly right about the cappuccino cup being good evidence. I would have never guessed that. And Hovinga was right about the truck being a dually. This information alone probably solved the poaching case. I got the details from Heather of where they worked and thanked her immensely. I couldn't wait to call Brad and Brian and tell them the great news. Both of them were on cloud nine and wanted to meet at the cappuccino place at 8:00. They were more than ready to go catch the bad guys, and so was I.

We drove out to the suspects' job site. Parked in a large parking lot was a silver Dodge dually truck. We checked out the truck and the tire pattern matched what we were looking for. We also noticed small drops of blood in the bed of the truck and a few small deer hairs. The rifle between the seats appeared to be a scoped .17 HMR. We definitely had our suspects' truck. The owner of the truck was operating a backhoe nearby. Brad and Brian approached the backhoe in their redshirts and motioned for the guy to shut it down and come visit with them. The man crawled out of the backhoe and walked towards them. His face color drained from normal to white in about two seconds.

Brad looked at the man and said, "Well, I guess you know why we're here."

The man dropped his head and said, "Yeah, I poached a deer the other night and I'm sorry for that."

The man was cooperative about poaching the deer but did not want to give up his buddy's name that was with him that night. Brad and Brian advised him that his truck would be confiscated and a search warrant obtained to go through his truck. The man agreed to this and said, "Just get whatever you need, you don't need no damn search warrant." Well, they got a search warrant anyways and went through the truck. They found everything that they needed, including the knife that was used to cut the head off the deer. They collected blood and hair samples from the back of the truck to match to the deer that was shot and wasted.

Stuck in the passenger seat was a down feather that matched the feather that was found earlier between the hooves of the headless deer. This only told us that the passenger may have been wearing a down filled vest when the deer was shot. There was also some marijuana and other paraphernalia found in the console of the truck.

The man's story was that they had been partying at the Green River Bar on Halloween night. He and his friend left the bar around midnight to go spotlight some jackrabbits on the Rye Grass Road. They had been drinking heavily when they noticed a large buck mule deer standing off the side of the road. They turned their truck hard to the right and centered the deer in their headlights. The passenger shot twice at the deer, missing him both times. The driver then took the rifle and shot the deer in the head with one shot. The deer dropped dead. The driver walked out and cut the head off the deer and returned to the truck. Once they sobered up, they decided to bury the deer head on a friend's ranch located about five miles away.

I'm not sure how the down feather ended up between the deer's front hooves since the passenger never left the vehicle. Wardens Nesvik and Hovinga would then interview patrons at the Green River Bar to figure out who the other suspect was. They were successful and found out the name of the other suspect. He lived in Riverton. Warden Hovinga drove to Riverton and found the man he was looking for. The man denied everything and told Hovinga that he had not even been in the Pinedale/Daniel area ever.

The man was wearing a down vest. Hovinga seized the vest as evidence and told the man that he had collected down feathers at the crime scene and would need to determine if the feathers in his vest matched the feathers at the crime scene. The man dropped his head and said, "Please give me my vest back. I was with the driver of the vehicle when he poached the deer." The man would not admit that he had also shot at the deer. Warden Hovinga also learned that the man had prior drug charges and was on probation. Hovinga also let the man know that drugs were found in the vehicle during the search. The suspect became very cooperative after learning that drugs were found in the vehicle and that they belonged to him. He eventually told the whole story and collaborated the story from the other suspect.

At the end of the day this was a great case solved by good old-fashioned game warden work. I learned something very valuable from this case that would help solve many more poaching cases in the future. What I learned was to use a teamwork approach to solve these cases. Take several of your best wardens and let them all investigate these cases together. Every warden will look at the crime scene differently and everyone will add a different perspective to what may have happened. Each of them will also come up with different ideas and different evidence to solve the case. I would have never believed that we could solve a case over a stupid cappuccino cup lying in a sage brush plant. Many wardens want to solve these kinds of cases on their own with no help from others. I don't know if it's a pride or ego sort of thing. But I did learn that teamwork and good communication are key, and work very well.

We went out to the remote ranch and dug up the deer head. This buck was a 4x4 and about 25" wide. Nothing special, for what it ended up costing these two nimrods. I returned home that evening tired again but had lots of new stories to tell Lana when she got home. We had a date night and got caught up on stories about our careers. One thing about it, we lived some interesting times with never a dull moment.

The next morning, I slept in. I did not leave the house until around 9:00AM. I was headed to the office to check email and write up a poaching report on our Case Management System (CMS.) I hated writing reports on this system. If you didn't save your work every five minutes the computer screen would flash and I would lose everything that I had just spent hours writing and thinking about. I would later name it the PMS system. Brad had just called me on his bag phone. He had already met with the County Attorney in Pinedale and was headed back to Big Piney. I told him that I would meet up with him along the highway and he could tell me all about his interview with the Riverton poacher.

I had my FM radio cranked and was singing along to the song *Don't worry be happy, Doo-Doo-Doo-Doo, don't worry just be happy!* This was one of my favorite songs. I looked up and observed a white oil field truck parked off the edge of the highway. It was backed up to the right-of-way fence. There was a man wearing a florescent orange hat carrying a scoped rifle on the other side of the fence. I thought that was weird because deer season had been closed for several weeks now. I quickly turned the radio down and whipped my patrol truck around and pulled up next to the white truck. What I saw next, I couldn't believe. The man had just killed a nice buck mule deer on the winter range during late morning hours. The dead deer was lying on the ground right behind his truck on the other side of the fence. I jumped out of my truck and approached the man.

I said, "Good morning! Looks like you have killed a nice buck deer!"

The man was in his mid-forties and replied, "Yup, I got lucky on this one and killed him right over there." The man pointed to the north. I asked the man for his hunting license and he produced one. It hadn't been filled out yet.

I asked the man, "Do you have permission to hunt on this private property?"

The man replied, "No, I thought this was all BLM land out here."

I explained to the man that the hunting season had been closed for three weeks and he had just killed a buck deer on private property without permission during a closed season. I also got the man to admit that he had shot from his vehicle off a public road. After further questioning, the man admitted to shooting the deer in his work truck while he was supposed to be working in the oil field. About that time, I heard a vehicle pull up next to us. I turned around and it was Brad. He walked over and whispered, "Did this guy just kill this buck?"

I replied, "He sure did."

Brad winked at me and said, "Good one, buddy; do you need any help from me?"

I replied, "I think we are about done here; if you could help me load the deer in the back of my truck that would be nice."

Brad helped me load the deer and headed down the road. I don't think he could believe that I had just caught a man shooting a trophy buck deer off the main highway essentially on its winter range. I issued the man several citations for nearly two thousand dollars in fines. I jumped back in my truck with a smile on my face and was hoping my favorite song was still on the radio. Don't worry be happy! I sang and whistled that song over and over in my head as I drove to Pinedale. I would later end up using the antlers off this deer for a brand-new remote control deer decoy. We named the decoy 'BE-HAPPY'.

If I hadn't slept in that morning and had a late start to work, this man would have probably got away with poaching this deer. Over my career, I have learned that everything happens for a reason and to just go with the flow. Sometimes certain people are doomed to get caught poaching. I "Must Appeared" the man into court. The judge took away the man's hunting privileges for two years. I also learned that the man was later fired from his job for poaching in his work truck while he was supposed to be working.

Poached deer out of season

Chapter 13

Mule Deer Poaching in the Prospect Mountains

It was December 2006. There would be various wardens patrolling the winter ranges 24/7 from November 1 through December 31. After years of investigating headless deer on the crucial mule deer winter ranges we discovered a few patterns. Most deer were poached sometime between Thursday and Sunday of each week. The majority of the deer that had been poached were shot late Friday and Saturday nights. Some deer were discovered to have been poached on holidays such as Thanksgiving and Christmas Day. In most cases alcohol and drugs were involved and it was typically two male subjects from the ages of about 18-35. With this information we decided to narrow our patrols down to Thursday through Sunday and focus on night patrols. So, in addition to the local wardens that patrolled every day we brought other wardens from all over the state to patrol from Thursday through Sunday each week between November 1 through the end of December. I would meet with each warden every Thursday afternoon to have a briefing meeting. I would also meet with the same warden on Monday morning to have a debriefing meeting. These meetings were designed to pass on important information each week to the new wardens patrolling the areas.

Each warden would carry a log book and evidence kit. The log book would document everyone that was contacted on the winter range. In this log book wardens would document vehicle license plates, location, name of registered owner, and any firearm calibers and serial numbers that may be found in their vehicles. Keep in mind it was still legal for people to be out on the winter range taking photographs, shooting predators, rabbit hunting, lion hunting, or just looking at big buck deer. Everyone that we contacted was generally photographing large mule deer bucks or coyote hunting, or both. But it was also these people that we were contacting daily that may be poaching large bucks. So, we were suspicious of everyone that we contacted on the winter ranges. The log book was full of information for the other wardens that were patrolling. Such information included names and phone numbers of all the local wardens in the area. The log also contained names and phone numbers of other law enforcement officers in the area and maps of all crucial winter ranges.

Each Thursday I would meet with the new warden patrolling the area. I would pass on information of where large mule deer bucks had been observed. We called these bucks 'High Risk Deer'. Most of these deer were over thirty inches wide and may even have non-typical points. We would essentially babysit all these high-risk bucks while patrolling. I would also pass on any information of highly suspect people and their vehicle description. We just gathered as much intel as possible each week and passed the information along to the new warden patrolling the area. Wardens were instructed to report any headless/poached deer that they came across to me. We would then bring out several other wardens to assist with the investigations. These wardens had extensive experience with winter range poaching over the years. Now that we had recently solved several winter range poaching cases, the local wardens were much more confident in catching the suspects than ever before.

I would meet with Riverton Game Warden Brad Gibb on Thursday afternoon. Brad was a great guy and a seasoned game warden. I always looked forward to working with Brad. He had one of the cleanest Game and Fish patrol trucks in the entire state, and equipped with every cool game warden gadget that you could ever imagine. He even got in trouble one year for putting pin stripes and chrome wheels on his department truck. Every game warden in the state received an email from the Chief Game Warden that they were not to pinstripe any trucks or put really cool looking wheels on their trucks. This was deemed as a poor public perception that Game and Fish trucks should not look too cool or too expensive. Keep in mind, we were still all driving regular cab trucks at this time. One of our administrators was dead set against game wardens driving extended cab trucks. He felt that the public wouldn't support the idea of more expensive trucks and he wanted to make sure that we were spending sportsmen dollars wisely. All these trucks were paid for with license sells from our constituents. At this time just about everyone that I knew was driving an extended cab truck, except game wardens.

While meeting with Brad. I told him to make sure that he got the license plate of every truck observed while patrolling on the winter range and document it in the daily log book. I shook Brad's hand and thanked him for his assistance over the weekend. It was really nice to have help from other regions in the state. The local wardens were getting burned out from patrolling 24/7 and occasionally needed a day off. I told Brad to call me if he ran into anything and that I would plan on meeting him Monday morning at 8:00 if I did not see him sooner. I wished him luck and told him not to get his new patrol truck too dirty.

It was late Friday night when I received a voice message from Warden Gibbs. His voice was shaky and I could tell his adrenaline was running high. This is what the message sounded like.

"Hey, Swerb, this is Brad. Hey, I was sitting along the main county road south of Buckskin Crossing, glassing some nice bucks. As I was looking through my spotting scope, I heard the sound of a vehicle approaching. I looked up to see a white Chevy pick-up go by me at a high rate of speed. I looked in my rearview mirror and only got a partial plate number. It was definitely a 4-County plate and I only got the first three numbers off the plate. I didn't think much about it at the time. Then about one hour later I was assisting some fish division personnel at Buckskin Crossing when I heard a gunshot go off right behind me to the south. I jumped in my patrol truck and headed south. I noticed the same white Chevy truck parked down in a draw several hundred yards away. I zoomed my binoculars in to see a man get into the passenger side of the truck. I then noticed the driver was looking back at me through his binoculars out of his rearview sliding window. The truck then took off at a high rate of speed and I have been looking for it for more than hour now. It is an absolute blizzard out here right now and the roads are drifting shut quickly. Every road that I have traveled on has their tire tracks in the snow. It's an older model white Chevy pick-up with big tires. And all I got off the truck earlier was a partial plate number. I called Big Piney Game Warden Brad Hovinga and he is headed out to assist me right now. I will call you when I learn more. Thanks. Brad."

I felt horrible. I had somehow missed this message earlier. Now I had two wardens out in a blizzard chasing down a white Chevy pick-up. I didn't even know if they had actually poached anything. Maybe they were shooting at a coyote or a rabbit or something. Heck, I didn't know any more about it. I then tried to call both Brads and no answer from either of them. I got worried and put on my redshirt and pistol and told Lana that I was headed out to the Buckskin Crossing area to help chase down a possible poacher. I jumped in my truck and headed towards Pinedale. About that time my bag phone rang and it was Warden Gibb. He filled me on more of the details. He told me that he and Warden

Hovinga had traveled every road in the area trying to catch up to this truck but no luck. He also told me that he didn't go down to where their truck was parked yet to look for a dead deer. He also told me that due to the darkness and drifting blowing snow that he and Warden Hovinga were going to drive down to the area at first light and see what they could find. I thanked Brad for his update and told him to call me first thing in morning when they had more information.

I went to bed running the whole scenario through my head. Did they really poach a deer? What else would they be shooting at? Why would they poach a deer after seeing a game warden in the area earlier? If they did poach a deer, this would take some huge balls to do it right in front of a game warden. I had a hard time sleeping that night and felt guilty that I was not out there with my fellow wardens assisting them. It drove me crazy not to be involved with everything all the time. I later learned as a supervisor that you have to trust your guys to do their job and you simply can't be involved with everything all the time.

Warden Gibbs called me the next morning at about 7:00. He told me that he and Warden Hovinga drove down to the area where the truck had been parked last night and where he had heard the sound of a gunshot. He said that they had found a large mule deer carcass that was missing its head right where the truck had been parked. The passenger of the truck more than likely had cut the deer head off while Brad was watching him. That is when they blew out of the area to never be seen again. It had snowed a great deal that night and most of the roads in the area were drifted shut. Brad didn't think that the truck could have traveled all the way across the Lander Cutoff over to South Pass due to deep drifting snow. I told Brad that I would head that direction to provide assistance with the investigation.

This deer poaching happened in the South Pinedale game warden's district. Brian Nesvik was out of town the previous night but was now also helping with the investigation. We showed up at the area at about the same time. I told Brian to assist both Brads with the investigation and that I would wait at the main road and stop any vehicles that may try and enter that road to prevent them from screwing up any evidence that we may have. I also decided to stop every vehicle on the main road and question them to see if anyone may have additional information. The first vehicle that I stopped was a man that I knew well and considered to be a good friend. He owned an auto-body shop in Pinedale. I told the man that we were investigating a poached deer and that the road was closed.

He replied, "Oh really? Well, you might want to drive down the road a couple miles and take the first left and go up to the top of the hill. On your left side you will see some magpies on a deer carcass. My wife and I hiked out there to check it out and it's a large buck deer that looks like it may have been shot."

I thanked the man for the information and continued to block the road until the investigation was completed. Once the investigation was completed, I learned that they had recovered a .270 caliber bullet out of the front shoulder of the deer. All the evidence that we had was tire tracks, a bullet, and a partial plate number. We then all traveled up to the location of the second dead deer. We located the same tire impressions at this sight. We could tell where someone had pulled off the road, probably to shoot the deer. I was amazed after the blizzard that we could still see the tire tracks well enough to match them to the suspects' vehicle. Now we knew that the suspects killed at least two deer that night and did not retrieve the head off one of them. Our next move was to contact SALECS, our dispatch, and have them run the partial plate number every way possible to see if they could come up with an older white Chevy pick-up with 4-County plates. Warden Gibb had the first three numbers but was sure there was at least one other number behind the first three.

We got a hold of our infamous dispatcher named Joe. She had solved many poaching cases for the entire department over her 30+

years as a dispatcher. Jo would work hard for hours and hours to help solve a poaching case. She seemed excited to get the information and replied, "Just give me a few hours and I will see what I can come up with." Several hours passed and we finally heard back from Joe. She had found four different older model white Chevy pickups in the town of Rocksprings based off a partial license plate number. We made a few phone calls to the game wardens in the Rocksprings and Green River area and asked them to check out the address of all four matches to see if we could find the truck that matched the tires tracks that we had.

The very last truck that the wardens looked at in the Rocksprings area matched our tire description. And, it also had a box of .270 shells sitting on the front seat. The front bumper was torn off the truck and the front end of the truck was still packed full with snow, probably from busting through deep snow drifts to get out of the area. I was pretty sure we had the right truck. Now we would have to figure out the registered owner's information, address, and any prior convictions. Once we figured out who this person was, we met with our local County Attorney, Ralf Boyten. He quickly drew up a search warrant and an arrest warrant for our suspect. Brian Nesvik received the judge's signature and called me with the good news at approximately 6:00PM.

He said, "Hey, buddy, are you ready to roll to Rocksprings to serve a search warrant and arrest a bad guy?"

I replied, "Hell, yeah! Let's get rolling before it gets any later."

I will never forget trying to keep up with Brian that night. I was following him in the dark with both of our red and blue lights flashing. Cars would pull over for him and then pull right back out in the highway right in front of me. They must have not been able to see my red and blue lights, because every single one of them pulled right out in front of me, nearly causing an accident. I would mash on the brakes, swerve hard to my left, and give it the onion again. I know we did at least 94mph all the way to Rocksprings and would have gone faster if we didn't have a governor installed in our trucks. We soon arrive in Rocksprings at approximately 7:00PM. We stopped by the local police department to see if anyone was interested in providing us with backup. Man, was this a learning curve for me. I soon realized that there are special force officers that do nothing except bash doors open with a posthole pounder that they had named 'Ugly Stick'. This post hole pounder was painted black with yellow and red fire flames all up and down the sides of it. This group of officers sat around waiting for these sorts of calls. They were all very eager to take us to the suspect's house and assist us with anything that we needed. They all had bullet proof vests and fingerless gloves, dressed in complete black attire. They packed AR-15s, taser guns, and any piece of law enforcement gear that you could imagine on their duty belts. These duty belts must have weighed at least fifty pounds. I felt pretty silly with only having a 9mm Glock and my pepper spray strapped to my western belt.

It was after 8:00 p.m. when we arrived at the suspect's house. One of the Rocksprings officers carrying the posthole pounder knocked on the front door of the house. He yelled, "POLICE, OPEN THE DOOR!" He gave the man about three seconds to open the door and then proceeded to bash the door open with his Ugly Stick. Two strikes with the flamed posthole pounder absolutely demolished the front door of the house. He quickly entered the house, followed by me and other officers with flashlights. We found the man in bed and arrested him, yelling, "PUT YOUR HANDS IN THE AIR, PUT YOUR HANDS IN THE AIR." As about five flashlights completely blinded the man. I was really hoping that we had the right guy after all of this. I was not used to using this sort of tactic to arrest someone. These guys didn't mess around. I was always Mr. Nice Guy and rarely used my authority to manhandle people. But I guess if you don't want to get shot, you need to move in quick and fast and get the suspect arrested. Come to find out, this man was in his late twenties and was living with his mother.

The police officers arrested the man and transported him to jail while the other wardens and I executed the search warrant. All we wanted was a .270 rifle, ammunition, and maybe the knife used to cut the head off the deer. What we found was horrible. This man was into porno and had drawers full of porno videos, dildos, women's underwear, and other things that you don't want to even know about. His mother was upset and crying and wanting to know what her dear son had done wrong. I hated doing search warrants. I believe in people's privacy rights and hate to ever infringe on all their personal stuff. Generally, whenever I did a search warrant, I would just tell the person what I was looking for and ask them to bring it to me. I would tell them, "Just bring me what I need and don't make me go through your wife's panty drawers." They would say, "Yes, sir, I will be right back with everything that you need."

We found everything that we needed and headed back down to the police department. They had the man dressed in a pumpkin suit and sitting in an interview room. The man was handcuffed to a single chair sitting in the middle of the room. The room had multiple cameras and the interview would be recorded. We read the man his rights and started asking him questions. The man lied about everything and had no idea what we were even talking about. Brian and I had been through many of these interviews before and were well trained on how to deal with these kinds of suspects. We gave the man every chance in the world to be honest and talk to us, but he refused.

Finally, Brian said, "Sir, do you see that camera up in the ceiling tiles?"

The man looked up and said "Yes, I do."

"Could you please hold both your boots in the air for that camera to take a picture?"

The man held both his feet high in the air.

Brian said, "Thank you, you see we have pictures of foot prints at the crime scene. This camera will take pictures of your boots and analyze the soles of your boots. If they match the pictures of the tracks that we have, it will let us know if it's a match. Do you think that there would be any reason that the tracks will match what we have on file?"

The man responded, "I don't think so, I don't even know what you guys are talking about."

The man was clearly lying and kept trying to scoot his chair around, except it was bolted to the floor and would go nowhere. After several more questions and lies from the suspect, Brian finally got serious. He got out of his chair and knelt down on one knee right in front of the suspect.

Brian said. "Sir, have you ever played Texas Hold 'Em?

The man's eyes lit up, he replied, "Yes, sir, I love that game."

"Well, this is exactly what we are doing right now. You have two down cards and I have two down cards. Now, I'm going to show you one of my cards but you have to also show me one of your cards. I'm going to show you one of my cards and tell you that we just received information from our lab that your foot prints match the foot prints that we have at the poached deer near Buckskin Crossing. Now you need to show me one of your cards."

The man looked at the ground and confessed to the whole thing. I couldn't believe my eyes. He admitted to killing both deer and admitted who was with him. He claimed that after seeing the game warden they drove through a horrible blizzard all the way across the Lander cut across road all the way to South Pass and on to Rocksprings. They tore the hell out of their truck, busting deep snow drifts all the way. Once back in Rocksprings they partied it up and decided to drive all the way back to the kill site to retrieve the deer heads around 2:00AM. They arrived near the area and noticed nobody had traveled down the two-track road where they had poached the second deer. He admitted that they had decided if there were tire tracks over their tire tracks that they wouldn't retrieve the head. They went down and retrieved the head in the middle of the night after being chased around all night by the two Brads. They couldn't find the location of the first deer that they had actually poached several days earlier so they decided to come back another time.

I couldn't believe that we had made this case over a partial plate number and a white Chevy truck. The wardens did an awesome job working this case and brought it to an end quickly. The suspects ended up with jail time, loss of hunting privileges, and thousands of dollars in fines. I don't think the guy would have ever cracked if Brian hadn't brought up the Texas Hold 'Em scenario. That was brilliant. One thing that I have learned about poachers over the years, they are not always the sharpest crayon in the box.

By the time that we had got done interviewing the suspect and issuing citations it was past midnight. We could not find a motel room in the entire town of Rocksprings. We ended up finding a rat hole motel in Green River in the wee hours of the night. Thankfully Warden Brad Gibb got a partial plate number in his rearview mirror from a truck traveling over 50mph on a county road or this case would not have been solved. Thankfully a Pinedale resident reported another dead buck deer in the area or we may not have known about that one. It takes great teamwork and good communication to catch poachers. I have also learned that some poachers are destined to be caught at some point in time.

I finally returned home Sunday morning. I didn't get much sleep the night before with all the mice running around in the walls of the motel room that we had stayed in. No wonder the room was only $39.00/night. I walked in the front door and gave Lana a hug. I had to tell her the story about the poacher and Brian playing Texas Hold 'Em with two down cards. She laughed and said, "That guy sure doesn't sound very smart, what a big ol' sack of dumbass to poach a deer in front of a game warden. You should check your voice messages; SALECS just called and left a message a few minutes ago."

South Pinedale game warden Brian Nesvik with poached deer from Buckskin Crossing

I didn't want to listen to the message. I just wanted to sit down in my recliner and take about a 12- hour nap. It seemed like all I did for the past several weeks was run my butt off from call to call. It was Sunday and I just wanted to watch an NFL game for once. I reached over and hit the play button on my answering machine. The message played "Hello Scott, this is Jo at SALECS. Hope you made it home safely. Hey, I just received a call of a moose hung up in a fence along the Horse Creek Road near mile marker four. Please call me back and let me know if you are available to take this call before I try someone else. Thank you and hope you enjoy your Sunday."

I called Jo back and let her know that I could handle the call. Heck this was within five miles of my house. I gave my wife a hug and kiss and said, "See you in a bit, honey. I will be right back." I headed down the road several miles and came across a yearling moose hung up in a barbed wire fence. The poor moose was standing there with his right hind leg sticking straight up in the air. Most generally when I come across calls like these, they almost always have a broken hip or pelvic bone and need to be put down. The yearling moose was on the opposite side of the fence from me, allowing me to walk right up to the moose and look it over for broken bones or other injuries. I did not observe any obvious injuries so I decided to cut the moose's leg out of the wire. As soon as the moose was free it ran off into the knee-high snow into a thick patch of willows. As it ran off, I could see that his right rear leg was broken high at the hip joint. I would need to put this moose down so that it didn't suffer trying to survive in deep snow with a broken hip or pelvis. I also wanted to donate the meat to any needy people in the community. I was mad at myself for not just shooting the moose while it was in the fence close to my truck. Now I would have to follow the moose tracks into the thick willows and try and get a shot with my pistol at close range.

I walked through the first patch of willows and observed the injured moose running ahead of me into another patch of willows about one hundred yards away. I slowly waded through the deep snow over to the next patch of willows to see the moose stop. I was breathing hard as I pulled out my 9mm Beretta pistol. The moose was standing broadside about seventy-five yards away. I put my front sight right behind the moose's left ear and slowly pulled the trigger. BANG! The moose dropped dead in his tracks. I could not believe I had made that shot and killed the moose instantly. I was pretty proud of my shot and wishing at least one other person in the world could have witnessed it. Generally, when other people are around to watch it never goes this well. I waded through the deep snow and walked up to the dead moose. I would need to gut the moose and get it back to my truck. All I had was a pocket knife on me. I had a better skinning knife in my truck but I didn't want to take the time to walk all the way back to the truck and then have to turn around and do it again. I rolled the moose onto his back and started to cut up the middle of his belly. While cutting I got this terrible feeling that somebody or something was watching me. I stood up and turned around to see a cow moose coming towards me very quickly, with both ears laid back. She was only about twenty yards away and coming quick. I jumped up and ran behind a large cottonwood tree. Thank God there happened to be a large tree right near the dead yearling moose.

The cow moose stopped and sniffed the dead moose. She then laid her ears back and came full blown towards me. We went around the tree several times. She was now standing on her hind feet and striking at me with her sharp front hooves. I was scared to death and didn't really want to have to shoot this moose in self-defense. This yearling moose was probably her baby from last year. I hadn't even thought about having this problem when I walked out to put the moose down or I would have been better prepared. I wasn't sure how long that she was going to try and kick my ass and I wasn't so sure that she might not just get it done. I had my pistol drawn and yelled at her, "GO AWAY, GET OUT OF HERE!" She finally stood still and looked at me. I holstered my pistol and broke a large dead branch off the tree and smacked her hard right in the nose. She put her head high in the air and her eyes bulged out as large as silver dollars. She then turned and trotted off into a nearby patch of willows. I didn't know if she was going to return and I didn't take any chances. I ran as fast as I could through the knee-deep snow all the way back to my truck. I ran so hard that I thought I was going to have a heart attack. I jumped in my truck and headed home to get my snowmachine and a rope. I couldn't leave all this good moose meat to go to waste.

I returned to the area and unloaded my snowmachine. I could not find a gate in the fence anywhere to drive my snowmachine through. So, I cut all five wires and headed back to the location of the dead moose. Once I arrived, the mother moose was standing over the dead moose. She looked at me and put her ears back and held her head high in the air. She was not going to give up her baby very easily. I ran right towards her at a high rate of speed, hoping to scare her off. She did not scare and neither did I. It was like a game of chicken with a moose, and I was the chicken. I veered hard to the right as she charged me. She nearly got me. I stopped about thirty yards away and tied my lariat onto the back bumper of my snowmachine. With the lariat in my left hand, I hit the loud lever and gave it the onion headed right for the cow moose. She did not scare again. This time I parked the snowmachine between her and the dead moose and quickly put the lariat around the moose's neck as the mother stomped the shit out of me and my snowmachine. I crawled back onto my machine and hit the loud level wide open. When the moose hit the end of the rope it was nearly air-born for about ten feet. Away we went through the deep snow and willows with a half-dressed yearling moose at tow.

The mother followed me clear back to the Horse Creek Road. I went through the opening that I had cut in the fence. She heard a truck go by on the highway and thankfully turned and went back into the willows. Now I was soaking wet, tired, and still had to repair the fence and dress out the moose. Once dressed out I used my snowmachine to drag the moose up on my trailer. I then parked my machine beside the dead moose and headed for home to hopefully catch the end of the football game. I hoped that whoever I donated this moose to would appreciate what I went through to put food on their table. Sometimes the general public does not know or understand everything that happens in the process of getting some free wild game. I ran through the front door of our house to hopefully catch the end of the fourth quarter of the game. I was soaking wet and covered in blood and moose hair. Lana looked at me as I grabbed the remote to turn on the TV and said, "Don't worry about watching the Denver Bronco game, they got their asses kicked again and the game is over. What in the hell have you been doing out there? I thought all you had to do was put down an injured moose caught in a fence?"

Thursday afternoon came quick. I would end up meeting with Lovell Game Warden John Hyde to discuss the winter range patrol briefing. John was a veteran game warden and knew his job very well. I suggested a few good areas for him to patrol and told him where I had seen several nice bucks in the last few days. I gave him my phone number and South Pinedale Game Warden Brian Nesvik's phone number if he needed help with anything.

John patrolled the area near Buckskin Crossing on Friday morning. While patrolling, a man in a pick-up truck stopped John on the road and told him that he was concerned about a large buck deer that he hadn't seen in a few days. Apparently, this man drove this road daily and had seen a large buck along the road for several days. There was a fresh snow and the man could see where a truck had turned around in the snow near the location of where he had been seeing the large buck daily. The man was concerned that someone may have poached the deer so he reported the information to John. John thanked the man for the information and followed up on the fresh tracks in the snow. While doing so, John noticed fresh boot tracks in the snow. The tracks left the main road and headed up a steep sage brush hill to the south. Once John reached the top of the hill he noticed a large buck deer dead behind a large boulder. It appeared that someone had tried to hide the carcass of the buck deer. The large rack was still attached to the head of the deer. The deer rack was a heavy 5x5 approximately 28" wide. This deer would later score 190 Boone and Crocket points.

John knew from experience that whoever poached the deer would more than likely return to the area within twenty-four hours to retrieve the large rack. John went back down to the main road and collected all the evidence that he could. All he ended up with for evidence was a tire impression of the vehicle as it turned around on the road and a picture of the boot track that had hiked up the steep hill. John didn't have much for evidence but decided to patrol that area for the rest of the day and into the evening hours. John would end up parking his Game and Fish truck along the road near the area where the deer had been poached. Just before dark a dark colored truck with a topper came towards John as he was parked off the edge of the road. The truck was also pulling a long flatbed trailer loaded with carpentry equipment and ladders, and had Utah license plates. John rolled down his window and held out his hand for the vehicle to stop. A heavyset man driving the truck slowed down and rolled his window down. John asked the man a few questions and he seemed very nervous. John picked up on the nervousness and asked the man to please pull forward off the road, as he would like to ask him a few more questions.

The man slowly drove by John and then gave it the onion. Did this man really think that he could outrun a game warden pulling a twenty-foot flatbed trailer on slick roads? Apparently so. By the time John got turned around the vehicle was out of sight. There was a four-way intersection just down the road and John didn't know for sure what direction they had gone. John called Warden Brian Nesvik on the radio and informed him of what was happening. Brian answered the radio and told John that he would be 10-76 (en-route) and that he was already in the immediate area.

Warden Nesvik actually ended up ahead of John in the high-speed pursuit. As Nesvik went around a sharp corner he nearly hit the twenty-foot flatbed trailer that was stretched across the road in front of him. He swerved hard and went flying off the road around the trailer. Apparently, they had lost their trailer from traveling at a high rate of speed. Nesvik quickly got on the radio to warn John of the trailer blocking the road. Nesvik slid sideways as he entered back up on the road and kept in the high-speed pursuit. As Warden Nesvik went around the next sharp corner, he noticed the truck lying on its side. There was shit scattered everywhere along and in the roadway. It looked like someone was having a yard sale. He mashed on his brakes and came to a quick stop. Two male subjects eventually crawled out of the wrecked vehicle. The truck had rolled several times and Nesvik found a .22-250 caliber rifle lying in the road next to the wrecked truck.

While Nesvik was asking the two men questions one of them was holding a flip phone in his hand. Nesvik heard the phone go DING, indicating that someone had just sent a text message to that phone. Nesvik asked the man for the flip phone and the man handed it over. Nesvik opened the phone and an incoming text message read, "Hey where are you guys at? I have the deer head and I'm coming down to the main road." At this point in time texting was a new thing and I didn't even know how to text someone back. Nesvik smiled and sent the man a reply text that read, "Hey there, this is the local game warden, please bring the deer head down to the main road and I will meet you there." Nesvik never received a response from the man but he soon showed up along the main road about two miles away, holding the large rack of the poached deer. So, there were three male subjects involved with poaching this deer and thankfully none of them were very intelligent. It was a miracle that neither the driver nor the passenger was seriously hurt in the accident.

I learned from this case that there are people on the winter range that watch these large bucks daily. Some of the deer are even named and famous to this day. Such as Popeye, Goliath, and Cactus Head. Photographers film these large bucks daily and later show up on the May 1 shed antler opener with hopes of finding the shed antlers that belong to the buck that they filmed all winter long. Thankfully, someone had been watching this large buck and noticed it missing for only one day when they reported it to Game and Fish. It's this kind of help that helps us catch some of the most serious poachers.

The three men were fined over $12,000 for the poaching of this deer. Two men also had to perform over 100 hours of community service and were placed on unsupervised probation for two years.

Both men wrote apology letters that were published in the local newspaper, apologizing for their actions. The truck was totaled and the rifle that killed the deer was seized and forfeited to the Game and Fish Department. We would have also seized the truck if it hadn't been totaled.

Poachers total their truck while running from game wardens

Chapter 14

RUDDY DUCKS AND TROPHY ANTELOPE

We were in the second year of the five-year test and slaughter program. We would be trapping elk on Muddy Creek and Fall Creek feed grounds. Brian Nesvik was in his second year as the South Pinedale Game Warden. He wrote and developed a very comprehensive plan to run the entire test and slaughter program. I was very impressed with his abilities to do this with very little experience actually trapping elk. This skill must have been learned through his leadership roles in the Wyoming National Guard. I felt like he was taking over the coordination of the entire project and I was all right with that. I was also still heavily involved with meetings with the Governor's Brucellosis Coordination Team and traveling all over the state. Lana was still working for the Antelope Run Ranch and feeding elk at Jewett feed ground. The feeding contract was now in her name and not the ranch manager's name. But both she and the ranch manager fed elk together each morning. Lana was still loving her job training high dollar horses at the ranch each day. She also got to rope, brand, and doctor cows, which she really enjoyed.

Pinedale is cold for nine months out of the year. The average growing season is twenty-eight days. So, no garden and no tomatoes. Over time I discovered that Lana and I burned somewhere between 10-15 cords of firewood each year. We heated the entire house with a wood stove. Part of Lana's job was to cut down all the dead trees pine trees off the large ranch each year. She had a four-wheel drive versatile Ford tractor with a bucket and grapplers to load the wood. She and Charlie would cut the wood into small blocks and load the tractor bucket full of cut wood. She would then dump the blocked wood into a large two-ton dump truck with a hydraulic tilt bed. Once the truck was full, she would drive it home and dump it next to the house. Don't fool yourself, I helped her with this whole operation by backing her up in the yard and telling her where to dump the wood. The first couple years we would split and stack the wood neatly next to the house. After year three I would leave all the split firewood in a large pile next to the living room window. We would load the wood rack in the house through the living room window almost daily. By the end of the winter the wood would be gone and there was no reason to neatly stack the wood each year next to the house. I would rent a hydraulic log splitter and literally run it for two days straight to split all the wood. I ran it so much that my arm got soar from just pulling the lever on the splitter. I can't imagine how much work this would have been splitting it by hand with a sledge hammer and wedge.

Over time I learned that we were burning at least thirty full grown pine trees a year. These trees were over 24 inches in diameter. The wood stove ran 24/7 for nearly nine months. You can't beat wood heat, but dammit that's a lot of wood! One day I was tired after spending two straight days splitting wood. I was going to take the log splitter back to the rental place in Pinedale before 5:00PM. It dawned on me that my neighbor had lost her husband and was taking care of her ninety old father-in law. I had seen her in Faler's general store buying a splitting maul a few days earlier. I decided to hook up the log splitter onto to my ATV and travel over to her house a few miles away. Once I arrived, her ninety-year-old father in-law was standing out in a heaping log pile splitting wood with an ax. He had only split a small amount of wood and was sitting down, resting on a log stump. He was wearing a white straw cowboy hat and a faded blue denim long sleeve shirt with sweat dripping off his eyebrows. I pulled up and offered to split the rest of the wood for him. He smiled and shook my hand but did not say anything. I split the entire stack of wood and finished just before dark. I was exhausted and told the man, "Don't tell your daughter-in-law that I split all this wood. Just tell her that you did it all by yourself today while she was at work." He smiled, shook my hand and said, "Thank you very much, young man." I knew that he appreciated everything that I had done. I never did get a thank you from the daughter-in-law so I can only assume that he told her that he split all that wood by himself. It made my heart smile to help this family in need. The best thing that you can do for someone else is help them with something that they can't repay you for. I tear up today thinking of that old man standing out there trying to split over five cords of wood at ninety years old. Some kids today don't have a clue what hard work is all about.

It was winter time. It seemed like Lana and I were doing less and less together all the time. She was wrapped up in her job at the Antelope Run Ranch and I was wrapped up in my job with the Game and Fish Department. She was one of the toughest and healthiest women that I had ever met. I didn't know a man that could outwork her. I would generally hold the post upright to make sure it was straight while she tamped it into the ground with a heavy spud bar. Her biceps were huge and she had a turtle shell stomach. As healthy as she was, she started having heart problems. Her heart would race a million miles an hour, to the point that it would scare her. I knew she was healthy, but what was wrong with her? I ended up taking her to a heart specialist in Idaho. He checked her out and said, "Lana, you are extremely healthy and you are not going to die, but I have no idea why your heart is behaving this way." I felt like she was very stressed out over something. I was very worried about her because she had never had any health problems before.

My son Wesley was playing basketball and was very successful at it. I decided one evening that we should go into the new multimillion-dollar Aquatic Center in Pinedale and enjoy the facility as a family. We decided to play a game called 'Lightning'. This is where you stand on the free throw line and shoot a basket. If you miss it the person behind you shoots quickly before you can rebound your ball. If that person makes the shot before you get your rebound you are out of the game. Wesley was standing behind Lana. She missed her shot and took off running quickly to get her rebound. She stumbled and nearly fell down for no reason. I could see the pain in her face and eyes as she stumbled nearly to the ground. She walked off the gym floor to go sit down on a nearby bench. I could tell she was in a great deal of pain. I thought maybe she had twisted her ankle or something. I walked over to her and asked her if she was all right. She replied, "Did Wes step on my ankle or something? I feel like I have severely twisted my ankle." I replied, "No, he did not step on your ankle at all."

Her face started to drain to a white in color. I asked her if she would like to go home and she said, "Yes, I think that would be a good idea."

I grabbed her by the arm and assisted her out of the building. She nearly passed out and fell to the ground. It brought tears to my eyes that my wife was in so much pain and I didn't know what was wrong with her. She was a tough gal and something was seriously wrong. We arrived at home and I took her shoe and sock off while she sat in the recliner. I felt the back of her foot and it felt mooshy and soft.

I said, "Honey, I'm not a doctor but I think you have completely ruptured your Achilles tendon."

She felt the back of her foot and tears rushed down her cheeks.

"I have to feed the elk in the morning and then I will go to the doctor in Jackson Hole."

I didn't know what to do or say. I took her to bed and elevated her foot and wrapped it in ice. She woke up the next morning and left before daylight to go feed more than 650 elk. After feeding she drove herself to Jackson Hole nearly sixty miles away to visit the doctor. It was even her right foot so I have no idea how she pressed the gas pedal to drive. The doctor x-rayed her foot and came out and said, "Oh my God, you have completely ruptured your Achilles tendon. Do you mind if I share your x-rays with my students to show them what a completely ruptured Achilles tendon looks like?"

The doctor performed surgery immediately. Lana ended up driving home after surgery with a cast on her right foot. The next morning, I heard a noise in the kitchen at 5:00. Lana was sitting on the kitchen counter duct tapping a black plastic garbage bag around her cast. I walked into the kitchen and turned on the light and said, "Honey, what in the hell are you doing?"

She responded, "I need to feed my elk and I'm not going to let no ruptured Achilles tendon slow me down!"

She had tears streaming down her cheeks as she wrapped the top of the black glad bag with duct tape.

I said, "Honey, please just take a few days off and heal yourself before going back to work."

She replied, "I'll be fine, the elk are depending on me today for food and I won't ever let them down."

I just shook my head in disbelief. Lana completely ruptured her Achilles tendon and never missed a day of feeding elk. This required her to drive a pick-up truck about thirty miles on a snow drifted county road, snowmachine another couple of miles, and harness a team of draft horses to feed over 650 elk. She would need to load nearly eighty small bales of hay to feed the elk each day. She did this every day for weeks until the cast was off. Once the cast was off, I would help her bend her foot back down each evening to gain mobility. I would pull her foot down with both hands until tears streamed out of her eyes. Her face would wince and she would say, "Please stop, I can't take no more." I had never met a tougher woman in my life. Those elk meant the world to her and she never let them down, not a single day.

Over time, I had become good friends with her boss Charlie, the ranch manager. We had Thanksgiving and Christmas dinners together. We also went to the NFR in Las Vegas together and went boating on area lakes in the summer. I had a great deal of respect for Charlie. He was a tough, good old-fashioned Wyoming cowboy. One day we went boating on Half Moon Lake. I was waterskiing and asked him to shoot me towards shore, as I didn't want to get wet. The water in the Pinedale area is very cold in the summer time. I let go of the rope and went gliding towards shore. I didn't have enough momentum and ended up sinking in the cold water about thirty feet from the shore line. Man, was that water cold! I started swimming towards shore and put my face down in the water while swimming. I looked down and observed a perfect arrowhead lying in the sand about six feet down. So, I dove down and collected the arrowhead. Charlie swung the boat right next to me so that I could get in. I raised the arrowhead in my hand out of the water and handed it to Charlie. I said, "Here, take this arrowhead that I just found." Charlie laughed and couldn't believe that I had actually found an arrowhead in the lake while waterskiing. This was the only arrowhead that I ever found in Sublette County after living there for over fifteen years.

That same year I drew a limited quota area 88 antelope license. The Antelope Run Ranch was named after all the antelope that occupied the ranch. I swore every antelope in the hunt area was on the ranch during hunting season. The ranch did not allow hunting and I never asked Charlie for permission to hunt, as I respected the decision of the owners of the ranch. One day I was up at the ranch and was visiting (bullshitting) with Charlie. I told him that I was going to run home and go do some antelope hunting. Charlie asked me what area I had drawn and I told him area 88. He said, "Well hell, go get your gun and shoot one on the ranch if you would like." I couldn't believe what I had just heard. Nobody ever got permission to hunt this ranch, ever! I thanked Charlie and headed home to get my rifle. I thought to myself, *Man, this is an opportunity of a lifetime to kill a Boone and Crockett trophy antelope.* I was so excited! I loved hunting trophy antelope and this would be a hunt of a lifetime.

I would guess that there were well over one thousand antelope on the property, with many large bucks. I would end up hunting several days and turned down at least ten bucks bigger than I had ever harvested before. I truly wanted a Boone and Crockett buck and was not going to kill anything unless it scored over 85 points. Every evening, I would stop in and visit with Charlie. He would pour me a whiskey and say, "Well, big guy, did you kill a buck today?"

I would respond, "Nope, not yet. I'm still looking for that Boone and Crockett buck."

Charlie would laugh and say, "Well, be sure and stop by the house when you get him; I really want to see a Boone and Crockett buck. I know they are out there."

I hunted and hunted. Finally, I spotted a large buck up on top of a huge sage brush covered hill. The buck was fighting with another buck about one thousand yards away. There were at least four hundred other antelope in the area. The bucks were rutting and running everywhere. But it seemed like the big bucks would never come down off the tall hill. It would be nearly impossible to stalk one of them and get within shooting range with all the other antelope in the area. There were only about eight hundred eyes watching over the landscape as I began my stalk on the large buck. I would have to crawl on my belly down a steep hill in sage brush that only stood up about one foot tall. I would need to crawl approximately one hundred yards to get to the bottom of the draw. Then I would need to crawl at least five hundred yards up the steep hill to maybe get within shooting distance of the buck. Not only that, but there were antelope running everywhere and the bucks may be gone by the time I reach the top of the hill.

I had watched the buck in my spotting scope from my truck for nearly an hour before deciding to try and stalk him. I estimated the antelope would score at least 85 Boone and Crockett points. I left my spotting scope in the truck and grabbed my binoculars. After about one hour of crawling very slowly I reached the bottom of the draw. I looked up over the tall sagebrush. Shit, a doe had me spotted and she was only about thirty yards away. I didn't move a muscle for about ten minutes and had my head raised up high so that I could see over the sage brush, when she spotted me. I slowly lowered my head and put face to the ground. The pain in my neck was slowly going away as my face lay on the ground.

I don't know what happened, but I was so comfortable that I fell asleep for over an hour. I woke up and couldn't even remember why I was lying on the ground in the middle of nowhere. I slowly raised my head and the doe antelope was still nearby but had forgotten about me. I slowly grabbed my binoculars and looked up above me on the tall hill. Believe it or not the large buck was still in the area. About that time, I observed a doe antelope about three to four hundred yards straight up the hill from me. The large buck saw the doe and came running towards me. I got excited and put a shell in the chamber of my .280 Rugar. There was a chance that this buck was going to run within shooting range of me and I wanted to be ready. I pulled out my binoculars and made sure that it was the big buck that I wanted. The big buck disappeared in a steep draw ahead of me. I waited patiently for the buck to step out of the draw above me. Finally, he stepped out and stood broadside at about four hundred yards. I felt like this was as close as I was going to get to him, but further than I wanted to shoot. I got a good rest and got my breathing under control. I held my crosshairs in my scope right on top of the antelopes back behind his shoulder.

I slowly pulled the trigger and BOOM the gun went off and the antelope dropped dead in his tracks. I couldn't believe the shot that I had just made. I was so excited I had finally killed a Boone and Crockett buck. About that time, I observed another antelope run out of the same steep draw ahead of me. I grabbed my binoculars to look at the antelope as it ran away from. *SHIT,* I thought to myself. *I think the big buck that I was hunting is running away from me and I shot the wrong buck!* As I walked up the steep hill, I was hoping that I had not shot the wrong buck. When you look at an antelope at four hundred yards in the scope of your rifle it can be tough to see much detail of their horns. I walked up to the dead buck antelope. I nearly puked as I observed his 12" long horns and tiny prongs. Not only did I shoot the wrong buck on a hunt of a lifetime, I shot one of the smallest bucks on the whole damn ranch. I was sick to my stomach and extremely embarrassed. I was going to gut that antelope and get him out of the area before Charlie could see him and give me a hard time for the rest of my life.

I got the buck dressed and loaded into my truck and met Charlie on my way out. Shit, I was hoping to avoid Charlie and get the antelope out of there without him ever seeing it. He stopped in the road and rolled his window down. "Well, big guy, did you have any luck today?"

I replied, "Yup, I finally got one."

Charlie jumped out of the truck and said, "Good for you, big guy! I have got to see this Boone and Crockett buck that you have been after for all these days."

He looked into the back of the truck and said, "What the hell did you shoot that buck for?"

I was embarrassed and hung my head down and replied, "I shot the wrong buck."

Charlie laughed and said, "Well, he will be a good eater. Come on up to the house and I will pour you whiskey. I want to hear this story."

I just wanted to go home but decided to follow Charlie up to the house. I told him the whole story and we both just sat there and laughed.

That's really all that I could do. You have no idea how many trophy antelope I had passed up to shoot this 12" buck. I had wasted stock after stock, day after day to finally bring this little guy home. Charlie laughed as he sipped a beer and said, "Well you just saved yourself about $600.00, since you damn sure won't need to mount this one!"

A few days later I noticed my neighbor drive by with a large bull elk in the back of his truck. I walked over to his house to check out the elk. It was a dandy 7x7 bull. After visiting for a few minutes my neighbor said, "Scott, would you like to see a hell of a buck antelope that my daughter shot yesterday near the Antelope Run Ranch?"

I replied, "Yes, I have a story to tell you about the Antelope Run Ranch."

I walked into his garage and quickly recognized the buck as the one that I had been hunting a few days earlier.

He said, "Yeah, it was the damnedest thing I ever seen. We got that snow storm the other day, so I took my fourteen-year-old daughter out hunting. The antelope were just streaming off the Antelope Run Ranch onto some BLM property. This was the first buck that we saw, so I told her to go ahead and shoot. Heck, she made a perfect shot and down he went. I just scored him this morning and he scored 87 points."

I was so happy for his daughter but a little sick to my stomach. This was the biggest antelope that I had ever seen in my career of checking antelope hunters. I guess I just wasn't destined to kill a trophy antelope that year. I told him the whole story and he just laughed and said, "Yup, you are not the only one who has ever done that before."

I walked back over to the house and seen that I had a message on my answering machine. It was Pinedale biologist Dean Clause. It sounded like he had a bull moose caught up in a tire swing somewhere up North Piney Creek. Dean asked me if I had time to assist him with the call. I agreed to meet him up there at a predetermined location. It took us forever to find the moose. I expected it to be in someone's front yard but it was actually found up the creek a long distance from anyone's house. Someone had hung a tire swing off a large cottonwood tree next to the creek in a remote location. The bull moose found the swing and somehow got one antler poked through the tire and was hung up pretty tight. This was the craziest thing that I had ever seen. The moose would take off running until he hit the end of the rope. This would jerk his entire body completely off the ground several feet into the air. The moose would then hit the ground and run the other direction until he hit the end of the rope and fly back up high into the air. Back and forth he went for several minutes. It was difficult to get a shot at him with our dart gun because the moose just kept running back and forth and flying high into the air.

The moose finally stopped for a second to catch his breath and Dean shot a dart right in his left hindquarter. Perfect shot. The moose

finally laid down with his head hanging high up in the tire. We were able to cut the tire off his head and release him back into the wild unharmed.

Dean was a great guy and one of the best biologists that I had ever worked with. He truly knew his area and spent hours in the backcountry learning his district and all the wildlife that he was responsible for managing. We have a handful of biologists that try to manage wildlife from their offices. Dean was not one of those biologists. He knew every year what was going on with all the big game populations that he managed, because he was in the field seeing what was going on with his own eyes and not just crunching numbers in his office to look good on paper.

It seemed like Dean and I didn't work that much together in the field. But when he called for assistance, it was always interesting. The previous summer Dean called me for assistance to get a duck out of a porta potty up at CC Ponds north of Pinedale. Some low life had actually placed a Ruddy duck in the septic vault of the outhouse. A lady went in there to do her business and the Ruddy duck flew up between her legs and tried to escape. I can't imagine how loud a scream that must have been. She reported it to Game and Fish and Dean got the call. We would end up having to take the toilet off the cement pad and fish down into the deep vault with a long fish net to try and locate the duck. A Ruddy duck is definitely a diving duck. I can tell you this from my own experience. The duck would dive down to the bottom of the tank and would not surface so that we could catch it in the net. We finally got lucky and it swam into our net about six feet down. We gave it a bath in a nearby canal and successfully released it back into the wild.

Ruddy Duck rescue operation

Safely released back into the wild

Summer had come and gone. It was already time for fall hunting seasons again. It always seemed like we had just got done setting seasons and having public season setting meetings and, bang, it was hunting season again. I was never ready for them to start but they showed up anyways. I was always eager to get out in the field each year. I especially loved checking antelope hunters. The weather was always nice and you could actually see people out hunting instead of just checking camps and game all day. But by the end of October working long hours every day would start to wear on a guy. I would even start to get cranky with stupid hunters doing stupid stuff. I always tried to remain professional with everyone that I contacted in the field, but sometimes it was very difficult.

I stopped by the office to check my messages and say hi to Des. While in the office a man brought in a mountain lion to have it registered. Des said, "Swerb, can you please check in a mountain lion in the back room?" I agreed and walked to the back room of the office where we checked bears, mountain lions, and plugged bighorn sheep heads. The man who killed the lion was middle aged and had only lived in Wyoming for a little over a year. I looked at his license and it appeared that he had bought the license on the same day that he harvested the mountain lion. This actually happens a fair amount. Generally, hunters are out hunting other big game animals when they opportunistically come across a mountain lion. They get excited, kill the lion, and then head to town and buy a license. Some people don't realize that the date and time of when they purchased the license is printed right on the license. This guy was one of them. I asked him when he purchased the license and when he harvested the mountain lion. He lied to me and told me that he had purchased the license a few days ago. If you looked at the time that he purchased his license and the time that he told me that he killed the lion, it was physically impossible to drive to that area and harvest a mountain lion.

He told me the location where he had killed the lion and claimed that he did not take any pictures nor was anyone else with him when he killed it. He also told me that he brought the lion to a taxidermist to have it mounted and the taxidermist told him that he needed to register it at the office within 72 hours of killing it. I asked him many questions about his hunt and he was simply lying to me. I told him that I had hunted lions myself and it would be very rare for me to buy a license at 10:00 in the morning and actually kill a lion two hours later. He just smiled and looked me right in the eyes and said, "Well, that's exactly what happened."

I requested that the man step back into our interview room and I called North Pinedale Game Warden Hubba Healy to assist me with the interview. There were few wardens in the whole state that could interview people like Hubba. He had bright baby blue eyes that would burn a hole in your soul if you stared at him long enough. Hubba was happy to assist and we met alone for a few minutes before stepping into the interview room. We had decided that if this guy was going to lie to us we would use the Reid Interview and Interrogation training that both of us had been through.

We asked the man several questions in a row. It was clear to both of us that the man was lying based on our training. We went back and forth with the man for over an hour and he simply was not going to tell us the truth. Hubba stood up and said, "Sir, would you like a cup of coffee?"

The man responded, "Yes please, that sounds good."

Hubba brought the man a cup of coffee and placed it in front of him and said, "We will return in a few minutes with the results of our investigation."

Hubba and I went and stood in the coffee room for about ten minutes and talked about nothing important. We both walked back into the interview room and sat on each side of the man. Hubba said, "Sir, we have concluded our investigation and it is very clear to us that you are being deceitful with us. Now we are going to give you one more chance to tell us the truth about what happened." The man looked at the table and replied, "I am telling you guys the truth, but what would the penalties be if I had done something illegal and killed a mountain lion without a license?"

From my experience, anytime a guy asks you that question they are guilty. I explained to the man the most severe penalty and the least severe penalty. I told the man that if he would cooperate with us and tell the truth that we would work with him. I told him that the fine would be $450.00 and that I would confiscate the lion and recommend to the judge to not take any of his hunting privileges. We went back and forth for another hour. The man finally admitted that he shot the lion but he also told us that he didn't even know what it was. He just seen something brown in a bush and pulled the trigger. When he realized that it was a mountain lion he went to town and bought a license. I couldn't believe the man had shot something with a high-powered rifle in a bush because he saw movement. What if that had been a person or someone's horse?

I confiscated the mountain lion and issued the man a citation for taking a mountain lion without a license. I also gave the man a court date in case he wanted to fight the case. He told me that he would likely just pay the fine and not go to court. I shook his hand and we parted ways. A few weeks later the man showed up in court. I was not present but Hubba was. The man pled guilty and told the judge his story. I think the man was hoping for some leniency from the judge. That did not happen.

The man stopped by my office after leaving the courtroom. He came into the office, very upset. He said, "I just got out of court and you lied to me. The judge took two years of my hunting privileges and ordered me to perform 100 hours of community service. You told me that the fine for this was only $450.00. Well, I'm a carpenter and I make $40.00/hour. So, my community service will end up costing me $4000.00 at the end of the day."

I responded to the man and said, "Sir, we didn't recommend to the judge to take your hunting, fishing and trapping privileges, but a judge can do whatever he wants. I told you this earlier. We also didn't recommend any community service but again the judge can decide whatever he feels is appropriate. You could have just paid your $450.00 fine and been done with it, but you chose to go to court and speak to the judge. That is not my problem."

The man put both of his hands on my desk and responded, "Did I just lose my hunting privileges in Wyoming?"

I replied, "Yup and, I think you lost your hunting privileges in 48 other states as well."

The man fainted and hit his head on my desk. It happened so quick. All I heard was DONK, and the next thing I knew the man was face down on my office floor. I jumped out of my chair and rolled the guy over. He was breathing but unconscious. I didn't know what to do so I slapped his face a few times back and forth with one hand. The man came to and started coughing. I assisted the man into the chair that I had in the corner of my office. He was pale but breathing again. We visited for a few more minutes and the man left my office, still upset.

A couple of weeks later the man stopped back by my office and told me that his church and local community was going to disown him if he didn't do something good for the community. He wanted to know if I had any recommendations for him. I recommended that he write a letter to the editor and apologize to other sportsmen for taking a mountain lion illegally. I also recommended that he go to the next hunter safety class and tell the whole class what he had done and what his punishment was. The man agreed to all of my recommendations and actually followed through with them. He also showed up at my office again months later and apologized for lying to me and Hubba and asked for forgiveness. I later became good friends with this man and I think this case changed him into a better person. I have told many violators over the years: It's not the mistake that you made, it's how you own the mistake after it has happened. If you hunt long enough you will eventually screw up, just own it and move on.

Chapter 15

BEAR BAITING

It was spring of 2007. Black bear baiting was very popular in the Jackson and Pinedale regions. Any hunter who wished to bait black bears on public lands would need to register the location of their bear bait sites at the regional office by a certain date each spring. Between the Jackson and Pinedale offices it was common for office managers to register over 650 bait sites each spring. Outfitters could register as many sites as they wished. The general public could only register up to two bait sites per person per year. A bait site consisted of one section or 640 acres of public land. Once you had your bait site registered no one else could bait bears in your section. Hunters could keep the same sections each year as long as they actively baited and hunted each site each year. They could hunt bears in your section but they could not legally bait them. You could even actually kill a bear off someone else's bait and that was completely legal, just not very ethical. Bear baiting is a very highly regulated activity. A hunter can't place a bear bait near campgrounds, hiking trails, roads, etc. The hunter must give the exact location of the bait site when registering it. The bait site must have the hunter's name attached to the fifty-five-gallon barrel. You can't use any processed foods to bait in areas that have grizzly bears. The department felt that they didn't want to acclimate bears to human foods.

If a hunter documented a grizzly bear on their bait site, they would need to report it immediately and a game warden would be responsible to remove the bait. Or the hunter could remove it themselves if willing to do so. There was danger when walking into a baited area knowing that a grizzly bear was in the area. As a game warden, this was never a fun job to perform. Wardens typically took backup in with them so that there were at least two armed wardens involved in case they encountered a grizzly bear while removing the bait. The Upper Green River area and the Wyoming Range were starting to document increased numbers of grizzly bears. In some areas it was nearly impossible for the hunter to bait black bears because a grizzly would always show up. This was frustrating for the hunter because they were now done hunting and were required to immediately remove their bait site. Baits can be a huge amount of work for hunters to haul in all the bait and containers. Often times hunters would haul their bait in backpacks for many miles to place in their fifty-five-gallon barrel. Once bears are active on a bait, they can literally clean the bait up overnight. The hunter would then have to haul more bait back into the remote areas.

Hunting bears off baits can be a great deal of work, especially if you also hold down a full-time job. Bears typically only feed on baits during nighttime, late evening, and early morning hours. So, many black bear hunters go to work all day and get home in the evening hours. They then drive to their bait site in a remote location in the mountains and hike another mile or two to get to their bait site. They then sit at a distance or in a tree stand until dark and walk out of the area in the dark back to their vehicle. This can be very scary in the night. Especially if you sat and watched bears feeding on your bait all evening or even maybe observed a grizzly bear feeding on your bait. How remote your bait site is will determine what time you will crawl back into bed with your lovely wife later that night. Often times, it's after 11:00 p.m. Then you get up early and go to work and turn around and go bear hunting again the next night and the next, etc. It's probably a good thing that the bear season is only a couple of months long.

So, in order for a game warden to enforce bear bait sites, he/she needs an accurate location of the site based on the hunter registering the site. This was back before GPS units that provide legal descriptions and probably before about 90% of the hunters knew how to actually read a topo map and give an accurate description. So, for a game warden this can be an absolute treasure hunt trying to find these bear bait locations in the remote mountains of Wyoming. I have actually spent many days looking for one bear bait to find out that it never was in the correct section that they registered it in. It's somewhat stressful walking through the thick trees looking for a barrel full of maggots that reeks to high heaven and has attracted every bear for over one hundred miles. You just know you are going to walk around a tree and come face to face with a bear feeding on a bait. And hopefully not a grizzly bear.

Warden Healy received a call that someone in the Upper Green River had observed a large grizzly bear feeding on their bait. Warden Healy called Warden Nesvik to provide some back-up while removing the bait. They showed up near the bait site in the early morning hours to remove the bait. Both wardens were carrying 12-gauge shotguns loaded full with slugs and 00 buck. They also each had a can of bear spray and .40 caliber Glock pistols. Warden Healy led the charge as they slowly walked through the thick trees to find the bait site. Warden Healy heard a tree branch break to his right side. He quickly turned to his right and aimed his shotgun towards the thick trees where the sound had come from. He then slowly and cautiously moved forward one step at a time, trying not to make any noise. Meantime, Warden Nesvik had jacked in a live round into his 12-gauge shotgun and followed close behind Warden Healy. When all of a sudden, out of nowhere, BOOM went Warden Nesvik's shotgun right behind Warden Healy. This scared Warden Healy so bad that he jumped straight into the air and turned around and looked at Warden Nesvik with his eyes wide open and whispered, "Where is the bear? Did you shoot at the bear?"

Nesvik responded with a smirk on his face, "No, my damn shotgun just went off. Sorry; I don't know what in the hell happened." Warden Healy was not impressed this nearly scared the shit right out of him. Thank God, Warden Nesvik had the barrel of the shotgun pointed in a safe direction when the gun discharged or he may have killed Warden Healy. Needless to say, silence had been broken that quiet morning and any bear within a mile was probably long gone.

Due to the sheer number of bear bait sites that were registered, I decided to put together a Bear Bait Task Force. We would do this each spring in one of the three warden districts in the Pinedale area. The warden in that district was responsible for putting together maps and locations of all of the bear baits that were registered in their warden district. All the other wardens in the Jackson/Pinedale region would assist with this task force. This task force was meant to be fun and also accomplish a great deal of work checking bear baits over a three-to-four-day period. The warden responsible for the task force was also responsible for finding the camping spot and purchasing camp groceries. Other wardens could decide if they wanted to check bear baits via horseback, ATV, motorcycle, or their patrol truck. Each warden was given ten to twenty bear bait site locations to find and check for compliance over the next several days.

Baits were often difficult and hard to find for wardens. Sometimes you may only check one or two baits per day depending on how difficult they were to find and how remote they were in the rugged mountains. The first year that we did this task force we determined that only about 10% of the baits were not in violation. Word got out quick with the public that wardens were checking bear baits for compliance. Most bear baiters also had trail cameras. So, when they looked at their sims card on the trail camera it would show a picture of the warden wearing their bright red shirt checking the bait. Many bear hunters became angry with this approach. They simply didn't want anyone to walk up to their bear bait and leave human scent on the ground. They felt that wardens were tampering with their bait sites and bears would not come in with all the new human activity in the area. They were probably right to some degree. But how else would wardens check for compliance without actually visiting their site?

Over the next several years, this bear bait task force became a tradition and wardens looked forward to it each year. Compliance from hunters went from very poor to the point that we couldn't hardly find a bear baiting violation because the bear hunters knew we were out checking their baits. And they knew we were checking baits because they saw us on their trail cameras or were later contacted by a warden due to a violation.

Bear bait task force fire pit

This task force built great working relations over the years with all the wardens working together. Often wardens were placed in teams of two and would have a competition each day to see who could check the most bait sites in a given day. We would then build a huge bonfire and cook big fat delicious steaks on a grill over the hot coals. Of course, no crazy stories were told and no whiskey was ever drunk over the bonfires. Stories usually involved horse wrecks, grizzly bear charges, stuck trucks, and even a few motorcycle wrecks. This was the best part of the whole trip. I believe Hubba Healy held the record for most bear baits checked in one day. He rode his horse over thirty miles and checked nearly thirty bear baits in the Bondurant area.

Bear bait task force sleeping quarters

On that particular day I had only checked three baits on my motorcycle. I spent the better part of the entire day looking for a bear bait that was registered to a known poacher. I found his vehicle tracks and foot prints on a game trail, but never could find his bait site. I ended up hiking clear to the top of the highest mountain to look for the bear bait in an isolated heavy patch of timber. Once I reached the timber, I was so tired and out of breath. I sat down on a rotten tree stump to catch my breath. While breathing heavily, I looked down at the ground in front of me and observed one of the coolest things that I had ever seen. Sitting right in front of me was the largest set of moose sheds that I have ever found. And both sheds had their points stuck down in the ground with the base of each antler sticking straight up in the air. That moose had poked the sharp tines of each antler into the ground and popped both off at the same time, leaving them stuck in the ground approximately three feet from one another. I never did find the bait site. But I still have that large set of moose antlers to remind me of that great day.

I brought the antlers back to the campfire that night. Hubba was not impressed with me only checking three baits that day and bringing home a large set of moose antlers. I explained to Hubba that it really was not that important that he checked thirty bait sites in one day and rode his horse over thirty miles. What was really important was finding a set of moose sheds. Everyone laughed except Hubba.

Big Piney Game Warden Brad Hovinga was having a whiskey and smoking a cigar. He picked up both moose antlers and said, "I have a story to tell you about ol' Swerb: if there is an antler of any kind within about five miles, Swerb will find it." There was more to this story than anyone else knew, except Brad.

The previous winter I had asked Brad if he could help me investigate a headless elk up on the Soda Lake feed ground. There was nothing left except a pile of white bones. We hiked up Fremont Ridge to look at the carcass of the elk. Brad taught me how to identify a bull versus a cow elk by looking at their pelvic bone. He had determined that it was a bull elk and someone had taken its head. On the way back to the truck Brad was walking in front of me and walked right by a huge seven-point elk horn. Just as he walked by it, I spoke up and said, "Hey, Brad, aren't you going to pick up that huge elk antler that you just walked right by?"

Brad turned around and said, "Damnit, I can never seem to find an antler."

Later that day we drove into the Forrest Park feed ground which was located about thirty-five miles up the Grey's River. It was spring of the year and I needed to pick up all the antlers that the elk feeder had collected on the feed ground that winter. Brad rode along with me to see some new country. Once we arrived at the feed ground Brad said, "Drop me off here, I'm going to go look for a shed elk horn while you drive into the cabin and clean things up. Just pick me up down here when you are done."

I sat in my patrol truck and watched Brad walking off across the feed ground. He wasn't thirty yards from my truck when I watched him walk right by a set of rag horn elk sheds. I yelled, "Hey Brad, aren't you going to pick up those antlers off to your right side?"

Brad turned to his right and observed both antlers on the ground right next to him. He yelled back at me, "You have got to be shitting me right now, how come I can't seem to find an antler!"

Brad picked up the antlers and kept walking. I drove into the feed ground and cleaned stuff up and loaded up the pile of antlers into the back of my patrol truck. Brad had been gone for quite a while. I sat on my tailgate in the warm spring sun and ate my sandwich, waiting for Brad to return. While sitting there waiting for Brad, I came up with a funny idea. I took one of the elk antlers from the back of my truck and hiked down the road away from the cabin. I observed a little open patch of grass in the middle of thick pine trees about one hundred yards from the road that we would be leaving on. I then hiked into the trees and placed that antler in the small meadow where maybe Brad could see it while he was hiking back to the cabin. I quickly ran back to the cabin and sat on my tailgate and waited for Brad to return.

Pretty quick, here came Brad walking down the road towards the cabin. He walked right by the antler that I had placed in the open meadow. He got back to my truck and said, "Man, I didn't find a damn thing. But heck, I probably walked right by ten of them or more. I just can't seem to find antlers."

I just laughed and replied, "Well, my work is done here; let's make a mile."

I purposely drove kind of fast on the two-track road to get us back on the main road. As soon as I drove slightly past the open meadow where I had stashed the antler I mashed on my brakes. Brad's head nearly hit the front window. He looked around and said, "What in the hell are you doing?" I looked over towards the meadow and said, "I think I see an elk antler way over there in that little meadow in the trees."

Brad replied, "Oh, bullshit, it's probably a tree branch or something."

I said, "Well, grab those binoculars and look and tell me what you see."

Brad looked through the binoculars and said, "You have got to be shitting me right now. How in the hell did you ever see that antler? That is frickin' crazy!"

I replied, "I don't know, I guess I just use my good eye once in a while."

Brad jumped out of the truck and went back into the trees to gather up the antler. He absolutely could not believe that I had found that antler while driving fast down a two-track road. I was going to tell him the real story but decided to have some fun with it for a while. We drove down the road about ten miles. Brad said, "Hey, could you stop at this little creek so I can fill my canteen?" I stopped the truck and hiked a short distance up into the trees with Brad. While he was filling his canteen I said, "I have to be honest with you, buddy. I stashed that antler earlier so that you could find it. But you didn't find it, so I decided to pretend that I found it on our way out."

Brad started laughing and said, "Oh, you devil! You got me good on that one, buddy."

I bent down and was getting a drink of water out of the creek when I heard Brad yell from upstream, "You better hurry up buddy!" I looked up to see Brad peeing in the creek right above me while I was lapping up the pure mountain spring water. Yup, he got me good on that one. Everyone around the camp fire laughed so hard that I thought they were going to hyperventilate. And so, this story started many, many more game warden stories that went on into the wee hours of the night. This is what I absolutely loved about my job. There is nothing better than good old-fashioned true game warden stories. It ended up raining cats and dogs that night. We all went to sleep at about 3:00AM in a wall tent that had about one inch of rain water on the floor. It was raining so hard that it nearly put out our bonfire. Nesvik was talking like John Wayne and crawling on his hands and knees back to the wall tent. From my experiences with Brian, when he starts talking like John Wayne he is going to pass out within about ten minutes.

I yelled at Brian while he was crawling away and said, "Where are you going buddy?"

Brian stopped crawling for a minute and looked back and replied with a slur, "I'm going to bed and I don't want to risk falling down and having a head injury. Good night you F-----s.

The next morning at about 5:30 Hubba poked his head into the main wall tent. He was wearing a yellow slicker and a dirty felt cowboy hat with a plastic condom over the top to keep it dry. I'll never forget, it was still pouring rain and the wind was blowing hard. Hubba yelled into the tent, "Where in the hell are all the horses? They are not in the corral?"

Brian flew out of his sleeping bag with a very concerned look on his face supported by a hangover and replied, "Shit I don't know, they were all there when we went to bed."

Hubba was not impressed. "Well, the gate is wide damn open and there is not a horse to be found anywhere. If you guys hadn't got so damn drunk last night we wouldn't have this problem."

I looked up and said, "What do you mean 'we'? I don't have a problem; my motorcycle is parked right where I left it."

Everyone flew out of their fart-soaked shorts and rain-soaked sleeping bags to go search for missing horses. Heck, it wasn't even daylight yet. I could have used a few more hours of sleep and maybe some breakfast. None of the missing horses were mine, so that's exactly what I did. Brad and I stayed together, built another fire, and made breakfast while Brian and Hubba searched for horses on ATVs in the rain. About one hour later Brad and I had another great fire going and we were drying out our clothes and cooking breakfast. I looked up to see Hubba coming towards us. He was traveling at a high rate of speed on a rough road full of deep puddles from the heavy rain. He went right by Brad and me at about 40mph and hit a huge mud hole full of water right next to our camp. His ATV hydroplaned across the puddle and sprayed water so far and high that it soaked both Brad and me and nearly put our campfire out. Hubba never even looked our way or stopped to visit. Brad took a sip of his coffee and said, "I'm guessing Hubba hasn't found his horses yet."

Swerb's Honda horse

255

The horses were all later found, caught, and brought back to camp. We spent most of the day drying things out. Hubba had found an illegal bear bait near Bondurant. The bait barrel did not have the owner's name on it, nor had the bait been registered at all. The bait had other violations such as too close to the main highway and too close to a stream. When wardens find something like this it can be very time consuming to catch the person who placed the bait. You end up waiting at the bait site mornings and evenings, hoping for the person to show up and sit on the bait. Well, Hubba had spent several weeks trying to catch up with this person and no success.

Brad stuck while checking bear baits

Several weeks later Hubba was headed to a meeting in Jackson during the early morning hours. He noticed a truck parked in the area of the illegal bear bait. Hubba knew where the bait was located so he snuck through the trees to get a better look at the bait site. While glassing the area over Hubba noticed something orange out in the sage brush near the bear bait. Hubba assumed this was the hunter lying on the ground with his florescent orange hat on waiting for a bear to arrive. After watching the orange hat with his binoculars for quite some time, it never moved in the sage brush. Hubba decided to sneak out in the meadow and check the guy's hunting license. As he got near the man, he saw something that nobody should ever have to see. There was a man lying in the sagebrush face down with an orange cap on. Except he wasn't hunting, he was dead. The man had drunk his last beer and placed the empty beer can on a stump next to him and shot himself in the head with a pistol. Hubba called the Sheriff's Office and reported what he had found. Hubba went on to attend his meeting in Jackson after seeing such a horrible thing. In a game warden's job, it is quite common to come across people who have committed suicide in remote areas. This is never something that you want to see or ever come across.

It was mid-June, the last day of bear season. I had received a phone call at about 10:30 p.m. from a very distressed bear hunter. The man was whispering in the phone and I could tell he was very upset. He asked me if it was legal to shoot a sow black bear with cubs at her side in self-defense. I could hear the sound of a bear growling in the background. It sounded very close to him. I asked the man what was going on.

He responded with a shaky voice, "I'm in my tree stand down on Dry Piney Creek, archery- hunting bears. I had a sow with two cubs of the year feeding on my bait. I watched them until after dark and they won't leave the area. I yelled and threw sticks at the sow to try and scare her off. I thought they had left the area so I crawled down out of my tree stand to walk back to my truck. As soon as my feet hit the ground the sow charged me and ran me back up the tree in my stand. She has climbed the tree now and is snapping her jaws at me just under my tree stand. I know it's illegal to shoot a sow with cubs at her side, but what if it's self-defense?"

I then heard the man yell, "GET OUT OF HERE, DAMN IT!"

Then I heard the bear growling very loudly. It sounded like the bear was within a few feet of his phone. I replied, "Sir, you certainly can kill the bear to protect yourself, just make sure it's self-defense if you decide to shoot her."

The man replied, "Oh shit, I have to let you go!"

I heard the man yell and I heard the bear growling in the background. The call dropped. I could now hear nothing. I was sitting in my recliner at home, feeling absolutely helpless for this poor man. I couldn't imagine being treed by a sow bear with cubs in the night. The poor man probably didn't even have a flashlight. He was archery-hunting. I wondered if he even had a pistol or bear spray. The call happened so fast I was not able to ask important questions. He had told me that his truck was parked about one mile away. If the man had bear spray, he probably would have used it by now. Lana came walking into the room and said, "Who was that, honey?"

I replied, "I don't know. A sow black bear is trying to eat the ass off some archery hunter in a tree stand somewhere. He never gave me his name and I don't have any idea where he is, except somewhere up Dry Piney Creek. I don't even know if he is still alive." I tried calling the man's phone back for nearly thirty minutes and no answer. I tried calling the Big Piney game warden and no answer. I called the Sheriff's Office and gave them a heads up, but I couldn't even tell them the guy's location other than Dry Piney Creek. I would need to drive to the office in the middle of the night to look up the black bear database and see if anyone had registered a bait site up Dry Piney Creek. More than likely, there would be a whole list of registered sites and I would have to contact hunters one by one to figure out who this guy was. *Welcome to being a game warden supervisor*, I thought to myself. I thought my day was about to end and now it was just beginning. (But this book has now ended. :)

Orphaned black bear cubs

Thank you all for following my crazy life journey over the years. There will more than likely be a book #5 that finishes this story and continues on with my 33-year journey as a Wyoming game warden/ game warden supervisor. I officially retired on March 21, 2025. I will now have more time to write;) Thank you all for your support and friendships over the years. Keep your powder dry, you might need it someday! And give it the onion once in a while or you are truly not living. When in doubt, punch it out!

Scott C. Werbelow
Game Warden Supervisor

If you enjoyed this book, please consider leaving a review on Amazon.

Order other books by Scott C. Werbelow at: scottwerbelow.com

Son of a Poacher: Wyoming Warden in the Making
Son of a Poacher II: Blast From My Past
Son of a Poacher III: No Time to Rest

www.ingramcontent.com/pod-product-compliance
Lightning Source LLC
Chambersburg PA
CBHW070909130626

46555CB00001B/71